BICYCLI
Atlantic Coast

A COMPLETE ROUTE GUIDE,
FLORIDA TO MAINE

Donna Ikenberry Aitkenhead

The Mountaineers

To my Mom, Beverly Bruer Ikenberry,
the most caring, honest, thoughtful, supportive mother and friend
any daughter could hope for.

Published by The Mountaineers
1011 SW Klickitat Way, Seattle, Washington 98134

Published simultaneously in Canada by Douglas & McIntyre, Ltd., 1615 Venables Street, Vancouver, B.C. V5L 2H1

Published simultaneously in Great Britain by Cordee, 3a DeMontfort Street, Leicester, England, LE1 7HD

Manufactured in the United States of America

Edited by Kris Fulsaas
Maps by Evelyn Phillips and Beth Duke
All photographs by Donna Aitkenhead
Cover design by Watson Graphics
Book layout by Michelle Taverniti
Typesetting by The Mountaineers Books

Cover photograph: Somes Sound in Acadia National Park, Maine. Inset: Bicycling across the Venetian Causeway, Miami, Florida
Title page: Sunrise at Delaware Seashore State Park

Library of Congress Cataloging in Publication Data
Aitkenhead, Donna Ikenbarry
  Bicycling the Atlantic Coast: a complete route guide, Florida to Maine / Donna Ikenberry Aitkenhead.
      p. cm.
  Published simultaneously in Great Britain.
  ISBN 0-89886-303-1
  1. Bicycle touring--United States--Atlantic Coast--Guidebooks.
2. Atlantic Coast (U.S.)--Guidebooks.   I. Title.
GV1045.5.A85A58 1993
796.6'473--dc20   92-41896
                                                                  CIP

CONTENTS

Preface . . . 5
Acknowledgments . . . 6
Introduction . . . 7

SOUTH ATLANTIC STATES

MIDDLE ATLANTIC STATES

NEW ENGLAND STATES

PREFACE

As an avid bicyclist, one who particularly enjoys touring, I'm always thinking of and planning my next cycling adventure. When a trip along the Atlantic Coast first entered my mind, later becoming a reality of which I could speak, my fellow southern Californians responded with many negative statements. Although my family supported me, even they were skeptical, tending to side with the locals.

"It's so crowded," most people said, a surprising statement from those trapped in the congestion and pollution of the Golden State. Others spoke of the heat and humidity, hurricanes, tropical storms, bugs, and unfriendly Easterners.

They complained about Florida and I had to wonder why. Would a state be bursting at the seams with people if it was such a bad place to live? Would tourists think it worth visiting? Others warned of New York and its masses, of New Jersey's ugly terrain.

Although a full-time traveler for the past nine years, I had never been to the Atlantic Coast, spending all of my time in the West, yet always craving to see the East. No matter what the critics said, I was determined to cycle the Atlantic Coast.

I spent months researching the area, gathering a box full of maps and brochures and requesting information from Atlantic Coast cyclists and various state and city agencies. Maps were my friends for months as I planned my route. In addition, I studied *The Weather Almanac* for the predominant spring-through-fall wind directions. Within a few months I was ready to roll.

I flew into Miami, Florida, choosing to cycle from south to north as the prevailing winds blow primarily to the north from April through October. In corresponding with about a dozen cyclists familiar with the Atlantic Coast, I found the majority agreed with my decision.

My trip ended two and a half months later in Bangor, Maine.

I did find my share of biting bugs and endured days of record heat and high humidity, but I enjoyed cool, bug-free conditions as well. Regarding traffic and crowds, I battled a maze of automobiles and trucks on some occasions, but overall I found quiet country roads to pedal. And I found peace and contentment in many small towns.

Best of all, I found friendly, helpful people, some offering me a room for the night, others stopping to ask if they could guide me along whenever it looked as though I needed help. Still others simply waved as I rolled by.

The trip proved to be a memorable one, with a mass of lightning bugs providing a spectacular show one night in New Jersey (which wasn't ugly at all). Although lightning bugs enchanted me on many occasions, their "lights" flickering in the night, it seemed as though the entire lightning bug population joined forces at my camp one night along the Delaware River. It was an evening I'll never forget.

In fact, my trip along the Atlantic Coast was one I will always have fond memories of. It was an adventure I can't wait to repeat.

ACKNOWLEDGMENTS

As with each and every project I pursue, I must first give thanks to God, for it is He who leads me along the various paths in life.

Next, I must thank my family. I get a lot of joy out of biking and writing, but the biggest thrill of the book-writing process for me is being able to dedicate my work to someone special. This book is dedicated to someone very dear to me, my mom, Beverly Bruer Ikenberry.

I thank God for my mom and family each day; for my dad, Don Ikenberry, and my two wonderful brothers, Don and David. They are a constant source of inspiration; with their love and support, I feel as though I can do anything.

In addition to my assortment of special friends who have never let me down, I'd like to express my gratitude to the various bicyclists who provided information so willingly when I put out a request in *BikeReport* magazine. Sally and Cliff Brody even offered me a place to sleep for a couple of nights when I first arrived in Miami. My trip began with two nights on their lovely yacht.

Various agencies—city, county, state, and federal—and some private businesses, as well, provided gobs of information and answered my many questions, and to them I must say thanks.

And last, I mustn't forget Donna DeShazo, and the staff at The Mountaineers Books. Thanks for your patience, guidance, and the opportunity to combine work with pleasure.

INTRODUCTION

From the warm, tropical beaches of southern Florida, to North Carolina's Outer Banks and Maine's spectacular, rugged coastline, you'll find a potpourri of cycling delights spanning nearly 2,700 miles. Along this maze of highways and an occasional bike path, you'll observe flatlands and forests, mountains and marshlands, and a variety of animal life, including turtles and alligators, robins and herons, deer and armadillo, and maybe even a doughlike manatee, or an impressive whale.

It's an adventure where the present blends with a very old past. You'll pedal through St. Augustine, Florida, the oldest permanent European settlement in the continental United States, and Williamsburg, Virginia, where an admission ticket allows you entrance to the restored world of the colonial Virginians.

As you pedal along the Atlantic Coast, you'll pass by and have the option of visiting an assortment of forts where you can relive early military history. Other famous sites include Savannah, Georgia; Plymouth Rock, a Massachusetts landmark; and Boston Harbor, site of the famous Boston Tea Party.

Rolling Right Along

Fifty-two daily mileage logs or segments link together the 2,697.7-mile route that begins in Miami, Florida, and ends in Mount Desert Island, Maine. Daily segments range anywhere from 25.5 to 92.5 miles, with the average being 51.8 miles. Side trips mentioned in the text provide additional miles.

Mileage logs also include detailed descriptions of the route and road conditions, and any other necessary information such as the location of towns and the services they supply. Campgrounds and points of interest are noted as well.

Markets, cafes, motels, and other services are listed for the various cities and towns you'll pedal through. If a town offers all of the above, plus a post office, it's noted as offering "all services" or something to that effect. If a town only harbors a cafe or market or convenience store, it is noted as such. Bike shops are mentioned as well.

The route traverses portions of fifteen states, which are divided (though not equally) into three chapters: the South Atlantic States (Florida to Maryland); the Middle Atlantic States (Delaware to New York); and the New England States (Connecticut to Maine). At the beginning of each chapter you'll find important information regarding weather and road conditions, and an overall review of what to see and expect during that specific portion of the ride.

Although you can cycle, drive, fly, or take the bus or train into Miami for the start of your adventure, you'll have fewer options upon

Cyclist photographing brown pelicans along the northern Florida coast

reaching Mount Desert Island. Possibilities include having a support vehicle meet you there in Mount Desert Island, bicycling home (depending on where you live), or taking the bus to the Bangor International Airport. A final 39.3-mile segment, Barcadia Campground to Bangor International Airport, provides detailed information for those who'd rather ride than take the bus.

The quest begins in pancake-flat Miami and boasts of flatlands (with a few rolling hills) for the first half of the ride, from Florida to New Jersey. Rolling hills and some steep grades—the kind that are bound to get your heart pumping—garnish the second half of the ride.

Portions of the journey lead along busy highways where vehicles whiz by at high speeds. At other times, you'll enjoy pedaling secluded country roads where nary a car passes. Regardless of where you travel, always use caution and wear a helmet!

Although you'll pedal close to the Atlantic Ocean whenever possible (providing it's a relatively safe route), there are numerous occasions where the route heads inland. For instance, in Georgia and Maine it's tough to stay right along the coast. With numerous fingers of land stretching into the Atlantic, you'd have to cycle out to the tip of each finger to see the coast, then turn right back around and head back to the main highway. A person could spend a lifetime exploring all the nooks and crannies of the Atlantic Coast.

In some states, like South Carolina and New York, the route wanders inland for safety's sake. Instead of riding the narrow, busy road leading along the popular South Carolina coast, you'll travel inland through rural South Carolina, rolling along roads that are free of crowds even during the holidays. And instead of hassling the swarms of people and chaos found in New York City, you'll ride along the Delaware River, where spectacular scenery and lonely roads are yours for the asking. Also, the route provides an excellent opportunity to explore portions of Pennsylvania.

Why South to North?

Although you can ride north to south by reading this guide backward, you'll definitely want to consider riding in a northerly direction. This guide was written in a south-to-north format because those all-important prevailing winds are usually blowing from the south in the spring and summer. From April to October you can expect the wind at your back, something every cyclist prays for. (Of course, you know the wind can't read *The Weather Almanac*, so it'll blow from the north on occasion.) Starting in October, the wind shifts, blasting in from the north for most of the fall and winter.

Maps and Other Information

Maps and other types of information, including additional bicycling information, may come in handy. For information regarding specific cities, write to the local chamber of commerce, using the city, state, and zip code for each specific town. Maps are available from many sources, including the Automobile Association of America (AAA). For biking information, write to the various agencies listed at the end of each specific chapter. Six states offer free bicycling maps—South Carolina, Maryland, Delaware, Pennsylvania, Connecticut, and Massachusetts. Georgia, Florida, North Carolina, and New Jersey offer free touring guides.

Accommodations

Although nearly all segments end at a campground, this guide was not written specifically for the self-contained touring cyclist. It was written with a wide range of cyclists in mind. If staying in motels or American Youth Hostels, and eating out in restaurants is your preference, you'll find these amenities pointed out along the way.

Due to a lack of campgrounds in some areas, three daily segments end in a city: Fort Lauderdale, Florida, Andrews, South Carolina, and Hightstown, New Jersey. You'll have to decide whether you'd rather rent a motel room for the night, or ask a local resident or church member if you can pitch your tent on their lawn or in the churchyard. If you ask permission, baseball fields may also work to your advantage.

Campsite at Buzzard's Point Marina, near Fair Port, Virginia

If you've ever cycled the Pacific Coast, you're familiar with the special hiker–biker campsites in Washington, Oregon, and California, where sites cost a mere $2 to $3 per person. Unfortunately, you won't find anything so reasonable on the Atlantic Coast.

State parks and national forests all along the route charge bicyclists the standard fee of anywhere from $8 to $21 per site. Because fees are high, I recommend sharing a site with at least one, and perhaps two or three, other persons whenever possible. In areas where state parks are priced particularly high and motels are reasonable, you may be able to find a motel room for two or three persons for about the same cost as a campsite.

Nearly all of the campgrounds in this guide provide hot showers (sometimes they are cold, sometimes they cost extra), water, picnic tables, grills, and a nearly flat area for camping. These are noted as offering "all amenities," or they are named as a "full-service facility," or something close to that. If they boast a laundromat, pool, recreation room, or some other amenity, then it is noted as such. (Day-use areas listed in this guide usually consist of picnic tables, grills, rest rooms, and water fountains, and sometimes even showers.)

Be sure to ask for special reduced rates for bicyclists at each campground. Although I found a few (you'll find each of them listed in the text), there is still a lot of room for improvement and perhaps more campground owners will find it in their hearts to reduce their rates.

Do I Need to Ride the Entire Coast?

This book is for anyone from a day tripper to a full-fledged, self-contained traveler.

If you can't ride 2,697.7 miles in 52 days, why not divide the daily mileage logs in half, spending 104 days to do the same ride? Can't take off 52 to 104 days for cycling? Why not ride the Florida section one year, Maine the next, then North Carolina, and so on? Out for a day ride? Choose one segment and ride to your heart's content.

Touring and Safety

As you may have guessed, you'll have a lot more fun if you're in good shape before you begin your ride. If time passes you by and you've had little time for riding beforehand, plan on riding fewer miles in the first few days of your ride, allowing time to rest sore muscles. Those beginning their ride in the south will at least have flat terrain to start with, a definite advantage.

Before your trip, you'll also want to check your bike over, buying new tires if needed, and squirting your chain with a little chain lube. Even if you sport new tires, you may want to carry a spare. Many cyclists do. If you don't go with the extra tire, at least carry a pump, spare tubes, and a patch kit.

Other necessities include at least two water bottles, a helmet, a bike lock (which you should always use), and an orange safety triangle, vest, or flag (any of which is highly recommended). Other niceties include a mirror (one for your bike or helmet) and a small bike tool kit. Some type of insect repellent is a necessity.

In regards to panniers and other touring equipment, I suggest reading one of many numerous books on touring. For an extensive list of cycling books, contact Bikecentennial, P.O. Box 8308, Missoula, MT 59807. For a brief listing, see Recommended Reading near the Index.

Riding defensively is your best bet when you're out on the road. Always be aware of your surroundings. In tight situations, plan what to do in an emergency. If you see a car, truck, or large recreational vehicle (RV) coming up from behind, never assume it'll get over for you. Watch closely, pulling off to the side of the road and stopping if necessary, allowing them to pass.

Bicyclists must obey the same laws as those written for motorists, which means riding single file, pulling over for emergency vehicles, and stopping for red lights and stop signs. Regardless of where you ride, whether it be the Atlantic Coast or the Pacific Coast, or some place in between, please be careful, use caution, and most of all be sure to ride with great pleasure!

A Note About Safety

Safety is an important concern in all outdoor activities. No guidebook can alert you to every hazard or anticipate the limitations of every reader. Therefore, the descriptions of roads, trails, routes, and natural features in this book are not representations that a particular place or excursion will be safe for your party. When you follow any of the routes described in this book, you assume responsibility for your own safety. Under normal conditions, such excursions require the usual attention to traffic, road and trail conditions, weather, terrain, the capabilities of your party, and other factors. Keeping informed on current conditions and exercising common sense are the keys to a safe, enjoyable outing.

The Mountaineers

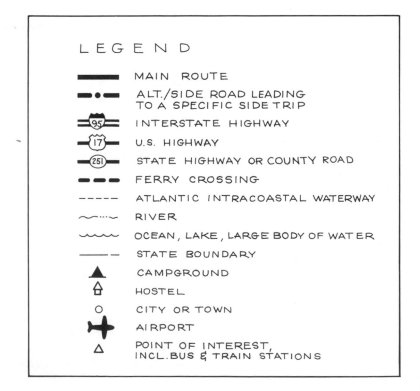

LEGEND

▬▬▬▬	MAIN ROUTE
▬•▬	ALT./SIDE ROAD LEADING TO A SPECIFIC SIDE TRIP
═(95)═	INTERSTATE HIGHWAY
▬(17)▬	U.S. HIGHWAY
▬(251)▬	STATE HIGHWAY OR COUNTY ROAD
▬ ▬ ▬	FERRY CROSSING
- - - - -	ATLANTIC INTRACOASTAL WATERWAY
∼⌇∼	RIVER
∿∿∿	OCEAN, LAKE, LARGE BODY OF WATER
——— -	STATE BOUNDARY
▲	CAMPGROUND
⚕	HOSTEL
○	CITY OR TOWN
✈	AIRPORT
△	POINT OF INTEREST, INCL. BUS & TRAIN STATIONS

SOUTH ATLANTIC STATES

Brown pelicans along the Florida coastline

Bicycle through the South Atlantic States and you'll enjoy almost perfectly flat terrain from Florida to North Carolina. Florida is so flat, in fact, that the highest point—some place in the panhandle—is but 345 feet. Upon reaching Virginia you'll encounter a few rolling hills, but level terrain still predominates.

In this region where history abounds, you'll cycle past many important historical sites with opportunities to explore and relive the days of old. Florida offers a peek into our future as well, with Spaceport USA a popular tourist attraction.

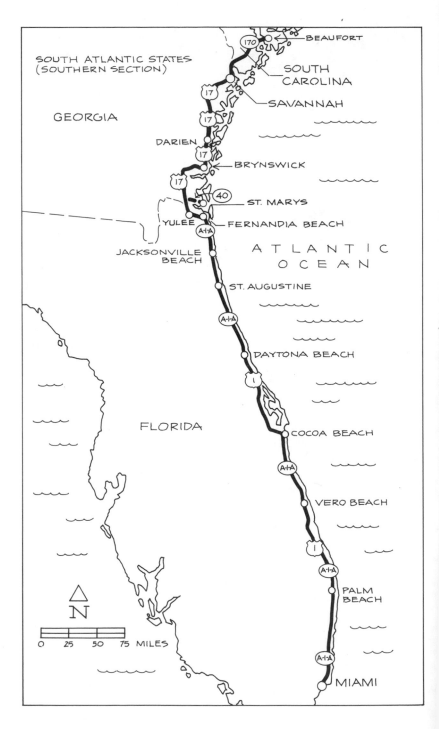

SOUTH ATLANTIC STATES
(SOUTHERN SECTION)

BEAUFORT

170

SOUTH
CAROLINA

17

SAVANNAH

GEORGIA

17

DARIEN

17

BRYNSWICK

17

40   ST. MARYS

YULEE   FERNANDIA BEACH

A-I-A

JACKSONVILLE
BEACH

ATLANTIC
OCEAN

ST. AUGUSTINE

A-I-A

DAYTONA BEACH

1

FLORIDA

COCOA BEACH

A-I-A

VERO BEACH

1

A-I-A

PALM
BEACH

N

0   25   50   75   MILES

A-I-A

MIAMI

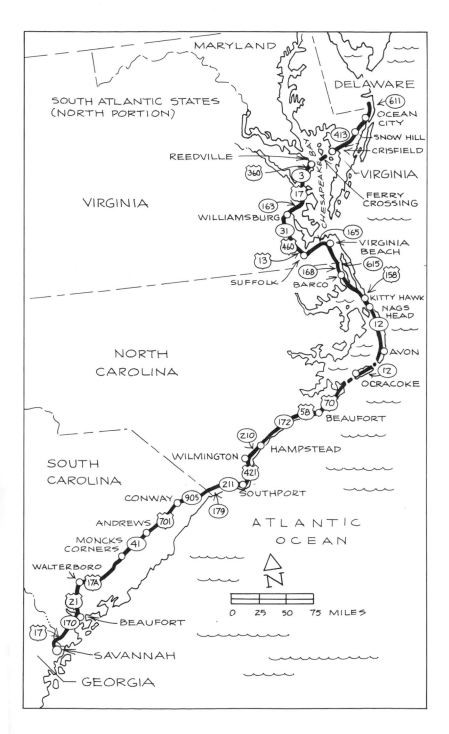

Along the way you'll experience everything from lonely country roads to cluttered cities. En route you'll alternate between the shore and inland areas, enjoying closeup views of the Atlantic, then pedaling through farm country rich in everything from corn to peanuts.

As mentioned in the introduction, this guide is divided into three chapters, the largest being this, the South Atlantic States, with 1,538.7 miles. It comprises six states—Florida (450 miles), Georgia (180 miles), South Carolina (264.8 miles), North Carolina (360.5 miles), Virginia (194.9 miles), and Maryland (88.5 miles).

The route begins at the Miami International Airport (bus and train passengers will find directions leading to the same path), aiming directly for Miami Beach and heading north to Fort Lauderdale, where you'll have to rent a motel room or make some other plans for the night. The first campground upon leaving the airport is 105 miles to the north, too far for most people to consider riding in one day.

If you'd rather spend time exploring Miami before heading north, there's a youth hostel near Miami Beach, right off the main route, less than 12 miles from the airport. Other options include a side trip to Key West, the southernmost point on the U.S. mainland.

Expect heavy traffic as you cycle out of Miami and on up to Fort Lauderdale. Fortunately, traffic thins out as you continue north along the Florida coast. Traffic lanes are often shoulderless, but basically wide enough for comfortable cycling, although you should be prepared for some busy, narrow sections of roadway. An intermittent bike path offers a necessary respite now and again.

Both Georgia and South Carolina offer some superb cycling, although you'll have to battle the masses upon entering Savannah, Georgia, and the roads leading to Skidaway Island State Park. South Carolina boasts quiet and scenic roads, although the roads leading into and out of Beaufort are often plagued with traffic. The route heads inland from Beaufort, South Carolina, due to reliable reports of heavy truck use on narrow Highway 17, which leads to substantial concentrations of traffic along the coast.

Road conditions are mostly favorable in North Carolina, Virginia, and Maryland, especially if you travel before the masses hit the beaches in July and August. North Carolina's Outer Banks are particular favorites, with heavy traffic making narrow roads hazardous for cyclists. Ride the Outer Banks in April or May if possible, or wait until September. Watch for heavy traffic around Beaufort, North Carolina, as well.

Virginia cycling is delightful except for the stint in Virginia Beach and west to Suffolk. From there, however, you'll travel quiet country roads to Jamestown. North of Yorktown, you'll experience some heavy traffic on Highway 17 before heading off onto a series of quieter roadways.

Again you'll be heading inland from Virginia Beach, as bicycles are not allowed on the bridges spanning Chesapeake Bay. Instead you'll ride west and then north to Smith Point, where you'll ferry over to Smith Island or Tangier Island en route to Crisfield, Maryland.

Maryland offers a delightful cycling adventure through farmland and small rural towns, with lonely roads and wide shoulders a definite treat.

Each segment ends at a campground, either public or private, except for one night in Andrews, South Carolina. Again, you'll have to rent a room or pitch your tent in someone's yard, as campgrounds are nonexistent in the nearby area. Most of the campgrounds and points of interest in the South Atlantic States remain open year-round, especially those visited in Florida, Georgia, South Carolina, and North Carolina.

Spring is a good time for cycling this region, as the heat and humidity, typical of this region, are not as oppressive as during the summer months, when temperatures rise to 100 degrees and the weather forecaster warns "tomorrow the heat will be dangerously hot."

Average summer highs are usually in the low 90s, although temperatures can reach up to 100 degrees. Thermometers drop to the low 70s at night.

Expect plenty of rain in the summer months, as most of the South Atlantic States receive more than half of their annual precipitation during the summer, mostly in the form of afternoon or early evening thunderstorms. Although rain often pours out of the sky in drenching amounts, the storms usually only last 1 or 2 hours. Average rainfall totals about three inches in April and eight inches in July.

Tornadoes and tropical storms also threaten the Atlantic Coast on occasion. Although tornadoes can strike all year, most occur in the spring. Tropical storms usually hit the coast from August through late October.

Upon corresponding with a dozen cyclists familiar with the Atlantic Coast, many spoke of a particular hazard in the South. They warned of dogs, saying they had been chased or scared by them. Although I had absolutely no problems whatsoever, you may want to come equipped with some sort of protection. Many cyclists recommended using a pepper-based aerosol spray that should temporarily "halt" any menacing dog.

For additional road or bicycling information, contact:

Dan Burden, state bicycle coordinator
Florida Department of Transportation
605 Suwannee St., Mail Station 19
Tallahassee, FL 32399-0450
(904) 488-8006

Steven Yost, bicycle coordinator
Georgia Department of Transportation
2 Capitol Square, Rm. 366
Atlanta, GA 30334
(404) 656-5351

Bicycle Affairs Coordinator
State Highway Administration
707 N. Calbert St., Rm. 218
Baltimore, MD 21202
(800) 252-8776

Mary Meletiou
The Bicycle Program
Department of Transportation
P.O. Box 25201
Raleigh, NC 27611
(919) 733-2804

South Carolina Department of Parks, Recreation and Tourism
1205 Pendleton St.
Columbia, SC 29201
(803) 734-0141

Richard C. Lockwood, state bicycle coordinator
Virginia Department of Transportation
1401 E. Broad St.
Richmond, VA 23219
(804) 786-2963

Miami to Fort Lauderdale (41.4 miles)

Although this guide begins at the Miami International Airport, bicyclists arriving by bus or train will find directions from those terminals leading to the same route described here. If arriving by bus, you'll meet up with the route at the 7.7-mile mark. Coming in by train? You'll begin riding the described route at the 16.1-mile mark.

To ensure the best path through Miami, state and local bike coordinators were contacted, and I drove dozens of streets in a rental car, hunting for wide, fairly uncrowded roads. Although traffic will undoubtedly be a problem in some areas, you'll find less traffic if you leave on a weekend morning.

You'll exit downtown Miami by way of the Venetian Causeway, where there are superb views of the city. The causeway links several islands with the mainland and the beach strip. As you pedal across the Venetian Causeway, you'll cross the first of many such bridges spanning the Atlantic Intracoastal Waterway, a toll-free navigable shipping route used mostly by pleasure craft in the south. This lovely ribbon of

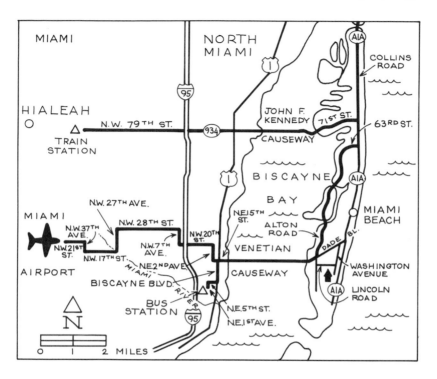

water, which comprises various bays, lagoons, canals, and rivers, stretches from Key West to Boston.

Although the Venetian Causeway sports a bike lane, you'll find bike paths and/or wide shoulders quite rare throughout the Sunshine State. This segment is no exception, although you will travel an occasional bike path and sometimes lanes are wide, providing room for cyclists.

Highway A-1-A hugs the coast at times, providing wonderful views of the Atlantic; at other times the ocean is obscured by row upon row of motels and restaurants. Motel accommodations, food sources, and bike shops are plentiful throughout this segment.

Campgrounds are nonexistent in this land of tall buildings and flat terrain, so the first segment ends in Fort Lauderdale, as those arriving in Miami in the morning should have no problem reaching Fort Lauderdale by evening. If you crave excitement, you'll want to spend time at the southern end of town. If you like peace and quiet, and inexpensive motels, try the north end.

If you arrive late in the afternoon, or if you just want to spend time exploring Miami Beach, try the youth hostel located just off the route near the 12-mile mark. Listed on the National Register of Historic Places, the hostel is two blocks from the beach in the Miami Beach Art Deco District.

MILEAGE LOG

0.0 From Miami International Airport (United Airlines terminal), follow the main road out of the terminal.

0.5 Take Exit 1 (N.W. 21st St.) toward downtown Miami, Hwy. 836 East, and Key Biscayne.

1.3 Turn right on N.W. 37th Ave.

1.7 Go left on N.W. 17th St., now pedaling through residential Miami.

2.7 Turn left on N.W. 27th Ave., a main thoroughfare. Cross the Miami River soon after turning.

3.4 Turn right on N.W. 28th St., now traveling residential streets again.

5.5 Make a right on N.W. 7th Ave.

6.0 Turn left on N.W. 20th St. Shortly after this turn, cross under I-95.

7.0 Go right on N.E. 2nd Ave., entering downtown Miami. Roads are busy, but the street is fairly wide.

7.4 Make a left on N.E. 15th St.

7.7 Continue straight on N.E. 15th St., which becomes the Venetian Causeway. (Those arriving by Greyhound will intersect with the route at this point. For complete directions, see "How to Get There," at the end of this segment.) There's a bike lane across the causeway with wonderful views of Miami. Enormous cruise ships are often seen in port. Cross several islands (Biscayne, San Marco, San Marino, Dilido, and Rivo Alto) as you travel over the Atlantic Intracoastal Waterway.

11.3 The road forks when you reach the other side of the Atlantic Intracoastal Causeway; go left on Dade Blvd.

11.5 Make another left on Alton Rd. A bike lane exists through this pretty residential area. **SIDE TRIP:** The Miami Beach International American Youth Hostel (AYH) is located nearby. Instead of turning left on Alton Rd., go right, then left on Lincoln Rd., and right on Washington Ave. It is open year-round. For further information, write or call 1438 Washington Ave., Miami Beach, FL 33139; (305) 534-2988.

12.2 Cross Arthur Godfrey Rd.

14.7 Alton Rd. becomes 63rd St. There's no shoulder now.

15.2 Junction with Hwy. A-1-A South. Go another 100 yards or so and make a left on Hwy. A-1-A North (Collins Rd.). Motels, hotels, and restaurants are plentiful.

16.1 Cross 71st St. (Hwy. 934). Bicyclists arriving by train will meet up with the route at this point. (See detailed instructions in "How to Get There," at the end of this segment.)

16.9 North Shore State Recreation Area; day use only, rest rooms, picnic facilities.

18.0 Surfside Recreation Center and Tourist Information. There's a library located here as well.

Cyclist viewing Miami from the Venetian Causeway

19.1 The road narrows upon entering Bal Harbour. Cross a bridge with ample shoulders, then it's back to riding a shoulderless road.

19.6 Haulover Beach County Park. A very scenic park, it boasts a picnic area and grand views of the Atlantic. To continue north, ride the Sunny Isles Ocean Walk, a wide bike/jogging/walking path that parallels the ocean.

21.0 The bike path ends at Hwy. A-1-A. Continue north.

24.9 Hallandale city limits.

27.9 Turn right on Johnson, then left at the alley. There's a sign pointing the way to a bike route, or you can ride the nearby boardwalk if you'd prefer. There's a bike rental shop off the alley at Hollywood Beach.

28.6 Make a right on Taft St., then a left onto the boardwalk.

29.3 The boardwalk ends; the bike route continues, eventually following Balboa St. to Hwy. A-1-A.

30.5 Junction with Hwy. A-1-A/N. Ocean Dr. Head north.

30.7 Pedal up and over the bridge toward Fort Lauderdale, now traveling Dania Beach Rd. There's a wide shoulder now.

31.9 Dania begins. This is a multilane road (three lanes each way), with no shoulders.

32.7 Turn right on US 1.

33.9 Junction with I-595 West. The Fort Lauderdale International Airport is less than 1 mile to the west. There's a good shoulder again.

36.5 Make a right on S.E. 17th St., which merges into Hwy. A-1-A. This is a crowded road with no shoulders.

37.6 Bridge over Turning Basin. There's a sidewalk for a safer crossing.

39.2 Hwy. A-1-A hugs the coast now, providing good views of the ocean from Fort Lauderdale, a motel-endowed city known as the "Venice of America." Here you can eat a romantic dinner at a restaurant overlooking the Atlantic, take a day cruise or a week-long cruise aboard an immense ocean liner, or explore underwater reefs from a glass-bottom boat.

41.4 Fork; keep left on Hwy. A-1-A. This segment ends here for one very important reason—there are inexpensive motels in the area.

How to Get There

Greyhound Bus Terminal: From the terminal located at the corner of N.E. 1st Ave. and N.E. 4th St., go one block north to N.E. 5th and make a right. Cycle 0.3 mile and turn left on Biscayne Blvd./US 1. Meet up with N.E. 15th St. and the Venetian Causeway in another 0.7 mile.

Amtrak Train Station: Amtrak is located off N.W. 79th St., about 9 miles to the west of Hwy. A-1-A in Hialeah. From the train station, go east on N.W. 79th St. This road becomes N.E. 79th St., the John F. Kennedy Causeway, and 71st St. (Hwy. 934) before reaching Hwy. A-1-A at the 16.1-mile mark.

Side Trips

If you'd like to do some bicycling before starting your ride, Key Biscayne is particularly nice and offers a wide bike path for its entirety.

The Florida Keys are especially popular with cyclists, although finding a safe route to the Keys can be a bit tricky. Many negative things have been said about cycling the Keys, the southernmost point of the U.S. mainland. I decided to check the route out for myself, my bike and gear stashed in the back of a rental car.

It's 155 miles from Miami to Key West. From Miami to Homestead, US 1 is three lanes and shoulderless, and carries a heavy load of traffic. True, this 28-mile segment would be nerve-wracking and dangerous, but the 127 miles from Homestead to Key West boasts a fairly wide shoulder of 4 feet or more, offering a pleasant ride.

If you decide to pedal to Key West, you'll cross forty-two bridges ranging in length from 140 feet to 35,380 feet (7 miles). Traffic can be heavy, especially during the high travel season from December to April, so plan your trip accordingly. There are many campgrounds along the route.

Fort Lauderdale to Jonathan Dickinson State Park (65.0 miles)

This portion of the ride leads through what must be one of the most exclusive residential areas in the world. Home to the Kennedys and other rich and famous people, it's like pedaling through a beachside version of California's Beverly Hills. Homes encompass thousands of square feet, manicured lawns are picture-perfect, and yachts rest at dockside, waiting for an ocean cruise.

The area is also known to provide some of the best salt- and freshwater fishing in the country. With its close proximity to the Gulf Stream, warm, oceanic currents bring an incredible array of offshore species to within less than 2 miles of four inlets located at Jupiter, Palm Beach, Boynton Beach, and Boca Raton.

Bicyclists will travel Highway A-1-A for the most part, pedaling through countless towns spread across flat terrain. Although some bike paths exist, you'll be riding two- to four-lane highways for the most part. Shoulders are usually nonexistent.

Highway A-1-A traces a narrow strip of land, sandwiched between the Atlantic and the Atlantic Intracoastal Waterway for much of its length. At times this strip of land is so narrow you'll be able to see both bodies of water at once. Although you might imagine countless markets along the way, the route passes through some regions where food is scarce. Stock up before heading north. While you'll enjoy many picnic areas off the route, the first campground upon leaving Miami is at segment's end—Jonathan Dickinson State Park.

MILEAGE LOG

0.0 From Fort Lauderdale, head left at the fork, following Hwy. A-1-A North. The highway passes through both the business and residential districts, sans shoulders.

7.8 After passing through Pompano, cross the Hillsboro Inlet via the Hillsboro Bridge.

9.9 A narrow shoulder begins.

11.7 The road curves to the right. There's a convenience store here.

12.1 Boca Raton town limits.

14.2 South Beach Park entrance; rest rooms, but no picnic facilities.

15.1 Red Reef Park; picnic facilities, rest rooms.

16.2 Spanish River Park; 46 wooded acres, nature trail, picnic facilities, rest rooms, showers. If you'd like to get off the main road for a while, there's a bike path that begins here and leads about 1 mile to the north.

20.1 Delray city limits. Settled by eight Michigan pioneers, Delray was named for a Detroit suburb in 1901. Today it is known for its miles of white sandy beaches.

23.1 Gulfstream city limits.

25.2 Visit Gulfstream Park, which is to the right and up the hill; picnic facilities, rest rooms. There's a convenience store just ahead.

25.9 Turn right on Beachway Dr. for a break from traffic.

26.1 Pedal left on Old Ocean Blvd., traveling parallel to the sea now.

26.6 The road curves back to Hwy. A-1-A. Head right.

27.3 Boynton Beach Oceanfront Park; picnic facilities, rest rooms, concessions.

28.2 Ocean Inlet Park; picnic facilities, rest rooms, snack bar. This park provides access to 600 feet of beach and 900 feet of Atlantic Intracoastal Waterway frontage.

28.4 Manalapan, an exclusive area where enormous homes predominate. Located between the Lake Worth and Boynton Beach inlets, Manalapan is a small, residential coastal community whose Indian name means "Good Bread."

31.2 South Palm Beach city limits. Lantana Public Beach is also located here; picnic facilities.

31.7 Palm Beach town limits. An occasional bike path will allow you a break from the main highway every so often. Be sure to look for the intermittent paths that parallel both sides of the street.

35.1 Phipps Ocean Park; picnic facilities, rest rooms, swimming pool, bike trail. According to the Palm Beach Visitor's Guide, "The Gulf Stream is closer to shore here than any other point in the United States."

37.6 Junction with US 98/Hwy. 80. Palm Beach International Airport is about 3 miles to the west via US 98.

38.3 Hwy. A-1-A curves to the left; exit it and continue straight on S. Ocean Blvd.

40.1 The road curves to the left and is now called Barton Ave.

40.4 Make a right on Hwy. A-1-A North.

40.9 Turn left on Poinciana Way/Hwy. A-1-A.

41.3 Begin crossing Flagler Memorial Bridge, which is two lanes and shoulderless. There's a sidewalk if you'd rather walk.

41.4 Turn off on the right fork to Flagler Dr.

43.4 Make a left on 36th St.

43.8 Head right on Hwy. A-1-A/US 1, also called Broadway.

46.4 Go right on Blue Heron Blvd./Hwy. A-1-A. **SIDE TRIP:** If you're hungry, you've probably noticed the shortage of inexpensive restaurants. Continue straight on US 1 for fast food, markets, et cetera. US 1 merges back with Hwy. A-1-A about 4 miles to the north.

47.1 Top of the Blue Heron Bridge. At about 100 feet high, it's one of the high points on the Florida coast. After exiting the bridge, Hwy. A-1-A, also called N. Ocean Blvd., curves to the north.

48.3 Ocean Reef Park on the right.

49.8 There's a shoulder now, but it narrows to nothing in 1 mile.

50.7 John B. MacArthur Beach State Park; 8,000 feet of ocean-front beach, picnic facilities, rest rooms, nature center, fishing and swimming opportunities.

View from a bridge between Palm Beach and West Palm Beach

52.8 Make a right on US 1, now called Federal Hwy.

54.0 Fork; take Hwy. A-1-A to the right to Juno Beach. There's a bike path now.

55.7 Junction with Donald Ross Rd. **SIDE TRIP:** For the nearest grocery store, go left on Donald Ross Rd. to nearby US 1.

55.9 Picnic area and rest rooms.

56.5 Jupiter city limits; end of bike lane at Juno Beach Park; picnic facilities, rest rooms, showers.

59.1 Carlin Park; 126 acres of beach-front area and hiking trails, picnic facilities, rest rooms, snack bar. Begin heading away from the beach now.

60.6 Turn right on US 1, a four- to six-lane highway where shoulders are nonexistent and traffic is often heavy. Use caution! There's a convenience store about 1 mile before the turn.

60.7 Cross the Loxahatchee River.

61.2 Stay straight instead of riding Hwy. 707, which is Alt. A-1-A. There are places to eat here in Tequesta, the last chance for food before the campground.

65.0 Jonathan Dickinson State Park. Here you'll find 10,328 acres of pine flatwoods, mangrove, sand pine scrub, river swamp, and the Loxahatchee River. Four scenic nature trails allow land exploration, while a thirty-passenger tour boat, the *Loxahatchee Queen*, provides a closer look at the Loxahatchee River and its animal life. Named for Jonathan Dickinson, a Quaker who was shipwrecked in this vicinity in 1696, the park is a sanctuary for bald eagles, manatees, and Florida sandhill cranes. Alligators also inhabit the area and should not be approached closely, frightened, or teased. Open year-round, there are two campgrounds within the park. Showers and picnic facilities are provided. Also, there are cabins for rent.

Jonathan Dickinson State Park to Sebastian Inlet State Recreation Area (73.3 miles)

Once again you'll pedal a flat route (it'd be hard to climb too high in a state where the highest elevation is 345 feet), following a section of US 1 before heading onto a lonely stretch of Highway A-1-A. This route leads through rural Florida, a place of great scenic beauty with green pastures and quiet roads. Be sure to stop at the Hobe Sound National Wildlife Refuge along the way.

Today's ride crosses the Indian River, which extends nearly 160 miles along Florida's east coast, separated from the Atlantic by a barrier island system. Home to more than 3,000 species of animals, 30 of which are listed as endangered species (such as the endearing

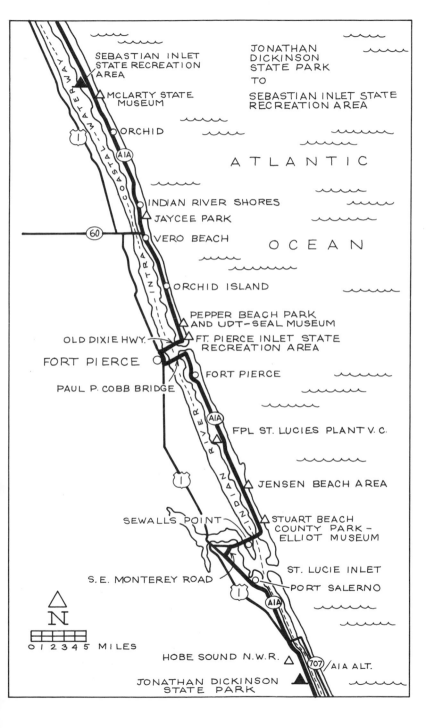

JONATHAN DICKINSON STATE PARK TO SEBASTIAN INLET STATE RECREATION AREA

manatee), 700 species of fish, and 310 kinds of birds, it is the most diverse estuary in the United States.

Once back near the ocean, the road crosses miles of desolate areas, some of it swampland where anxious bicyclists can look for alligators and other animal life.

Food stands and convenience stores are often a rarity. Be sure to carry enough food, water, and other supplies.

MILEAGE LOG

0.0 From Jonathan Dickinson State Park, continue north on US 1. Traffic can be heavy for the next few miles.

2.5 Hobe Sound National Wildlife Refuge. Rest rooms and water are available at headquarters. Managed by the U.S. Fish and Wildlife Service, the 968-acre refuge is one of the most productive sea turtle nesting areas in the United States. According to a refuge brochure, "In good years, over 100,000 hatchlings may be produced along the refuge's 3.5 miles of beach." In addition to being a prime nesting area for loggerhead, green, and leatherback sea turtles, it is also home to many species of birds, including brown pelicans, ospreys, and a variety of shorebirds. Manatees live in waters adjacent to the refuge.

3.2 Junction with Hwy. A-1-A (also called Dixie Hwy.); head right, toward Hobe Sound. The road is now two lanes with no shoulder, but traffic is light.

11.0 Bike path on the right.

11.5 Cove Road intersection.

12.1 S.E. Salerno Rd. junction and Port Salerno. There's a cafe with good food and prices, as well as a couple of small markets.

15.7 Turn right on S.E. Monterey Rd. The bike lane continues on the opposite side of the road.

17.1 Bike path ends. Road is now four lanes with narrow or nonexistent shoulders.

17.3 Merge back to Hwy. A-1-A (E. Ocean Blvd.). Make a right. Lanes are wide now.

18.2 Cross the St. Lucie River. The road narrows to two lanes.

18.7 Sewalls Point. If you're hungry, stock up on food. Amenities are few up ahead.

19.1 Cross the Indian River and begin riding a narrow strip of land where the Atlantic is sometimes visible on the right and the Atlantic Intracoastal Waterway (Indian River) on the left.

19.4 Stuart Jensen Park; picnic facilities, rest rooms.

20.0 Cross the bridge to South Hutchinson Island.

20.7 Stuart Beach County Park and the Elliott Museum. You'll find all the usual amenities at Stuart Beach, including picnic facilities, rest rooms, and showers. Also there's a concession stand and opportunities for fishing, swimming, and snorkeling. Harmon

Fishermen and brown pelicans along the Indian River near Stuart, Florida

Parker Elliott built the Elliott Museum in 1961 "to recognize the genius of his father, American inventor Sterling Elliott (1852–1922), of Massachusetts." Numerous wings house everything from Elliott's inventions to an apothecary shop, a miniature hand-carved circus, and Indian artifacts. As you head north from the park and museum, there are moderate shoulders. Farther north, a bike lane alternates with the shoulder to provide a good biking path.

24.7 Jensen Beach area; picnic facilities, rest rooms, concession stand. As you travel on, the beach is accessible from several points, all lacking rest-room facilities.

27.3 Shoulder/bike lane ends.

30.9 Florida Power and Light (FPL) St. Lucies Plant Visitor Center. There are rest rooms here and free tours of the plant.

37.7 Fort Pierce city limits.

38.0 There's a bike path or shoulder now.

40.0 Keep left on Hwy. A-1-A. There are markets, restaurants, and motels in the area.

41.6 Cross the Paul P. Cobb Bridge. **SIDE TRIP:** Turn off to St. Lucie County Historical Museum just before crossing the bridge. The museum is open Tuesday through Sunday and boasts Spanish shipwreck artifacts, a reconstructed Seminole

Indian encampment, and the 1907 Gardner House, to name a few items. There's a park here as well. You'll find picnic facilities, but no rest rooms.

42.5 Hwy. A-1-A joins US 1; go right.

43.2 Exit US 1 and go right on the Old Dixie Hwy., then merge back onto Hwy. A-1-A in 0.4 mile. Head right.

43.8 Cross the Indian River again.

44.2 Cable Crossing Picnic Area; picnic facilities, rest rooms. The road is now narrow with no shoulders.

45.7 Fort Pierce Inlet State Recreation Area. Situated on a barrier island, the 340-acre park offers nature trails and opportunities for fishing, swimming, and birding.

46.0 Keep to the left on Hwy. A-1-A North.

46.7 Pepper Beach Park and the Underwater Demolition Team (UDT)— SEAL Museum, birthplace of the Navy frogmen.

51.3 Orchid Island town limits.

56.0 Vero Beach city limits.

56.6 Convenience store.

58.5 Junction with Hwy. 60.

59.0 Shoulder begins, a welcome treat for rattled riders.

59.3 Jaycee Park; boardwalk, sandwich shop, picnic facilities, rest rooms, outdoor showers.

60.1 Indian River Shores city limits. There are markets in town.

67.1 Orchid city limits.

71.9 McLarty State Museum offers historic exhibits and treasures from a 1715 shipwreck.

72.8 Beach access area with rest rooms.

73.3 Sebastian Inlet State Recreation Area (south entrance). Located between the Atlantic Ocean and the Indian River, this 576-acre park is one of Florida's best and most popular surfing areas. It's also popular with those who enjoy fishing, snorkeling, and catching some rays. You'll find all services available at the campground.

Sebastian Inlet State Recreation Area to Jetty Park (41.9 miles)

Once again, Highway A-1-A comes through for bicyclists who enjoy flat pedaling with a pancakelike ride along the Atlantic Ocean and the Atlantic Intracoastal Waterway. The beginning of this segment passes through residential areas where markets and rest rooms are few. But unlike the previous segment, where markets were spaced miles apart, today there are many fast-food outlets, markets, motels, and so on.

Humans aren't the only ones that have taken a liking to this area. From

Sebastian Inlet to Spessard Holland Park, you'll find the largest sea turtle nesting area in the United States. Three species of sea turtles—loggerhead, green, and leatherback—come ashore from May until August to lay their eggs. Hatchlings make the long journey back to the sea until late October.

For bicyclists, the journey is an easy one, as the highway parallels the Atlantic for the most part. Although the ocean isn't always visible, there are side roads leading to it, and many nice parks for a picnic or a rest.

En route to Patrick Air Force Base, you'll appreciate a shoulder and/or a wider lane; however, the highway to Cocoa Beach sports four lanes and is shoulderless. Traffic can be heavy, so use care. There's a grass shoulder if needed.

The day ends via a bicycle path to Jetty Park, a quiet campground with all the services one could possibly hope for.

MILEAGE LOG

0.0 From Sebastian Inlet State Recreation Area, continue north on Hwy. A-1-A.

0.6 Sebastian Inlet Recreation Area (north entrance); picnic facilities, rest rooms. The shoulder ends, but a bike lane begins on the opposite side of the road.

2.1 Exit to Long Point County Park and Campground on the left. This full-service campground is about 1 mile away. A market/deli services this junction.

5.5 Sunnyland Beach city limits.

6.4 Floridana Beach city limits.

6.9 Market on the left.

8.1 Melbourne Shores city limits.

8.4 End of bike lane. The road is two lanes with no shoulder.

9.2 Restaurant and motel on the right.

13.1 Bike path on the left.

14.2 Convenience store, market.

14.7 Holland South Beach Park; rest rooms, picnic facilities.

15.0 Fork; keep right on Hwy. A-1-A. The bike path takes off to the left, but there's a shoulder on the main road now.

15.3 Spessard Holland North Beach Park; picnic facilities, rest rooms, 3,600 feet of splendid sand and beach.

15.5 Melbourne Beach city limits.

16.4 Ocean Park; picnic facilities, rest rooms. Hwy. A-1-A curves to the left. There are markets, motels, and restaurants for many miles to come now.

17.3 Indiatlantic city limits.

18.3 Junction with US 192. The shoulder ends; Hwy. A-1-A is four lanes now.

19.3 The bike path on the left is a welcome relief from the busy highway.

20.5 Paradise Beach Park; picnic facilities, rest rooms, snack bar.

21.2 Canova Beach town limits.

21.7 End of bike lane. The road is narrow now. There's a park on the right with rest rooms, and a large shopping center is on the left.

22.8 Bicentennial Beach Park; picnic facilities.

23.0 Satellite Beach city limits.

23.8 Pelican Beach Park; picnic facilities, rest rooms. There are numerous markets as you continue.

26.9 Junction with Hwy. 404. Enter Patrick Air Force Base, an Eastern Space and Missile Center.

28.4 Bike lane on the left, just past the central entrance to Patrick Air Force Base.

30.2 Bike lane ends.

30.8 Picnic tables and rest rooms on the right.

32.3 Cocoa Beach city limits; motels, restaurants, markets. A favorite with families, the beaches here are among the world's safest, as they slope at a gradual angle into the sea. While in town, be sure to ride on over to the Cocoa Beach Pier.

35.0 Bike lane on the right.

36.3 Fischer Park; picnic facilities, rest rooms.

37.4 Junction with Hwy. 520. Turn right, toward the beach, then left in 0.1 mile on Ocean Beach Blvd., which turns into Ridgewood Ave. along the way. Look for the Cocoa Beach Pier about 0.5 mile to the north after turning onto Ocean Beach Blvd. Stretching 800 feet over the Atlantic, the pier features restaurants and gift shops, and is a popular fishing spot, with bait, tackle, and fishing poles available. This is the last place for food before reaching Jetty Park.

38.4 Avon by the Sea.

38.9 Cape Canaveral city limits.

39.9 Cherie Down Park, a 5-acre facility; picnic areas, showers, rest rooms.

40.2 Turn left on Central; there's a bike lane now.

40.7 Make a right on N. Atlantic.

41.4 From the George J. King Blvd. junction, follow the bike lane and sign to Jetty Park.

41.9 Jetty Park is a scenic 35-acre Brevard County park offering picnic facilities and all camping services, including a laundromat and a market.

Jetty Park to Cape Kennedy KOA (38.2 miles)

Portions of the flat road from Jetty Park to the Cape Kennedy KOA Kampground can be very busy, but there are quiet places to pedal as well, places where moss-covered trees dip toward the earth, uncrowded roads where cars rarely pass by.

Today's segment is a short one, leaving plenty of time for interested cyclists to spend a few hours or more at NASA Kennedy Space Center's

Spaceport USA. Whether you have some curiosity about space or not, you may want to visit this popular attraction. There's an excellent IMAX film, *The Dream Is Alive,* that you won't want to miss. It includes footage shot by NASA astronauts in space. Also, there are interesting exhibits and a variety of bus tours. Admission is free and includes all exhibits, both indoors and outdoors, but there's a charge for the IMAX presentation and the bus tours. Spaceport USA is open every day except Christmas.

Afterward, you'll pass through Titusville and several small towns as you head to the Cape Kennedy KOA.

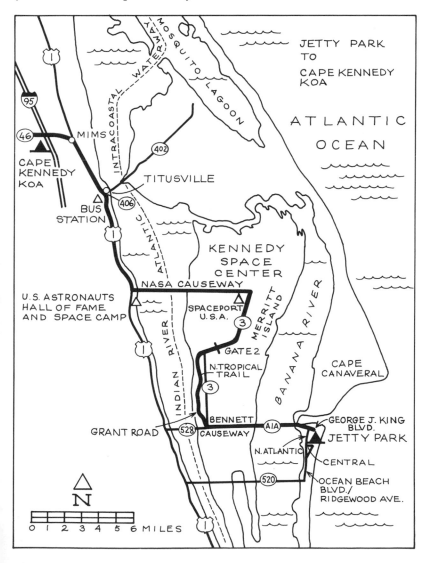

MILEAGE LOG

0.0 From Jetty Park, head back via the bike lane to George J. King Blvd., a four-lane, shoulderless road, reached in 0.5 mile; make a right.

1.6 Go left in 100 yards or so to Hwy. A-1-A/Hwy. 528. Turn right. There's a good shoulder now. As you continue, cross the Banana River via the Bennett Causeway.

6.8 Exit SR 3 (go right) toward Spaceport USA. SR 3 is very narrow with no shoulders. Traffic is heavy.

7.4 Make a left on Grant Rd.

7.8 Go right on N. Tropical Trail, an uncrowded two-lane road where groves of citrus and moss-covered trees decorate the landscape.

12.7 Head left, now traveling on SR 3 again.

14.4 Enter Gate 2 to the John Kennedy Space Center. There's a rest room on the right. The road improves to a four-lane highway.

14.6 Begin traveling through the Merritt Island National Wildlife Refuge on the Kennedy Space Center. The refuge is home to alligators—of which there are currently more than 4,000—roseate spoonbills, American bald eagles, loggerhead sea turtles, raccoons, armadillos, and bobcats. Gentle manatees are found in the waters surrounding Merritt Island. The main portion of the Merritt Island National Wildlife Refuge is located east of Titusville via Hwys. 406 and 402.

17.9 Go left on the NASA Causeway, following the signs to Spaceport USA.

18.8 Entrance to Spaceport USA; parking area is approximately 0.2 mile away. There are bike racks available near the entrance or you might be able to store your bikes in the free pet kennel. From this point on, the NASA Causeway can be extremely busy. Riding the grass shoulder is safer, although slower.

21.9 Leaving Merritt Island National Wildlife Refuge.

23.7 Cross the Indian River via the NASA Causeway, which bears a shoulder. The shoulder ends when the bridge ends, however.

25.1 U.S. Astronauts Hall of Fame and Space Camp on the left. At the Astronauts Hall of Fame, you'll see films of actual flights, interviews with various astronauts, and memorabilia showcasing America's first astronauts from their early training days to their historic missions during NASA's Mercury programs. Space Camp is a place where children, grades 4 through 7, can get hands-on astronaut training.

25.4 Turn right on US 1; there's a shoulder now.

29.2 William J. Manzo Park, located along the Indian River; picnic facilities, rest rooms.

30.8 US 1 forks to two one-way roads. There's no shoulder, but lanes are wide in Titusville.

Saturn V rocket, Spaceport USA

31.9 Greyhound bus station on the left. Sand Point Park on the right; picnic facilities, rest rooms. (There are plenty of stores, restaurants, and motels along most of US 1 to this point, then they begin to fade out.)

35.3 Mims city limits.

36.3 Junction with Hwy. 46. Turn left on Hwy. 46, passing a store and market before crossing under I-95 in 1.6 miles, where there's another market/deli.

38.2 Cape Kennedy KOA Kampground entrance. This full-service, privately owned campground offers shady or sunny sites, a recreation room, a laundromat, and a market. There are also Kamping Kabins.

Cape Kennedy KOA to Nova Family Campground (40.3 miles)

This portion of Highway A-1-A North is quite different from that traveled in the south, although it is still tortilla-flat. Instead of passing by sky-reaching hotels and condominiums, however, the road proceeds through lush pastures and several small towns, then continues on to Port Orange.

Occasional shoulders and wide lanes make life easier for some of the ride. Upon entering Port Orange, however, traffic is heavy, requiring extra caution. Fortunately, this segment ends at a quiet campground.

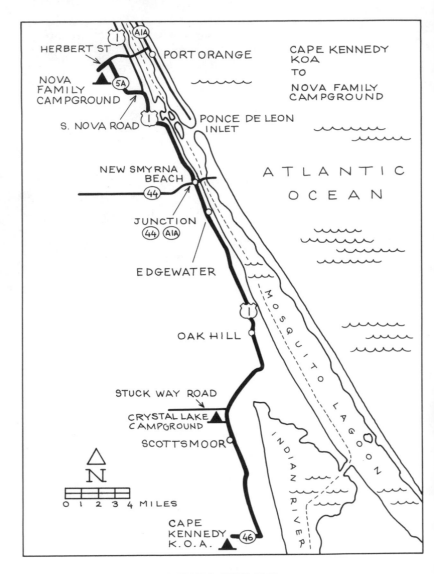

MILEAGE LOG

0.0   From Cape Kennedy KOA, head back to US 1 on Hwy. 46.

1.9   Junction of Hwy. 46 and US 1. There's a fabulous restaurant here with the biggest "small" pizzas you've ever seen. Delicious french-breadlike crusts melt in your mouth. Turn left on US 1, a four-lane highway with no shoulders. Pass two markets as you head north.

8.1   Scottsmoor city limits.

9.3   Motel and food store.

10.4   Junction with Stuck Way Rd. (formerly Hwy. 5A). **SIDE TRIP:** Privately owned Crystal Lake Campground is located to the left in 0.7 mile. Although there's little shade, you will find a pool, a laundromat, and all other services, and it's quiet. There's a convenience store nearby.

16.0   Oak Hill city limits.

17.4   There's a couple of convenience stores in this area.

17.9   There's a shoulder now. Later it ends, but the road remains wide. Just ahead is a place where you can buy souvenirs and see two live alligators.

20.2   Groceries, picnic tables, water on the right.

23.3   Edgewater city limits. As you proceed, there are plenty of markets and shops now.

28.1   New Smyrna Beach city limits.

29.4   Junction with Hwy. 44/Hwy. A-1-A. Keep straight on US 1.

29.7   Another Hwy. 44 junction; stay on US 1. **SIDE TRIP:** A visitor center is located to the right 0.3 mile on Hwy. 44. There's a bike shop en route through downtown.

31.6   Head out of town. The road narrows, and there's no shoulder.

34.8   First of three Spruce Creek crossings.

Brown pelicans

36.6 Junction with Hwy. 5A (S. Nova Rd.). Make a left on Hwy. 5A. The road begins with a wide shoulder, then narrows. Use caution.

37.3 Port Orange city limits; restaurant nearby.

39.9 Intersection. Make a left on Herbert St., riding the bike lane to the campground. There's a convenience store at this junction.

40.3 Nova Family Campground. Sites are shady at this privately owned, full-service campground. There's a laundromat as well.

Nova Family Campground to Anastasia State Park (60.2 miles)

Once out of Port Orange and back along the coast, you'll pedal for miles past enormous hotels, budget motels, and a wide array of restaurants and shops.

You'll pass the pier at famous Daytona Beach. Ride your bike on the sand if you like; it's as hard as stone. Nearby, the Daytona Speedway awaits a future race. The races began on the beach in 1902, when early auto pioneers topped out at speeds of 57 mph. Today they race around the oval track at more than 200 mph!

Afterward, you'll cycle through a peaceful landscape where homes and cars are few and far between. The road is always flat, often narrow, but usually not too busy. Ride along the beach for miles, where reddish orange sand paints a new and unique picture and pelicans glide in the wind, diving offshore.

Visit Washington Oaks Gardens, Marineland, and Fort Matanzas and end the day at beautiful Anastasia State Park.

MILEAGE LOG

0.0 From Nova Family Campground, head back to the intersection of Herbert St./S. Nova Rd. (Hwy. 5A) in 0.4 mile. Continue straight on Herbert St., a narrow road.

1.9 Make a right on US 1.

2.1 Go left on Hwy. A-1-A.

2.6 Begin crossing the Congressman William V. Chappel Jr. Bridge over the Halifax River (Atlantic Intracoastal Waterway). There's a shoulder over the bridge, which tops out at about 75 feet.

3.3 Keep left on Hwy. A-1-A. The road is four lanes, plenty wide for riding. Accommodations are many as you ride through Daytona Beach Shores.

7.8 Lanes narrow.

8.9 Junction with US 92 West to Deland.

9.3 Intersection with Main St., Daytona Beach. **SIDE TRIP:** Go right if you'd like to walk the pier, ride the boardwalk, shop, eat, et cetera.

Cyclist riding on the sand at Daytona Beach

12.3 Ormond Beach. Amenities are many.

14.1 Junction with Hwy. 40. There are quite a few beach access areas as you head north. After the junction, the road narrows to two lanes with no shoulder.

14.8 Sidewalk/bike lane on the left as you travel through residential areas now.

16.6 Hwy. A-1-A sports a shoulder now. There are motels and other services in this vicinity.

17.8 Ormond-by-the-Sea on the left. There are outhouses in the parking area.

18.3 Ocean Village Camper Resort, a private campground, is located across the street from the beach. They have a laundromat in addition to all the usual amenities.

18.9 Market on the left as the road continues for miles along the shore. The two-lane road is narrow, however, and shoulderless as well.

21.6 North Peninsula State Recreation Area. Look for strings of pelicans as you continue through this area rich in native vegetation and reddish orange sand.

24.4   Flagler Beach State Recreation Area begins and North Peninsula State Recreation Area ends.

25.0   Shoulder now.

25.3   Flagler Beach Campground entrance on the left. There's a picnic area on the west side of the highway, bathrooms and campsites on the east side.

25.7   End of shoulder.

27.1   Shoulder again, but it disappears, reappears, then disappears as you continue north. There are restaurants and motels in the area.

30.6   Beverly Beach city limits.

30.7   There are two private campgrounds near here, both located across the street from the beach. The first, Singing Surf, offers all services, including a laundromat and a limited supply of groceries. Just beyond is Picnickers Campground, with reduced rates for bicyclists. They're a full-service campground with a laundromat.

31.6   Beverly Beach, a private camp on the right. This full-service facility has a laundromat, a restaurant, and a store on the premises.

32.1   Flagler-by-the-Sea Campground, a full-service, privately owned camp on the right. Enter Painters Hill just beyond.

34.6   Hammock; continue through a residential area. The highway is still narrow, heading inland now and away from the ocean.

36.6   Junction to I-95 and the Palm Coast. There's a couple of little eating places and a motel as you travel along this area.

38.4   A sweet shop on the right. They have yogurt, ice cream, and delicious sausage dogs. Bing's Campground is across the street; services unknown. There's a pizza stand just down the road as you continue.

40.8   Turnoff to Washington Oaks State Gardens. A short **SIDE TRIP** to the gardens is possible by going left, pedaling 0.5 mile or so to a beautiful formal garden. You'll find picnic facilities and rest rooms as well. Washington Oaks State Gardens extends from the Atlantic Ocean to the Matanzas River, preserving 390 acres of Florida's original coastal scenery. This includes a stratum of coquina rock, boulders, tide pools, coastal scrub, lush coastal hammock, and tidal marshes. Also known for its camellias, roses, and azaleas, the garden boasts exotic plants from around the world. May is the best time to visit.

41.5   Granda Campground, a private facility located on the beach to the right, offers all services.

42.8   Marineland city limits.

43.0   Marineland's Yogi Bear Camp-Resort on the left. Situated next to Marineland, a marine park where whales and dolphins frolic, the privately owned, full-service campground offers a laundromat, a limited supply of groceries, and a trail leading to the beach.

44.3   Bridge crossing. As you head north, you'll travel through a scenic area where homes are built on stilts.

44.9 Pedal into the town of Summer Haven.

45.5 Another bridge crossing.

45.9 Market on the right.

46.0 Cross the Claude Varn Bridge over the Matanzas River, entering Fort Matanzas National Monument upon reaching land.

47.0 Fort Matanzas, a 298-acre park, is located on two islands—Rattlesnake Island, where the fort rests, and Anastasia Island, on which you are now bicycling. The visitor center is also on Anastasia Island. The fort, once a small Spanish outpost, is accessible by boat only, with ferry crossings made daily except for Tuesdays. Built in 1740, the fort's primary purpose was to prevent enemy vessels from passing through this inlet, which ultimately leads to St. Augustine. The fort served that purpose until 1821, when it became the property of the United States.

50.7 Crescent Beach. There's a market as you head north.

53.3 Shoulder begins.

54.5 Ocean Grove, a private camp resort offering all services, on the left.

54.6 St. Augustine Beach city limits.

55.0 Junction with Hwy. 3 to the left. Keep to the right on Hwy. A-1-A. Shoulder ends.

Rose at Washington Oaks State Garden

57.3 Visitor information center at the pier to your right. The road is narrow as you pedal to St. Augustine.
58.3 Fork; go right on Hwy. A-1-A North to historical St. Augustine. The road is four wide lanes now.
59.3 St. Augustine city limits.
59.8 Turnoff to Anastasia State Park. Go right; the entrance booth is reached in 0.4 mile. **ALTERNATE ROUTE:** If you'd rather stay in town for the night, there are motels and a youth hostel (it's open all year); continue straight to St. Augustine. The St. Augustine AYH is about 3 miles away, at 32 Treasury St., St. Augustine, FL 32084; (904) 829-6163.
60.2 Anastasia State Park. You'll find an all-service campground, with hiking trails, fishing, and swimming opportunities. Special features include lovely sand dunes and abundant birdlife.

Anastasia State Park to Fort Clinch State Park (67.2 miles)

Although narrow roads are often found on this segment, it is nonetheless pure pleasure. From Anastasia, you'll pedal a couple of miles to St. Augustine, a definite must-see. The oldest permanent European settlement in the continental United States, St. Augustine has so much to see and do that you might want to spend a day or two or even more. Most of the historical town is open every day except Christmas.

Ride north of St. Augustine and you'll travel through miles of sparse residential homes and the undeveloped lands of Florida's state parks. Look closely, and you may see cardinals, mockingbirds, armadillos, nighthawks, raccoons, and fox.

Crowds reappear as you reach Jacksonville Beach. If you don't need supplies, however, you can travel along residential roads. If you need some supplies, then it's onto busy Highway A-1-A for you. There's a bike lane for a portion of the ride as you head north. Although there's little commercial truck traffic, expect a considerable amount of traffic on the weekends.

Before reaching the ferry across the St. Johns River, the road narrows. Although it'll be hard to tear yourself away from watching enormous ships making their way up Florida's longest river, you'll want to keep an eye on the highway, as Mayport Road is a main thoroughfare and often heavily congested. After crossing the river, you'll travel flat, narrow Highway A-1-A to Fernandina Island and on up to Fort Clinch State Park.

MILEAGE LOG

0.0 Entrance to Anastasia State Park. Go right on Hwy. A-1-A toward historic St. Augustine.

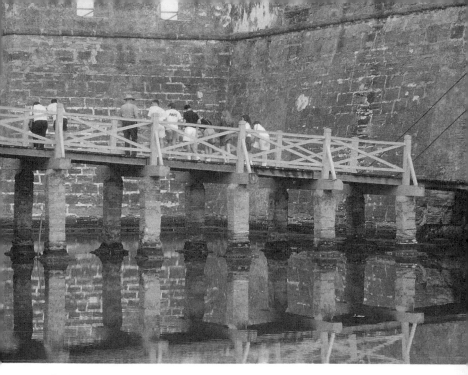

Castillo de San Marcos, St. Augustine

- **0.1** St. Augustine Alligator Farm on the left.
- **0.5** There are plenty of motels, restaurants, and stores as you continue on for the next few miles. You'll pass a couple of bike shops as well.
- **1.5** Begin crossing the Bridge of the Lions over the Matanzas River.
- **1.8** End of the bridge and beginning of historic St. Augustine. After crossing the bridge, keep right on Hwy. A-1-A, pedaling past Castillo de San Marcos, a fort built by the Spanish in 1672–95. Constructed of coquina, a native shell stone, the walls are 33 feet high and 14 feet thick. Surrounded by a moat, the fort is a definite must-see. **SIDE TRIP:** If you want to explore the city, you can do so and come back to this location when you're ready to ride on. Although you'll need to pay a fee to visit many of the attractions, some are free and much of the time the cost is minimal. If nothing else, you can always cycle up and down the narrow streets, admiring the distinctive architecture of the various buildings, including Flagler College and the Basilica-Cathedral of St. Augustine. Visit the Oldest House, built more than 250 years ago; see the Oldest Store, where you can buy snacks and other items; take a scenic cruise around Matanzas Bay, or store your bike and relax during one of many narrated sightseeing train tours or a horse-drawn carriage tour.
- **2.3** Extensive visitor information center on the left; Ripley's Believe It

Memorial Presbyterian Church, St. Augustine

or Not on the right. Ripley's is a collection of art, oddities, and curiosities.

- **2.8** Mission of Nombre de Dios on the right. This mission was not only the first in the United States, but the site of the nation's first Mass in 1565.
- **3.2** Keep right on Hwy. A-1-A North, heading out of town now. No services.
- **3.9** Vilano Beach; rest rooms, picnic facilities.
- **4.2** Begin crossing Atlantic Intracoastal Waterway.
- **4.8** Back on land; motels, restaurants, and markets are in the area.
- **5.1** Hwy. A-1-A curves to the left. End of motels.
- **5.6** Small park on the right next to the beach; picnic facilities, rest rooms.
- **7.6** North Beach, a private camp resort, offers all services, including a swimming pool.
- **8.5** South Ponte Vedra Beach city limits.
- **10.4** South Ponte Vedra Beach; picnic facilities, rest rooms.
- **12.6** Market on the left.
- **12.8** Access to Guana River State Park is to the left. A dirt road leads to the river.
- **17.1** Guana River State Park South Beach Use Area; outhouses in the parking area.
- **18.9** Guana River Wildlife Management Area on the left; great view of the river/marsh.

19.4 Guana River State Park North Beach Use Area; outhouses.

22.4 Junction with Hwy. 203. Hwy. A-1-A takes off to the left; keep to the right on Hwy. 203.

29.2 Fork; stay on Ponte Vedra Blvd.

29.6 Make a right on 1st St. S.; there's a bike lane now.

30.5 Go left on 19th Ave. S. **ALTERNATE ROUTE**: If you don't need any supplies, you can stay on 1st St. S., riding to Atlantic Blvd. and merging back onto the main route at the 34.9-mile mark.

30.6 Intersection. Just across the street is a grocery store and other shops. Go right on Hwy. A-1-A North, also called 3rd St. S. There are motels, restaurants, markets, and a couple of bike shops in the Jacksonville Beach area.

30.9 Bike lane disappears, but lanes remain wide.

33.6 Neptune Beach city limits.

34.8 Junction of Hwy. A-1-A and Atlantic Blvd. Go right on Atlantic, now traveling through a residential area of Atlantic Beach.

34.9 Go left on Ocean Blvd.

35.4 Make a left on 7th St.

35.5 Pedal right on East Coast Dr.

35.6 Head left on Plaza Rd., then continue straight.

36.7 Turn right on Mayport Rd., which is Hwy. A-1-A North. The highway is six lanes now, with no shoulder.

37.1 Road narrows to four lanes with no shoulder.

38.3 Fork; head left toward Mayport, continuing on Hwy. A-1-A North, which narrows to two lanes.

41.8 St. Johns River Ferry. Service from 6:20 A.M. to 10:00 P.M. daily. Ferries leave at 30-minute intervals, usually on the hour and half-hour. Fare is 10 cents for cyclists. No rest room here or on board.

42.0 Exit the ferry and head straight to Hwy. A-1-A. There's a convenience store across the street as you head north (right).

44.2 Cross a bridge.

44.3 Little Talbot State Park begins.

47.1 Entrance to Little Talbot State Park is on the right, the campground is across the street to the left via a dirt road. **SIDE TRIP:** Those with camping in mind should register at the entrance booth, about 0.2 mile to the right. Encompassing more than 2,500 acres of land, Little Talbot Island is but one link in a chain of unique islands off the northeastern coast of Florida. Many species of animal life make their home in and along the tidal creeks that meander through acres of extensive salt marshes. The full-facility campground and nearby picnic area offer more than 5 miles of beautiful beach, nature trails, and more.

48.1 Big Talbot Island State Park; picnic facilities on the left.

51.2 Big Talbot Island State Park day-use entry on the right. A dirt road leads to the park.

Cyclist boarding the St. Johns River Ferry

52.0 Cross a small bridge.

52.4 Begin crossing the Alexander G. "Sandy" McArthur and the Herbert Wm. "Heimey" Fishler Bridge. There's a grand view of the Nassau River from this point.

53.1 End of bridge; outhouses on the right. Horse stables are just ahead on the right.

55.6 Amelia Island Plantation, a private resort; the public is invited to visit its gift shops.

56.9 Convenience store.

57.9 Amelia City. There are a few restaurants here.

58.3 Hwy. A-1-A North curves to the right. Two markets dot the junction.

59.2 Peter Point Beachfront Park to the right; picnic facilities, rest rooms.

61.0 Junction with Hwy. 105B; motels, restaurants, markets.

64.1 Intersection. Turn left on Atlantic Ave. There's a couple of convenience stores here, as well as a few motels and a restaurant. Also,
there's an ocean-front park with picnic facilities and rest rooms.

64.2 Fort Clinch State Park entrance on the right. Fee booth is just
ahead. There are two types of camping at the 1,086-acre park: the
full-service campground is situated in the trees near Cumberland
Sound; beach camping is 2.9 miles away and consists of open
sites near the beach. A boardwalk leads over sand dunes to the
water. There are full facilities, including fruit juice and pop machines and a laundromat. A nearby pier is only 0.8 mile away.
The fort and full-service camping are about the same distance
from the fee booth. Along the way you'll pedal under a canopy
of live oaks as you travel past the Willow Pond Nature Trail,
where you might see alligators and various wading birds.

67.2 Either camp would put you at about this mileage. Fort Clinch is a
short distance from the full-service campground. A wonderful
place to visit, the fort is open daily. There are machines with pop,
juice, and snacks, as well as rest rooms and a gift shop. At Fort
Clinch, you'll learn about life at the fort through a living history
program wherein rangers (one or two a day) dress in the typical
Union garb of the 1864 garrison soldier and go about their daily
tasks of cooking meals or maintaining and guarding the fort. Pre-
tend it's 1864 and feel free to ask questions to your heart's content. On a special note, the first weekend of every month there
are civil war reenactments wherein rangers dress in proper attire
and cook, set up camp, et cetera.

Fort Clinch State Park to Jekyll Island State Park (74.9 miles)

Old town Fernandina Beach lies 3 miles west of Fort Clinch State Park,
so you'll want to leave the park around midmorning if exploring historic
downtown is on your agenda. Another possibility would be spending an
extra day at Fort Clinch and pedaling into town for the day.

Unfortunately, heavy truck traffic plagues Highway A-1-A as you
head south, then west to Yulee. Once you begin cycling US 17, however, you'll find the roadway is lined with trees and traffic is light.

Enter Georgia, the largest state east of the Mississippi, where you'll
travel along the uncrowded back lanes of time through small, quiet
towns. In fact, some towns are so small they don't even sport a market.

An excellent side trip leaves US 17 via Highway 40 and leads to historic St. Marys, a quiet southern town where time seems to stand still.
St. Marys is also the jumping-off point for those intent on exploring
nearby Cumberland Island.

If you opt for the side trip to St. Marys/Cumberland Island, you'll

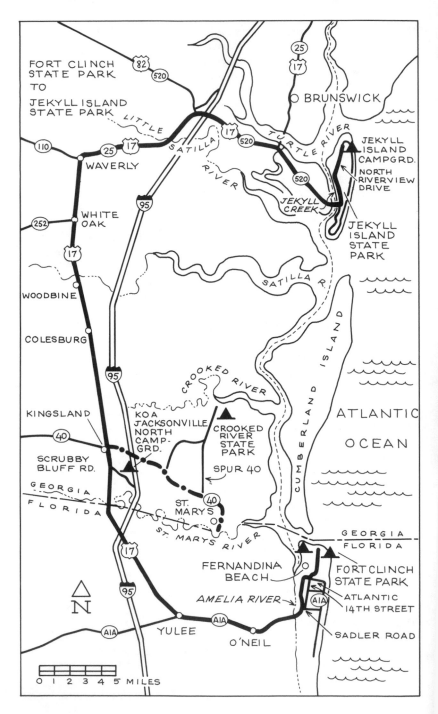

FORT CLINCH
STATE PARK
TO
JEKYLL ISLAND
STATE PARK

82
520

LITTLE

O BRUNSWICK

25
17

17
520

TURTLE RIVER

JEKYLL
ISLAND
CAMPGRD.

NORTH
RIVERVIEW
DRIVE

110
25
17
WAVERLY

SATILLA

RIVER

95

520

JEKYLL
CREEK

JEKYLL
ISLAND
STATE
PARK

252
WHITE
OAK

17

SATILLA R.

WOODBINE

COLESBURG

95

CROOKED RIVER

CUMBERLAND ISLAND

ATLANTIC

OCEAN

KINGSLAND

40
SCRUBBY
BLUFF RD.

KOA
JACKSONVILLE
NORTH
CAMP-
GRD.

CROOKED
RIVER
STATE
PARK

SPUR 40

40

GEORGIA
FLORIDA

ST.
MARYS

ST. MARYS RIVER

GEORGIA
FLORIDA

17

FERNANDINA
BEACH

FORT CLINCH
STATE PARK

N

AMELIA RIVER

A1A

ATLANTIC
14TH STREET

SADLER ROAD

A1A

95

A1A

YULEE

O'NEIL

0 1 2 3 4 5 MILES

probably want to spend the night some place other than Jekyll Island, as your daily total would be close to 100 miles. Crooked River State Park would probably be your best bet. If you take the St. Marys turnoff at the 26.6-mile mark, and cycle to St. Marys and back to Crooked River State Park, you'd do so in less than 50 miles. The next day's ride to Jekyll Island would total about 63 miles. Another alternative includes camping on Cumberland Island, although you won't be able to bicycle to your campsite. Bikes are prohibited and all travel must be done on foot.

If you forego seeing St. Marys and Cumberland Island, the long day's ride ends via a wide road leading to popular Jekyll Island, one of Georgia's barrier-island gems and a winter retreat for the Goodyears, Rockefellers, Pulitzers, and other elite families from 1886 until the beginning of World War II. Known as the Golden Isles, these offshore islands, dense with pines and palms, form a golden chain nearly 100 miles long and are enjoyed today by many.

MILEAGE LOG

0.0 Entrance to Fort Clinch State Park. Continue riding west on Hwy. A-1-A; there's a wide lane for riding now.

0.9 Road narrows to a small shoulder.

1.3 Convenience store on the right.

1.4 Hwy. A-1-A heads to the left now. You might want to visit the quaint town of Fernandina Beach before continuing on. There's a bike shop just past the corner.

2.1 The highway is now four lanes and narrow, with heavy truck traffic. **ALTERNATE ROUTE**: If you'd rather skip seeing downtown Fernandina, opting instead to pedal a quieter road, you might consider riding 14th St. Before turning left onto 8th St. (Hwy. A-1-A), turn left onto 14th St., then go right on Sadler Rd., eventually merging back onto Hwy. A-1-A.

3.4 There are many eating establishments in this area; you'll find all the usuals and convenience stores, too.

5.3 Begin crossing a bridge over the Amelia River. There's a shoulder over the bridge and a gorgeous view of the river valley.

5.9 End of bridge; the road narrows again.

7.2 O'Neil, a tiny town.

12.2 Bike path on the right.

13.0 Intersection. Turn right on US 17 in the town of Yulee. There are markets and restaurants here.

13.3 Motel on the right. The road narrows to two lanes with no shoulder. Traffic is usually light, however.

20.0 Cross under I-95; there are a couple of convenience stores, and a restaurant and motel.

20.5 There's a shoulder now.

22.2 Rest area on the left; picnic facilities, rest rooms.

22.4 Cross a narrow bridge over the St. Marys River.

22.5 Welcome to Georgia! Shoulder ends.

25.2 Junction with Scrubby Bluff Rd. **SIDE TRIP:** Turn right on Scrubby Bluff for less than 2 miles to KOA Jacksonville North Campground located near I-95. There are all services, including a laundromat, limited groceries, a swimming pool, and a game room.

25.6 Little Catfish Creek Park on the left; picnic facilities.

26.0 Town of Kingsland, elevation 35 feet, and the high elevation point of the day! There are motels, restaurants, markets, and a laundromat.

26.6 Junction with Hwy. 40. See "Side Trip to St. Marys" at the end of this segment. If you've decided to skip the trip to St. Marys, continue straight. The road is two lanes with narrow shoulders but uncrowded (I-95 carries the bulk of the traffic). As you pedal along, you'll travel through a region of slow-moving streams bordered by wide swamps and woods, with homes scattered here and there.

28.0 Convenience store.

28.8 Cross the Crooked River.

29.2 Cross North Fork Creek.

34.5 There's a shoulder now.

35.1 Colesburg, a town with no services.

35.8 Cross Walker Swamp.

37.1 Woodbine, site of Georgia's Crawfish Festival. There are restaurants and a laundromat.

38.6 Motel on the left.

38.8 Bridge over the Satilla River. There's a park with rest rooms just before the bridge.

39.8 Road on the left leads 2.8 miles to Refuge Plantation on the Satilla River. At one time it was one of the largest rice plantations in the south.

40.7 Cross Tower Swamp.

42.8 White Oak; no services.

43.0 Junction with Hwy. 252 to Folkston.

46.2 Cross Little Waverly Creek.

46.6 Cross Waverly Creek.

47.4 Junction with Hwy. 110. Waverly; convenience store.

53.7 Market on the right.

54.7 Cross Little Satilla River.

57.3 Junction with US 82/US 17/Hwy. 520. There's a market here as well. Turn right on US 17 North/Hwy. 520 East. There's a wide shoulder. (Special note: If using a map dated prior to 1988, US 82 may be listed as US 84.)

58.0 Travel under I-95. Stores, motels, fast food, and restaurants are in the area.

63.4 Junction with US 17 and Hwy. 520. Head right on Hwy. 520, riding the Jekyll Island Causeway to Jekyll Island. The shoulder narrows, but it's adequate as you cross an enormous saltwater marsh. Look for wood storks and various shorebirds, and watch for crushed turtles on the roadway as you pedal along. If you see a live turtle, you may want to stop and help it off the road, leaving it on the side of the road to which it was heading. Be careful, though, as turtles can bite.

67.8 Welcome center on the left. Maps, information, cold water, rest rooms, and a limited selection of gifts are available here.

69.4 Hwy. 520 ends as you begin crossing the M. E. Thompson Bridge over Jekyll Creek (Atlantic Intracoastal Waterway) to Jekyll Island, one of the finest resort islands on the Atlantic Coast.

70.0 Junction with Ben Fortson Pkwy./N. Riverview Dr. Turn left on N. Riverview Dr.

70.5 Head left at the fork, hugging Jekyll Creek while en route past the historic district, where you'll see the grand old Jekyll Island Club. Upon exploring the historic district, you'll want to make one of your first stops at the Museum Orientation Center on Stable Rd. The center offers a slide show depicting Jekyll Island's

Cyclist riding around Jekyll Island

history and you can purchase tickets for a tour of the village's restored homes. Eight of the thirty-two buildings still in existence are open for inspection.

71.8 Bike path begins now, with great views of the vast salt marsh.

74.0 Site of Georgia's first brewery on the left. Constructed by Major Horton, an aide to General Oglethorpe, Georgia's founder, the tabby ruins once supplied ale to troops and settlers at Fort Frederica on St. Simons Island. (Made of lime, sand, or gravel, and oyster shells, tabby was a cement used primarily along the Georgia and South Carolina Coast in the seventeenth and eighteenth centuries.)

74.9 Jekyll Island Campground on the right, Clam Creek Picnic Area on the left. Sites are shaded by regal, moss-covered live oaks and pines. This 18-acre, full-service campground offers a laundromat and a limited supply of groceries as well. As for other accommodations, island motels are a bit on the expensive side, although there are some moderately priced motels if you check around. Check at the visitor center for discount coupons, too. Also, there are many fine restaurants. The nearest market to the campground is 4.6 miles away as you wind around the island in a clockwise direction. Golf, tennis, jogging, beachcombing, shopping, and, of course, biking are all popular activities for island visitors. If you'd like to explore the island, you'll find 20 miles of paved biking/jogging trails.

Side Trip to St. Marys

0.0 From the 26.6-mile mark, turn right on Hwy. 40. The road is two lanes with no shoulder, but increases to four lanes with a small shoulder after 0.7 mile.

2.1 Pass under I-95. There are many motels, restaurants, and markets in the area now.

3.0 Camden County Library on the left.

4.4 Junction with road to Crooked River State Park on the left (one of two roads leading to the park).

7.5 Dark Entry Creek crossing.

7.8 More motels and food places in this area.

8.0 Junction with Spur 40, which leads to Crooked River State Park, located about 7 miles to the north. Located on the south bank of the Crooked River, facilities include an Olympic pool and bathhouse, tent sites, cottages, and a hiking trail.

9.6 St. Marys Public Library on the right.

10.0 Road narrows to two wide lanes.

10.9 Begin historic area of St. Marys.

11.0 Visitor center on the right. Also there's a First Presbyterian Church, which was built in 1808 and is one of the oldest churches in St. Marys and the oldest currently in use.

11.4   St. Marys River. Pass the a hotel/restaurant and two bed-and-breakfasts just before. This is the only lodging available in the historic area. St. Marys is also the take-off point for those interested in ferrying across to Cumberland Island National Seashore, established October 23, 1972. Ferries run daily from March 15 through September 30; daily except Tuesday and Wednesdays from October 1 through March 14. Cost is $7.50 for a round-trip ticket. Visitors may explore both beach and live-oak forest, and observe local animal life, but all must be done on foot. Vehicles, including bicycles, are not allowed. There are no stores on the island so you will have to bring food, insect repellent, and other necessities. Camping is allowed at developed campgrounds and several primitive backcountry sites. Whether you decide to camp overnight or explore the island for the day, you're bound to see an abundance of animal life. Eighteen miles long, Cumberland Island and the salt marsh that hugs its western, northern, and southern shores is home to many wading birds, including herons, egrets, wood storks, and ibises. On the eastern or Atlantic side, vast beaches invite female loggerhead turtles to come ashore in summer to lay their eggs.

Jekyll Island State Park to South Newport Campground (54.7 miles)

A bike path leads you back to the mainland, but in Brunswick all shoulders quickly disappear. Fortunately, US 17 isn't too crowded if ridden before or after the summer months, although caution is advised.

US 17 is grooved in some spots, so expect a bumpy ride at times. Although a nuisance, the road isn't grooved for the entire ride, it just seems like it.

It's a historic trip through time as you pedal US 17 through rural regions dotted with occasional homes and small towns. Pedaling through the South, you're bound to see more churches than people. If you enjoy lovely old churches, stop and admire these captivating works of art.

Other highlights include flat terrain (the norm from Florida to New Jersey), the Hofwyl-Broadfield Plantation, and Fort King George at Darien.

Located between Brunswick and Darien, the Hofwyl-Broadfield Plantation State Historic Site is a place where the evolution of a rice plantation comes to life.

Fort King George was the southernmost outpost of the British Colonies in 1721. Colonel John "Tuscarora Jack" Barnwell led his men here in 1721, at which time they constructed a cypress blockhouse, a moat, and other deterrents. The British soldiers endured incredible hardships

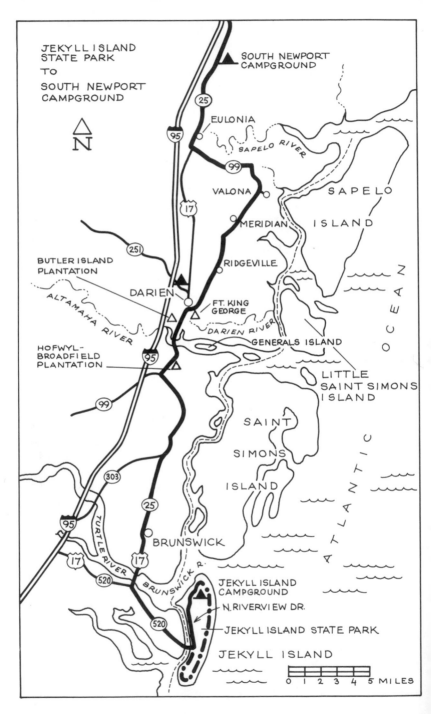

JEKYLL ISLAND
STATE PARK
TO
SOUTH NEWPORT
CAMPGROUND

N

SOUTH NEWPORT
CAMPGROUND

25

EULONIA

95

SAPELO RIVER

99

VALONA

17

MERIDIAN

SAPELO

ISLAND

251

BUTLER ISLAND
PLANTATION

RIDGEVILLE

DARIEN

FT. KING
GEORGE

ALTAMAHA RIVER

DARIEN RIVER

GENERALS ISLAND

O
C
E
A
N

95

LITTLE
SAINT SIMONS
ISLAND

HOFWYL-
BROADFIELD
PLANTATION

99

SAINT

SIMONS

ISLAND

303

25

95

17

TURTLE RIVER

17

520

BRUNSWICK

BRUNSWICK R.

A
T
L
A
N
T
I
C

JEKYLL ISLAND
CAMPGROUND

N. RIVERVIEW DR.

520

JEKYLL ISLAND STATE PARK

JEKYLL   ISLAND

0 1 2 3 4 5 MILES

from both disease and the harsh coastal environment, and the fort was abandoned after seven long years. Today, visitors view a replica of the fort, reconstructed from detailed accounts and drawings researched in the South Carolina and British public records offices.

MILEAGE LOG

0.0 From Jekyll Island State Park campground, you have two options. You can head back the way you came, or you can take a **SIDE TRIP** cruise around the perimeter of Jekyll Island. A bike path leads around much of the island. From the campground, continue in a clockwise direction along N. Beachview Dr., S. Beachview Dr., and S. Riverview Dr., back to the same junction (Ben Fortson Pkwy./N. Riverview Dr.) upon which you first entered Jekyll Island. It's approximately 10 miles around the island.

4.9 Junction with Ben Fortson Pkwy./N. Riverview Dr. Leave the island on Hwy. 520.

10.9 Junction of US 17 and Hwy. 520. Head north on US 17 toward Brunswick. The shoulder continues.

11.5 Begin crossing the Brunswick River via the Sidney Lanier Bridge, a long drawbridge with a nice view of the area.

12.3 Brunswick.

13.1 Shoulder ends; the road is four narrow lanes.

14.5 Glynn Waterfront Park on the right; picnic facilities. Markets, restaurants, and motels are in the area.

15.2 Visitor center on the right.

15.3 Junction with K St. **SIDE TRIP:** If you need a bike shop, turn left here. K St. eventually turns into L St. Go 1.2 miles to Norwich; make a right and travel 0.7 mile to the bike shop.

19.9 Junction with Hwy. 303.

20.0 Convenience store on the right.

26.4 **SIDE TRIP** leads to the Hofwyl-Broadfield Plantation State Historic Site. Turn off to the right and pedal 0.2 mile down a soft dirt road to the visitor center/museum. Founded by William Brailsford of Charleston, this once-flourishing rice plantation produced rice from the early 1800s until 1915. Hurricanes, war, and the lack of abundant labor led to the demise of the rice empire. Visitors will find a museum filled with memorabilia from a working rice plantation. A slide show describes the life of planters and slaves. Best of all, you'll walk beneath live oaks, past magnolias and camellias, to the antebellum home decorated with fine antiques.

28.0 Bridge over the Altamaha River.

28.8 James Allen Williamson Champney River Park on the right; rest rooms, picnic facilities. Cross the river just after the park.

30.2 Butler Island Plantation on the left. This scenic plantation makes for a great photo if taken in the early morning. The early to mid-nineteenth-century rice plantation was owned by Pierce Butler of Philadelphia. Of special interest is the 75-foot brick rice mill chimney, built by slaves in the 1850s. Fanny Kemble, the famous English actress, spent the winter of 1838–39 at Butler Island Plantation, writing her well-known book, *Journal of a Residence on a Georgian Plantation.* Cross another river just past the plantation.

30.8   Generals Island is visible to the east. This island was the property of General Lachlan McIntosh and his family by a grant of 1758. They lived in the home up to and during the early years of the American Revolution. The island was in rice cultivation for many years.

31.1   Bridge over the Darien River leads to historic Darien, founded in 1736.

31.4   Visitor center on the right. Stop here for a map of a self-guided walking tour of old-town Darien. The road also leads to Fort King George.

31.6   Junction with Hwy. 99. Make a right here. See the Darien Courthouse off to the right near here. Hwy. 99 leads to Fort King George as well. **SIDE TRIP:** There's a library and several motels and restaurants within 0.8 mile if you stay on US 17 at this point. Also there's a campground off I-95 and Hwy. 251, about 2 miles from this point. Darien Inland Harbor Campground offers all amenities, including a laundromat.

31.8   Grant House on the right. Thought to have been built in the 1840s, this was the only residence to have survived the destruction of the town by Union forces in 1863.

31.9   Fork; stay to the left.

32.4   **SIDE TRIP** to Fort King George State Historic Site on the right. It's a 0.6-mile ride to the three-story fort, where you'll find a museum and slide show. The historic site is closed Mondays.

34.2   Ridgeville; no services.

35.3   Road on the right leads to the Atlantic Intracoastal Waterway and the Blue N' Hall Boat Launch Area.

36.4   Small market on the left.

38.7   Meridian; convenience store, laundromat.

39.6   Road to the right leads (by boat) to Sapelo Island.

41.4   Road to the right leads to Valona; keep to the left.

44.8   Convenience store on the left.

47.6   Eulonia.

48.0   Make a right, once again traveling US 17/Hwy. 25.

48.5   Supermarket on the left, then the highway passes under some immense live oaks for a short distance.

49.1   Bridge over Sapelo River.

50.3   Market on the right.

54.7   South Newport Campground on the right. There's no shade, but tent sites are inexpensive and they have all services.

Fort King George Historic Site

South Newport Campground to Skidaway Island State Park (49.1 miles)

Today's ride continues through rural Georgia where you'll ride past seasoned homes and tiny towns. A special treat is visiting Christ Chapel, America's smallest church. While US 17 remains peaceful for the first half of the ride, traffic picks up some in Richmond Hill and continues to increase as you enter south Savannah. Roads leading to Skidaway Island State Park are also heavily trafficked. Fortunately, Skidaway Island State Park provides a pleasant respite to what may end as a rather hectic day.

You'll travel US 17 to the Savannah outskirts, where you'll head west on Highway 204, eventually riding the Diamond Causeway to Skidaway Island State Park.

Although US 17 is generally uncrowded, at least until reaching Richmond Hill, the highway is often bumpy, the result of grooved pavement. The grooves last for about 17 miles from the Interstate 95/US 17

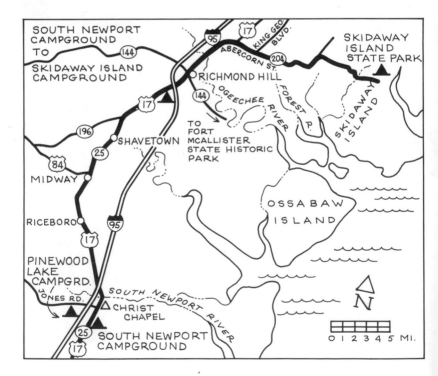

junction, just north of the campground, to the Highway 196 junction. Although a bit jarring, the bumps are bearable. The bumpiest ride of all, however, extends for about 1 mile as you pedal out of Savannah en route to Skidaway Island.

MILEAGE LOG

0.0 South Newport Campground. Continue north on US 17/Hwy. 25.

1.4 Junction to Pinewood Lake Campground. **SIDE TRIP:** To reach the campground, turn left, pedaling about 1.5 miles west on Jones Rd. It offers all services and boasts lake fishing and swimming.

1.7 Christ Chapel, the smallest church in America, on the right. Open 24 hours a day, Christ Chapel is located in little Memory Park. Constructed of whitewashed concrete blocks, the tiny church measures 10 feet by 15 feet, and seats 12 people. Stained glass windows and small pews adorn the chapel. The church, a dream of Mrs. Agnes Harper, a rural grocer, offers interdenominational worship services every third Sunday, and during the year a variety of programs are held. Sometimes, the church is even used for weddings. Mrs. Harper deeded the Little Church, as it was originally named, to Jesus Christ before her death to prevent its ever being sold.

2.1 South Newport River crossing.

2.9 Cross under I-95. The highway is grooved now. There are two convenience stores at this point.

6.4 Riceboro city limits.

9.6 Convenience store.

10.3 Cross Riceboro Creek. Picnic tables on the right.

12.1 Bridge over a creek.

14.0 Midway; restaurant on the left. Now the road is smooth again.

14.2 Junction with US 84. There are a couple of markets here. (If you're using a map dated prior to 1988, US 84 might be shown as US 82.)

14.4 Cay Creek crossing.

14.6 Motel on the right; restaurant on the left.

14.7 Lovely old church on the right with the Midway Museum just ahead on the same side of the road. The road is grooved again, with no shoulder.

15.1 Restaurant on the right.

18.7 Shavetown; no services.

20.4 Junction with Hwy. 196 to Hinesville. There's a shoulder now— no grooves.

22.3 Convenience store on the left.

24.9 Richmond Hill city limits. To the right is the Savannah KOA. If you enjoy fishing, drop a line into the KOA lake—no license required. There's also a store, an air-conditioned laundry, and all other services. Sites are shady. There are restaurants, fast-food establishments, and motels nearby.

25.6 Cross under I-95.

26.3 Road narrows to two lanes, no shoulder.

27.6 Shoulder begins. Also, this is the junction for Hwy. 144, which leads to Fort McAllister State Historic Park, 9 miles to the southeast. Sprawled along the south bank of the Great Ogeechee River, this park is "home of the best preserved earthwork fortification of the Confederacy," according to the Georgia Department of Natural Resources. It is closed on Mondays.

29.9 Cross the Ogeechee River.

30.1 Kings Ferry Park; picnic facilities, rest rooms.

32.6 Grocery store on the left.

32.9 Intersection. Turn right on Hwy. 204 East, which is also called Abercorn St. There's a wide but bumpy shoulder now.

35.0 Junction with King George Blvd.; convenience store.

37.0 Bridge over the Forest River.

37.4 Shoulder disappears. Road is six lanes and very busy. If it's terribly crowded, you can ride in the wide gutter.

38.9 Motels and food in this vicinity.

41.5 Turn right on Spur 204 East, known as Montgomery Cross Rd., following the signs to Skidaway Island. It's a narrow two-lane road with no shoulders. In the summer of 1991, Spur 204 was widened, but according to the Georgia Department of Transportation, "the project did not include bike lanes, and only isolated sections have wide shoulders or sidewalks." **ALTERNATE ROUTE**: If you'd rather skip going to Skidaway Island State Park, opting instead for a motel or continuing on to the next stop, you can continue on Hwy. 204 (Abercorn St.) at the Montgomery Cross Rd. junction. To do so, continue north on Abercorn St., which remains very busy, for about 5.7 miles. The last 0.7 mile passes through the historical district, a real treat. Go left on Liberty St. for about 0.5 mile to Martin Luther King Jr. Blvd. and the visitor center. This is the 14.2-mile mark on the next segment, Skidaway Island State Park to Kobuch's Campground.

42.9 Turn right on Spur 204 East, known as Waters Rd. This road is grooved and *very* bumpy with no shoulder. The name changes to Whitefield Ave.

43.9 Grooves end; now there's a narrow shoulder.

45.0 Fork; keep to the left on the Diamond Causeway.

45.6 Junction with Ferguson Ave. Restaurant/convenience store off to the right 0.1 mile.

46.4 Bridge over the Back River.

47.4 Skidaway Narrows Boat Ramp Park, on the right before crossing the Atlantic Intracoastal Waterway (Skidaway River).

48.4 Skidaway Island State Park. Turn left at the signed entrance to the 490-acre park. One of Georgia's barrier islands, Skidaway embraces both salt- and freshwater, which serve to support a variety of estuaries and marshes.

49.1 Information and park office. Register here. The campground is nearby and offers shaded sites with all services, including a laundromat. Also, there's a Junior Olympic swimming pool and concession stand (open Memorial Day through Labor Day) and a nature trail.

Skidaway Island State Park to Kobuch's Campground (54.1 miles)

The day begins with a trip through historic Savannah, a place definitely worthy of your time. You'll want to walk or ride the streets bordering the Savannah River (you'll probably have to walk, as the streets are made of cobblestone), explore the numerous shops, and admire the lovely antique buildings.

For those cyclists intent on using Savannah as a starting or ending point, you'll find air, train, and bus transportation in or near downtown Savannah.

From there, you'll pedal northwest before crossing the Savannah River and entering South Carolina's Low Country, a land characterized by nearly flat terrain, salt- and freshwater marshes, magnolia trees, and moss-strewn live oaks. It is also home to the Savannah National Wildlife Refuge, a place where wildlife is abundant.

After leaving the refuge, continue on through the Low Country, traveling across the scenic plains to Kobuch's Campground, a quiet site southwest of the lovely town of Beaufort.

The ride from Skidaway Island State Park to Savannah is often plagued with heavy traffic, but seeing the sights in downtown Savannah is well worth the effort. Just use caution! From Savannah, Georgia, to Beaufort, South Carolina, you'll often ride narrow roads, also heavily trafficked at times, but your reward is a beautiful ride through the Low Country.

MILEAGE LOG

0.0 From Skidaway Island State Park, begin heading back the way you came, aiming for Savannah.

3.5 Intersection of Ferguson Rd./Diamond Causeway. Turn right on Ferguson Rd. and go north. The road is two lanes and narrow, but relatively uncrowded. Pass a variety of farms before cycling into a residential area.

5.9 Turn left on Skidaway Rd. Services are plentiful from here throughout Savannah. Traffic is heavy.

11.2 Five-way intersection. Head left on Henry St., a one-way road

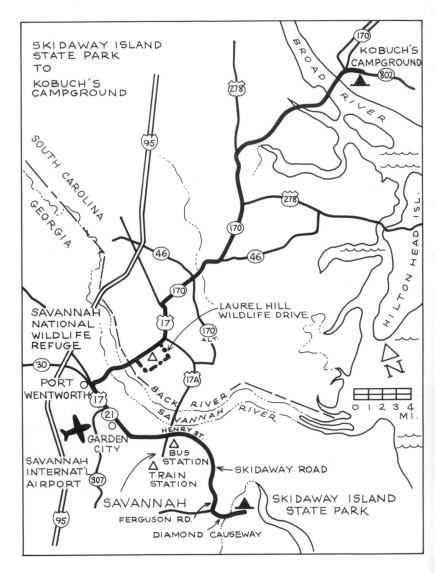

with wide lanes. It passes through a low-income neighborhood where you'll see some grand old homes.

13.4   Intersection. Make a right on Martin Luther King Jr. Blvd. (previously called and sometimes still signed W. Broad St.)

14.2   Intersection. Make a left on Louisville Rd., which is two lanes with no shoulders, but traffic is relatively light. There's a visitor center at this junction. **SIDE TRIP:** Before heading off to South Carolina, you'll undoubtedly want to cruise around downtown

Historic home in Savannah

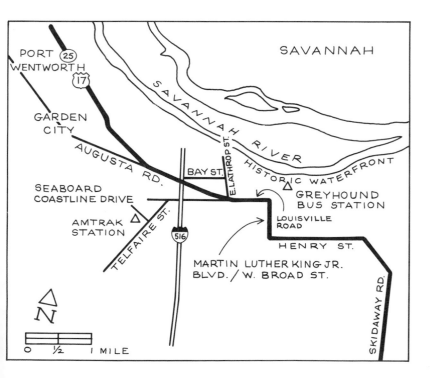

Savannah. To visit the historic waterfront, continue straight ahead 1 mile or so. You'll want to walk or pedal the 2.2-square-mile historic district, with its cobblestone streets and lovely squares. Established in 1733 by James Oglethorpe, Georgia's founder, the town was named after the river. Birthplace of the Georgia colony, Savannah was the state capital until 1786. The city was designed in squares, with twenty-one of the original twenty-four squares still intact. Decorated with a semitropical flora of azaleas, magnolias, and tall oaks, each square features a statue or monument in remembrance of one of Savannah's past heroes.

15.0 Make a right on E. Lathrop St., then go left on Augusta Rd. in about 100 yards or so.

16.1 Cross under I-516.

16.2 Turn right on US 17A North and US 80 West. In 100 yards, turn left on Bay St.

17.0 Garden City town limits; motels, restaurants, markets.

17.1 Turn right on US 17 North/Hwy. 21 North.

17.3 Turn left at the signal, staying on US 17 North. Hwy. 25 North merges together at this point. The road continues to be two lanes, with some truck traffic.

19.2 Junction with Hwy. 307.

19.4 Port Wentworth city limits; convenience store, motels, restaurants.

21.4 Junction with Hwy. 30.

22.3 Cross the James Houlihan Bridge over the Savannah River.

22.6 Enter the Savannah National Wildlife Refuge, a 25,608-acre reserve established April 6, 1927.

23.3 Cross another branch of the Savannah River.

23.8 South Carolina State Line. Welcome to South Carolina's Low Country, a stunning land of glorious open scenes and abundant wildlife, which includes bald eagles, egrets, herons, alligators, and turtles.

24.6 Savannah National Wildlife Refuge; rest rooms. **SIDE TRIP:** There's a 4-mile one-way packed-gravel drive (Laurel Hill Wildlife Dr.) that wide-tire enthusiasts are bound to enjoy. Birders will find good opportunities for pursuing their hobby (more than 260 species have been recorded on the refuge) all year, but best results are obtained from October through April, when temperatures are mild. Greatest concentrations of waterfowl exist from November through February. From March through October, you're likely to observe alligators and other reptiles.

25.8 Exit for the Laurel Hill Wildlife Dr.

26.9 Fork; go left on US 17, a four-lane, shoulderless highway. Alt. US 17 takes off to the right. Traffic is heavy.

28.5 Turn right on Hwy. 170. The road is two lanes, with no shoulder.

32.4 Junction with Hwy. 170 Alt. Keep straight on Hwy. 170. Convenience store here.

33.0 Cross the New River.

39.4 Junction with US 278, which leads to Hilton Head Island and also merges north with Hwy. 170 toward Beaufort. Keep straight.

42.2 Convenience stores, fruit stands, heavy traffic.

43.4 Keep right on Hwy. 170. US 278 continues north.

45.1 Country store on the right and another farther on down the road.

48.7 Lemon Island Marina on the left before crossing the Chechesee River via the G. G. Dowling Bridge.

51.3 Begin crossing the Broad River via the E. B. Rodgers Bridge. Although many bridges sport a slippery steel deck near the center of the bridge, this one has a particularly long steel deck and is extremely slippery when wet. There's a narrow shoulder.

53.1 Intersection. Turn right on Hwy. 802 East to Port Royal. The road is two lanes, with moderate traffic.

54.1 Kobuch's Campground on the right. Shady sites and all services are provided, with the nearest market and laundromat less than 1 mile up the road.

Kobuch's Campground to Givhans Ferry State Park (76.6 miles)

Today's trip begins with a ride through historic Beaufort, a gracious antebellum town where restored eighteenth- and nineteenth-century homes serve to form a fabulously compact historic district. Located on the banks of the Beaufort River, the town is a delightful must-see.

Upon leaving Beaufort, you'll pass vast marshlands and open fields where everything seems to be various shades of green. And later on, you'll roll past numerous fields of corn. In other words, you'll travel wide-open spaces.

Although this guide parallels the coast whenever possible, you'll head inland on several occasions due to unsafe highway conditions. South Carolina is one such place, with heavy traffic along US 17, which spans the coastline, leading to popular tourist towns like Charleston and Myrtle Beach. Reports of heavy truck use, and a highway so narrow that many motorists were complaining about driving it in a car, made the decision an easy one.

After exiting US 21, the ride is traffic-free for the most part. Travel along tree-covered Old Sheldon Church Road to the Sheldon Ruins. You'll see what remains of this church, built twice and burned down twice, once during the Revolutionary War and again during the Civil War. Later, pedal through rural South Carolina to Givhans Ferry State Park. Closed for two years after Hurricane Hugo devastated the area in September 1989, the park is once again open for business.

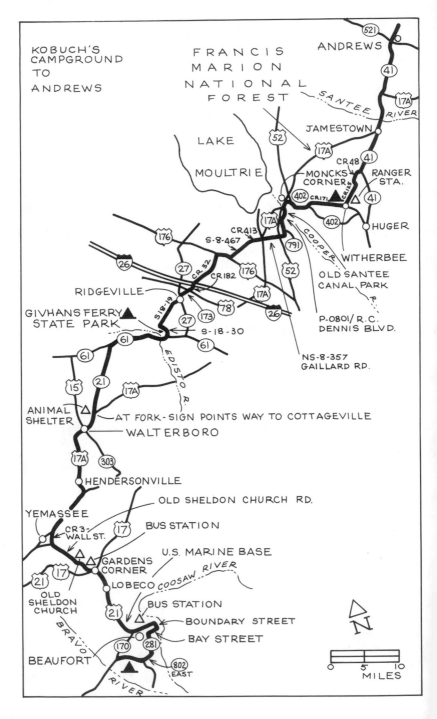

KOBUCH'S
CAMPGROUND
TO
ANDREWS

MILEAGE LOG

0.0 Kobuch's Campground. Continue to the right on Hwy. 802 East.

0.9 Market, laundromat, several restaurants. Junction with Hwy. 280 is just beyond. Traffic is heavy now.

2.2 Shopping center on the left.

2.3 Junction to Parris Island, which is just over 2 miles away.

2.4 Begin crossing Battery Creek. Enter Port Royal town limits.

3.3 Road is now four lanes; traffic is still heavy.

3.7 Market on the left.

4.9 Junction with Ladys Island Blvd. Continue straight on US 21 North/Hwy. 281. There are motels, restaurants, and markets in the area now.

5.4 Beaufort city limits.

7.6 To go through the historic district, turn right on Bay St. **ALTERNATE ROUTE**: If you'd rather skip this fascinating old town, continue north on Hwy. 281 (Ribaut Rd.) for less than 1 mile to US 21 North, the 10.1-mile mark.

8.4 Visitor center on the right. Inside you'll find a free map with a driving tour (easily adapted for cyclists) that is highly recommended. The tour pilots one past many beautiful homes and churches. There is a bike shop on Port Republic St., near the visitor center.

8.7 Ride through Beaufort and make a left on Boundary St. (US 21 North).

8.8 Library on the left.

9.6 Greyhound bus station on the right.

10.1 Junction with Ribaut Rd. Those skipping the historic part of town will rejoin this segment here.

10.9 Bike shop on the right.

11.2 Junction with Hwy. 170. Continue straight on US 21 North, passing a few motels and restaurants.

13.1 Cross Alvercotti Creek. The road continues to be four lanes; there's a grass shoulder if necessary.

13.6 Junction with Hwy. 116 West. U.S. Marine Air Base on the right.

16.1 Convenience store on the right.

16.4 Market on the left, then it's down tiny Gray's Hill, the first "real hill" of the entire Atlantic Coast ride.

18.7 Small market on the right.

19.6 Cross Whale Branch River via a shoulderless bridge.

20.2 Lobeco town limits.

21.3 Convenience store on the left.

23.9 Gardens Corner town limits.

24.1 Fork; keep to the left on US 21 North.

24.2 Stop sign. Head left on US 21 North. There's a motel, a country store, and a Greyhound bus station at the junction.

24.7 Turn right on Old Sheldon Church Rd. Now you'll enjoy a pleasant, ride along a magnificent tree-covered lane. Although the road is two lanes and narrow, traffic is light.

26.3 Ruins of the Old Sheldon Church on the right. This church,

Old Sheldon Church ruins

Prince William's Parish Church, was originally built in the years 1745–1755, but was burned down by the British in 1779. Rebuilt in 1826, it was again burned in 1865, this time by the Federal Army. Today, the ruins are the site of annual services held the second Sunday after Easter.

31.8 Yemassee town limits.

32.0 T-junction; turn right on CR 3.

32.8 Market on the left. At this point, turn right on Wall St.

33.2 Intersection. Turn right on US 17A. The road is two lanes and uncrowded. Convenience store on the corner.

35.1 Cross the Combahee River.

36.6 Market on the left.

40.3 Another market on the left.

43.0 Junction with Hwy. 303. Tiny store on the right.

44.1 Hendersonville; no services.

50.7 Walterboro city limits.

51.9 Fork; go right, continuing on US 17A. Hwy. 63 East joins the route now. The road is four lanes, with no shoulders. Traffic picks up some.

52.9 Motels, restaurants, and markets begin now.

53.1 Another junction for Hwy. 303.

53.9 Keep right on US North 17A. US 15 goes straight.

54.0 Grocery store on the right. Two wide lanes exist now.

54.7 Fork; continue left on US 17A. Hwy. 64 takes off to the right.

55.4 Bicycle shop on the left.

56.5 Look for an Industrial Area Recreation Complex sign soon after passing the airport. Next, you'll come to a fork with signs pointing to the right to Cottageville—9 miles. Go left on the unsigned road, traveling CR 21 for a wonderfully quiet ride. Although the road is two lanes and narrow, there is little traffic.

56.6 If you made the correct turn, you should be passing an animal shelter on the left now.

58.4 Convenience store on the left.

59.5 Tiny market on the right.

67.7 Intersection; go right on Hwy. 61; market on the left.

69.1 Junction with Hwy. 651.

76.1 Cross the Edisto River.

76.4 Market on the right. About 100 yards ahead, turn left on unsigned Road S-18-30. A sign, however, does point the way to Givhans Ferry State Park.

76.6 Givhans Ferry State Park. Turn left and head into the campground. The 988-acre park offers all services, although they don't have grills. There are four cabins for rent, nature trails, and fishing in the Edisto River.

Givhans Ferry State Park to Andrews (71.9 miles)

This ride is a real treat, as roads are relatively free from traffic except for a short ride on US 52 and a small stretch of US 176. Best of all, the route passes through many rural communities where the people are friendly, so much so that it's often difficult to pedal out of town once you stop for a rest or snack.

Along the way, you'll see the damage incurred by Hurricane Hugo, as downed trees still litter the area. Classified a 4, just below the most destructive hurricanes ever recorded, the 1989 hurricane was the most powerful to hit the United States in two decades, and the tenth strongest storm to hit the United States this century. As one Witherbee Ranger Station employee recounted, "Things will never be the same around here in my lifetime." Although she opted to stay home when Hurricane Hugo hit, she is prepared to leave in a second if prompted by another hurricane.

Staying in a motel or asking permission to stay in someone's yard or a local church, playground, et cetera, is recommended in Andrews, home of Chubby Checkers and the conclusion of this segment. There are markets and restaurants in town.

Unfortunately, campgrounds are nonexistent during this segment, although there is a primitive site at Little Hellhole Reserve. A dirt road leads to the one-tent site. Obtain a free use permit at the Witherbee District office, less than 1 mile away. Also, camping is allowed outside of the primitive campsite upon obtaining a free permit, also available at the district office.

If you choose to stay at Little Hellhole Reserve, however, you'll have an additional 30 miles to add to the next day's ride, the Andrews to Conway Marina Camping Area segment, or you can spend two days cycling this segment. If you'd rather not pay for a motel, though, or you're shy about asking to pitch your tent in town, this may be your best bet.

MILEAGE LOG

0.0 From Givhans Ferry State Park entrance, go left on Road S-18-30. This road, as well as the ones to come, are two lanes and uncrowded.

2.5 Make a right on Road S-18-19.

5.3 Market on the left.

8.2 Downtown Ridgeville. There's a general store on the right. Just past, turn left at the stop sign, traveling unsigned Hwy. 27.

8.6 Intersection. Go right on Hwy. 173.

10.2 Intersection. Ride across US 78 and continue on (unmarked) CR 182.

11.1 Fork; veer to the left.

11.9 Ride over I-26, now traveling CR 32.

17.7 Intersection. Turn right on US 176. Traffic is heavy, but only for a short distance.

19.5 Two markets in this area.

19.9 Turn left on Road S-8-467, an uncrowded but bumpy two-lane road.

24.2 Merge onto CR 413.

25.8 Intersection. Turn right on US 17A, then make an immediate left on Gaillard Rd. (NS-8-357).

27.6 Cross US 52.

28.4 Intersection. Make a left on Hwy. 791.

31.3 Moncks Corner town limits. You'll find grocery stores, laundromats, restaurants, and motels as you continue. Do you enjoy old churches? Moncks Corner is the site of numerous historic churches, so pedal to your heart's content.

31.5 Junction with US 52; make a right on R. C. Dennis Blvd. (P-0801). If you'd like to visit Lake Moultrie, a man-made lake world-famous for its landlocked striped bass, continue north on US 52, then go west on Hwy. 6 and north on Hwy. 21.

32.5 Junction; Old Santee Canal Park, open daily. This historic park contains the southern end of the Santee Canal, the first major canal constructed to facilitate river transportation in the United States. Completed in 1800, it is considered one of the earliest engineering achievements in American history. Horses and mules were used to pull boats and barges weighing up to twenty-two

Orange day-lily, found along the roadside from Florida to Maine

tons through the 22-mile-long, 30-foot-wide, and 5½-foot-deep, canal. Today, visitors may walk several miles of boardwalks and trails skirting along the Old Santee Canal and the wildlife-endowed Biggin Creek basin. The day-use facility also offers a picnic shelter and grill. In addition, there's the Stony Landing Plantation House, and an interpretive center with two theaters, numerous cultural and natural history displays, and a gift shop.

33.6 Junction; make a right on US 52. The road is now four lanes and traffic is heavy.

34.1 Dennis C. Bishop Bridge crossing over the Tail Race Canal.

34.6 Turn right on a road leading to Hwy. 402. This road and those to come are two lanes with no shoulders and uncrowded.

34.8 Make a right on Hwy. 402.

35.1 Biggins Church Ruins and cemetery on the right.

36.5 Ride the Wadboo Bridge over the Copper River. The road forks just after; keep to the left.

37.9 Intersection. There's a market just before the junction. Turn left on CR 171. A sign points the way to Witherbee.

40.2 Enter the Francis Marion National Forest. Comprised of more than 245,000 acres, the area was once a battleground wherein General Francis Marion opposed Colonel Banastre Tarleton's British troops. The only present-day signs of battle include numerous trees that lay scattered about after Hurricane Hugo swept through the area in 1989.

44.1 Fork; keep to the left as the road changes to CR 125. Just before the fork, a dirt road leads to the left to the Little Hellhole Reserve, a primitive tent site with no facilities. Obtain a free camping permit at the Witherbee District office less than 1 mile ahead.

44.3 Junction CR 125. This road leads 2.4 miles to Huger, an area now closed to camping due to damage incurred by Hurricane Hugo. The campground will not be reopened, according to Forest Service personnel.

44.7 Witherbee Ranger Station on the right; rest rooms. Obtain permits, maps, and other items here.

48.5 Road ends; turn right on CR 48. There's a small market on the right.

50.5 Junction; make a left on Hwy. 41.

56.4 Leave the Francis Marion Forest. Continue straight on Hwy. 41 and US 17A, which joins the route at this point.

56.8 Jamestown town limits. Located in the center of Hell Hole Swamp, this town, population 200, is the home of the Hell Hole Swamp Festival, held the first full weekend in May.

57.2 Convenience store on the left.

58.7 Begin crossing the Santee River. There's a shoulder on the bridge, although the road remains uncrowded.

63.0 Market on the left.

63.2 US 17A leaves the route at this point, taking off to the right. Continue on Hwy. 41.
71.2 Andrews town limits. You'll pass a motel (the only one in town) and grocery store en route to US 521.
71.9 Junction with US 521. This is downtown Andrews, where you'll find cafes and various shops.

Andrews to Conway Marina Camping Area (51.7 miles)

Travel this segment during the Memorial Day holiday and you'll have to convince yourself that somewhere out there, people are traveling in typical bumper-to-bumper fashion en route to a favorite retreat. Along the coastline, the beaches are undoubtedly crawling with people, and bicyclists are obviously stressed out from dodging heavy traffic.

But this route follows along a two-lane shoulderless road with nary a sprinkling of traffic. It's a delightful trip through rural South Carolina, a place where most of the homes, plain or fancy, are wrapped in enormous well-landscaped lawns.

Be sure to look for alligators, seen on occasion in some of the rivers, as you roll along. Black River is a particularly good place to look for them, although nighttime observations are often the most rewarding. "Go down to the bridge at night and bring a flashlight," offered one Andrews resident. "You'll see lots of eyeballs staring back at you."

Convenience stores dot today's path, although there are no cafes or restaurants until you reach the end of the route at Conway.

MILEAGE LOG

0.0 From the junction of US 521 and Hwy. 41 in Andrews, continue northeast on Hwy. 41. This road, along with the ones to come, are two lanes, mostly shoulderless, and usually uncrowded.
1.6 Cross Horsepen Creek.
2.8 Cross the Black River.
3.4 Junction with Hwy. 527.
4.6 Market/tackle shop.
12.7 Rhems.
13.0 Market on the right. Hwy. 51 now merges onto Hwy. 41. Continue straight.
14.9 Cross Black Mingo Creek.
15.4 Fork; stay straight on Hwy. 513. Hwys. 41 and 51 bear to the left.
16.2 Junction with Hwy. 512.
17.9 Pleasant Hill.
18.2 Tiny store on the right with another small market on the right in 2 miles.

Black River, near Andrews

21.9 Convenience store on the right.
24.3 Intersection. Turn right on Hwy. 261.
26.9 Gas station; snack items available.
33.4 Junction; go left on US 701 toward Conway.
35.5 Yauhannah. Begin pedaling over a bridge.
36.1 Great Pee Dee River crossing.
36.9 Cross Great Pee Dee overflow area.

Conway Marina Camping Area, Conway

37.4 Market on the left.
38.9 Cross Cowfort Swamp.
39.3 Small store on the left.
44.7 Another small store on the left.
48.3 Conway city limits.
48.8 Road widens to four lanes, no shoulder. As you enter Conway, US 701 is now known as 4th Ave. Traffic picks up now. Pass a laundromat as you head into town.
50.5 Pass under US 501. Continue straight to signed Hwy. 905.
50.9 Supermarkets, a motel, and restaurants are in the area. The Greyhound bus station is across from the Piggly Wiggly market and down a block.
51.2 Make a right on Elm.
51.7 Conway Marina Camping Area. Campers register here. Tent sites are located across from the marina, along the Waccamaw River. Sites are inexpensive and you'll find all services.

Conway Marina Camping Area to Waterway Family Campground (48.5 miles)

Once again you'll travel through South Carolina where friendly folks wave, often talking up a storm. After traveling inland for several days, you're bound to enjoy seeing the Atlantic Ocean once again. You'll see it in North Carolina upon taking a short side trip to Sunset

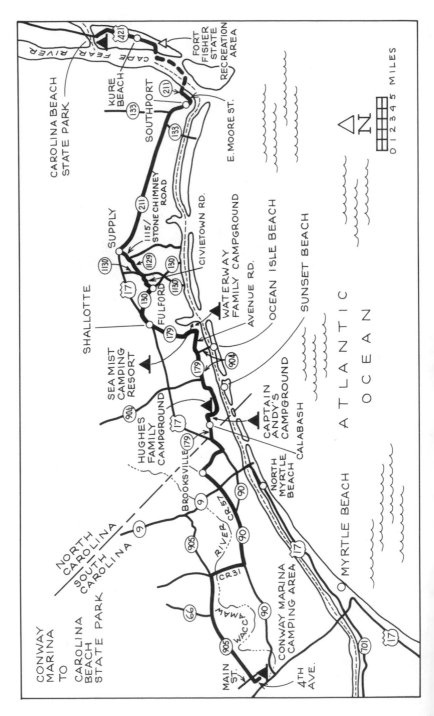

Beach. Along the way, you'll pedal across the only pontoon bridge spanning the Atlantic Intracoastal Waterway.

For the most part you'll travel rural roads once again, although traffic thickens immensely upon entering North Carolina. Quiet roads are the norm through South Carolina, although Highway 90 and US 17 do pump out a bit more traffic. Be prepared for heavy traffic, however, while cycling North Carolina's Highway 179, a narrow, two-lane, shoulderless road.

The segment ends at the Waterway Family Campground, located along the Shallotte River.

MILEAGE LOG

0.0 From Conway Marina Camping Area, ride back to 4th Ave. on Elm.

0.5 At the junction of Elm and 4th Ave., turn right on 4th Ave.

0.6 Ride across Main St. and continue onto Hwy. 905.

0.7 Cross Kingston Lake.

2.8 Convenience store on the right.

4.5 Small store on the left with another less than 0.5 mile ahead.

10.2 Junction with CR 66. There's a market on the left. There's another less than 1 mile ahead.

14.1 Junction; make a right on CR 31.

14.5 Cross the Waccamaw River. Ahead, cross Waccamaw Swamp on several occasions.

18.0 Turn left on Hwy. 90. Traffic is a bit heavier now.

19.2 Small store on the right.

20.2 Pizza shop on the left.

21.1 Supermarket on the left.

22.1 Sandwich stand on the right.

23.5 Fork; Hwy. 90 heads to the right, CR 57 to the left. Bear left on CR 57.

26.4 Junction with Hwy. 9; convenience store. Continue straight on CR 57.

28.6 Brooksville; market on the right.

28.8 Turn right on CR 111.

31.7 Turn right on Mineola Ave. (S-2650).

32.4 Turn left on US 17, a busy four-lane road. There's a motel, restaurants, and a grocery store.

33.5 Curve to the right on Hwy. 179. There's a rest area on the left. Traffic is heavy. There are no shoulders.

34.3 North Carolina state line.

34.9 Calabash. There's a laundromat on the right as you enter the town. There are all services here.

35.1 Visitor center on the right.

35.5 Bear right, staying on Hwy. 179.

Cyclists pedaling across a pontoon bridge near Sunset Beach

36.1 Turn right on Wilson Ave. if you'd like to check out or camp at Captain Andy's Campground. It's 0.5 mile away, along the Calabash River. There are shady sites at the full-service campground.

36.5 Hwy. 179 curves to the right.

37.1 Hughes Family Campground, an all-service camp, on the left.

38.2 Sunset Beach city limits.

40.0 Hwy. 179 curves to the left. There's a small store on the corner. **SIDE TRIP:** Begin by going right and across a unique pontoon bridge in 0.1 mile. "It's the only one of its kind anywhere," according to a local sheriff. Reach Sunset Beach, motels, gift shops, and the pier another mile down the road.

41.9 Hwy. 904 merges onto the route. There's a grocery store 0.2 mile to the left.

44.6 Hwy. 904 leaves the route, heading down to Ocean Isle Beach.

46.5 Turn right on an unsigned street (there is a sign for Waterway Family Campground, however). Later the road is signed Avenue Rd.

48.3 T-junction; cycle right. Pavement ends and a sandy road begins as you head left to the campground.

48.5 Waterway Family Campground office. The all-service campground offers open sites along the water. Sea Mist Camping Resort is 0.2 mile farther.

Waterway Family Campground to Carolina Beach State Park (42.9 miles)

The ride from Waterway Family Campground to Carolina Beach State Park is pleasant, with a fun-filled 30-minute ferry ride along the way.

Although the roads are usually shoulderless, traffic isn't too bad in some areas if you travel early in the morning. In others, it is often heavy and caution should be used. Heaviest traffic exists along US 421 between Kure Beach and Carolina Beach.

Those boarding the ferry to Pleasure Island should watch for a "resident" alligator. Seen regularly, the mouthy reptile is about 13 feet long.

Pleasure Island—surrounded by the Atlantic Ocean on the east and south, the Cape Fear River on the west, and the Atlantic Intracoastal Waterway on the north—boasts wonderful beaches, historic Fort Fisher, and the North Carolina Aquarium. A boardwalk in Carolina Beach awaits visitors with time to spare and a nature trail at Carolina Beach State Park provides a quiet respite from the masses, if desired.

MILEAGE LOG

0.0 From Waterway Family Campground, head back out to the pavement, going right and then continuing straight ahead.

1.3 Make a right on Hwy. 179. The road is two lanes, with no shoulder.

4.1 Shallotte city limits.

5.3 Junction; make a right on US 17. South Brunswick Islands Chamber of Commerce information center is on the left after you make the turn. There's a shoulder now as you pass some motels and restaurants.

6.6 Turn right on Hwy. 130. The road is two lanes, with no shoulder.

9.5 Turn left on Civietown Rd. There's a small market just before the turn. This road, as well as the next three, are all narrow but uncrowded.

11.8 Turn left on CR 1130.

12.1 Turn right on CR 1129.

13.7 Turn left on Stone Chimney Rd. (CR 1115).

14.9 Turn right on Hwy. 211. **SIDE TRIP:** If you need a store, go left on Hwy. 211 for 0.3 mile to a convenience store complete with hot grill. There's a shoulder now, but it's very rough, making for a bumpy ride.

15.3 Lockwood Folly River crossing.

23.7 A country store on the left. They sell snacks and some groceries. The paved shoulder ends, a grass shoulder begins. Hwy. 211 is a series of slightly rolling hills.

28.8 Junction with Hwy. 133, which takes off to the south. There are markets and restaurants here.

29.6 Junction with Hwy. 133, which takes off to the north (left). Keep straight on Hwy. 211.

30.5 Junction Hwy. 87.

31.9 Southport; all services. Make a left on E. Moore St. (Hwy. 211).

32.0 Visitor information center on the right. Another center is located across the road in City Hall. Both a fishing town and a military town since it was founded in 1792, Southport has long been known for its pleasant climate. It is listed on the National Register of Historic Places.

33.3 Keep right on Hwy. 211 to the ferry that crosses Cape Fear River.

34.1 Hwy. 211 ends at the ferry crossing. There's a $1 charge for bicyclists taking the half-hour ferry. Be sure to look for the resident alligator!

34.4 After departing the ferry, you'll find a picnic area before turning left toward Wilmington. Now you'll cycle US 421, a two-lane road with narrow shoulders. Traffic may be heavy.

35.7 Fort Fisher State Recreation Area on the right. Just beyond is the first of several beach access areas. Although camping is

Cape Fear River ferry crossing from Southport to Fort Fisher

not allowed, it's a good place for swimming, sunbathing, fishing, and hiking. This is also the entrance for the North Carolina Aquarium. One of three state aquariums along the coast, it contains sharks and horseshoe crabs, just a couple of the many fascinating forms of marine life found here. Also, there are films, speakers, and workshops.

36.1 Fort Fisher Civil War Museum on the left. Known as the "Last Major Stronghold of the Confederacy," Fort Fisher is free and offers 30-minute tours, priceless artifacts, and an orientation program in the form of a movie. Visit the fort during Living History Days, and you'll feel as though you've shot back in time. Why? Because, with a little imagination, it's the days of the American Civil War with actors parading around in authentic Confederate uniforms. Watch as they re-enact skirmishes with Union soldiers, fighting on grounds that were once the most important earthwork fortification in the South. Fort Fisher is open daily from April through October and closed Mondays the rest of the year.

36.2 Kure Beach city limits. A small, family-oriented beach, Kure Beach offers a large, uncrowded seaside where you can play in the ocean, saunter along the sand, or fish from the surf and/or the famous Kure Pier, located in the center of town. You'll find plenty of motels, restaurants, and markets in this land of white-sand beaches and warm sunny days.

40.3 Road curves; stay on US 421 as you pass Carolina Beach, where there are fine shopping and dining opportunities, rides at the boardwalk or family amusement park, and a variety of overnight accommodations.

41.6 Turn off to Carolina Beach State Park on unsigned Dow Rd. Make another left immediately upon turning, continuing on Dow Rd.

41.8 Turn right at the Carolina Beach State Park entrance.

42.4 Carolina Beach State Park's shaded 83-site campground is on the right.

42.9 Marina. Campers pay here. In addition to providing the usual picnic tables and hot showers, the 1,773-acre state park offers visitors 5 miles of hiking trails that wind through savanna, lime-sink ponds, and sand ridges. The trails pass through two unique areas as well—a large remnant sand dune known as Sugarloaf, and an insectivorous plant area called the Fly Trap Loop Trail. Explore the Fly Trap Loop Trail and you'll see several species of carnivorous plants, including the rare Venus flytrap, an unusual plant native only within a 60- to 75-mile radius of Wilmington. Bivalved like a clam shell, the Venus flytrap lures an unsuspecting insect in with its pale-yellow to bright-red interior. Trigger hairs note the insect's presence and the plant snaps shut in about one-half second, entrapping the prey. It takes the plant 3–5 days to absorb the prey, at which time the trap reopens. Although the trap dies after opening and closing three times, underground stems produce new traps in the spring.

Carolina Beach State Park to Rogers Bay Family Campground (59.4 miles)

This segment is a pleasant one. After leaving Carolina Beach State Park, you'll travel quiet River Road along Cape Fear River en route to Wilmington.

Enter Wilmington, one of the fastest-growing deep-water ports on the Atlantic Coast, and things liven up a bit. You'll travel through downtown historic Wilmington, past some spectacular seasoned buildings. Be sure to pick up a map describing the historic district at the visitor information center (located on the corner of Third and Princess Streets). *Guide Map of North Carolina's Cape Fear Coast* also highlights other area attractions.

Many Wilmington visitors opt to view the USS *North Carolina,* a beautifully restored battleship, open daily. Visitors look at a 10-minute orientation film, then take a self-guided tour of "The Showboat," as it is known, considered the greatest sea weapon in the world when it was commissioned in 1941.

The ride out of town is a bit hectic, but soon you're off on a series of quiet roads where you can hear the whir of your chain and the shifting of gears.

Brown pelican

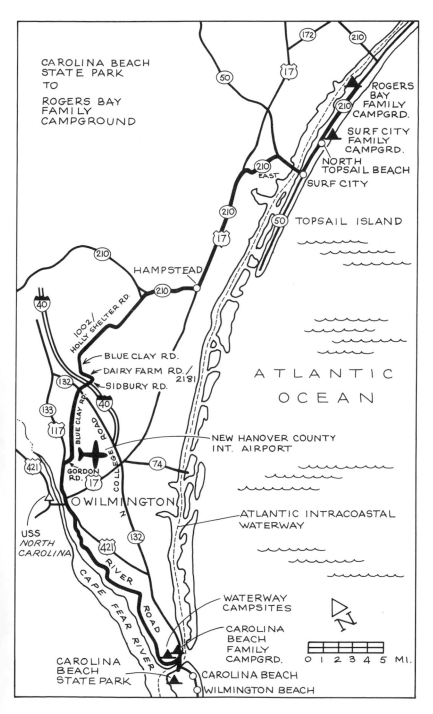

CAROLINA BEACH
STATE PARK
TO
ROGERS BAY
FAMILY
CAMPGROUND

ROGERS
BAY
FAMILY
CAMPGRD.

SURF CITY
FAMILY
CAMPGRD.

NORTH
TOPSAIL BEACH

SURF CITY

TOPSAIL ISLAND

HAMPSTEAD

1002/
HOLLY SHELTER RD.

BLUE CLAY RD.

DAIRY FARM RD./
2181

SIDBURY RD.

ATLANTIC
OCEAN

BLUE CLAY RD.

COLLEGE ROAD

NEW HANOVER COUNTY
INT. AIRPORT

GORDON
RD.

WILMINGTON

ATLANTIC INTRACOASTAL
WATERWAY

USS
NORTH
CAROLINA

CAPE FEAR RIVER

RIVER ROAD

WATERWAY
CAMPSITES

CAROLINA
BEACH
FAMILY
CAMPGRD.

N

0 1 2 3 4 5 MI.

CAROLINA
BEACH
STATE PARK

CAROLINA BEACH

WILMINGTON BEACH

All roads for the first portion of the segment are shoulderless, but most are uncrowded. The bakery at 36.6 miles makes an excellent stop after riding for miles sans a store or cafe. Enter Hampstead and soon you'll be on your way to Surf City, a popular vacation spot.

MILEAGE LOG

0.0 From the Carolina Beach State Park marina, head back the same way you came, to US 421.

1.3 Junction with US 421; head left toward Wilmington. There's a shoulder now.

1.7 Cross Snow's Cut Bridge over the Atlantic Intracoastal Waterway.

2.1 End of bridge; end of shoulder.

2.5 Make a left on CR 1576, then curve back, making a horseshoe turn riding parallel to US 421 for a short distance. The road is two lanes with no shoulder, but is uncrowded. There's a convenience store on the right before you turn.

2.9 Carolina Beach Family Campground on the right. It offers a laundromat in addition to all the typical services. A dirt road leads to shady sites.

3.1 The road, which turns into River Rd., curves along the Cape Fear River. Snow's Cut Park is on the left; picnic facilities, rest rooms. On the right, there's the Waterway Campsites, a full-service camp with a dirt road leading to shady sites.

12.7 Wilmington city limits. Soon after passing this sign, cross several sets of railroad tracks that at times run nearly parallel to the road, so use caution. Now you're pedaling through an industrial area.

14.8 Make a right on Shipyard Blvd.

15.0 Make a left on Burnett Blvd. You'll pass through some more industrial, then residential, areas. The road is two lanes, with no shoulder, but the speed limit is 25 mph and traffic isn't too heavy.

16.6 Cross Carolina Beach Rd., staying on Burnett Blvd., now a four-lane road. Greenfield Park is on the right just past the junction.

16.9 Burnett Blvd. becomes S. 3rd St. Keep to the left. Although riding through Wilmington is a bit hectic, traffic lanes are a bit wider than usual for the most part.

17.5 Junction with Dawson St. Although you won't see much in the way of motels, restaurants, or markets as you cycle along, Wilmington offers all of the above and there are several bike shops as well. For more information, stop by the visitor information center just ahead.

17.6 Junction with Wooster St. Turn left here for a **SIDE TRIP** to the USS *North Carolina*, located just across the Cape Fear River. Signs point the way to the memorial, dedicated in 1961 to the men and women of all U.S. military services who served our country during World War II.

18.2 Travel through downtown now. Those promised lovely old buildings are seen in this vicinity, as is the visitor information center, which is on the corner of Third and Princess Sts.

19.1 Greyhound/Trailways bus station on the left.

19.2 Make a right on Front St.

19.3 Go left on 4th St. (US 117 and Hwy. 133) as you head out of town. The road changes to Cornelius Harnett Rd. and then to Castle Hayne Rd. along the way.

21.0 Turn right on Gordon Rd. This road, like many to follow, is two lanes, with no shoulders, but is uncrowded.

21.4 Cross 23rd St., staying straight on what is now called Blue Clay Rd.

26.0 Cross Hwy. 132 (N. College Rd.).

26.2 Make a right on Sidbury Rd. (Blue Clay Rd. doesn't go through.)

26.7 Ride over I-40.

27.0 Make a left on the first road: Dairy Farm Rd. (CR 2181).

27.5 Road changes to Blue Clay Rd. again.

29.1 Make a right on Holly Shelter Rd. (CR 1002).

35.2 Keep straight, now traveling Hwy. 210 to Hampstead.

36.3 There's a bake shop is on the right. They have rest rooms and the best baked breads and cinnamon rolls in town, if not on the Atlantic Coast.

39.1 Make a left on Hwy. 210, joining US 17 in Hampstead. Now there's a shoulder. There are markets, restaurants, and a motel as you head through town.

41.7 Public library on the left.

41.8 Grill and groceries on the right.

45.8 Hill Top Grocery on the right.

46.4 Shoulder ends.

47.9 Head right on Hwy. 210 East, a two-lane, shoulderless road.

50.8 Hwy. 50 joins Hwy. 210; make a right.

51.9 Surf City city limits; restaurants, stores, motels.

52.3 Cross the Atlantic Intracoastal Waterway to Topsail Island.

52.7 Hwys. 210 and 50 split now; continue northeast on Hwy. 210.

53.1 Laundromat on the right; motels in the area.

55.2 North Topsail Beach city limits. Pronounced "Tops'l," this area is a natural nesting ground for the loggerhead sea turtle. Topsail Island also boasts of more than 100 species of birds.

55.8 Surf City Family Campground on the right. There are sunny sites, all services, and limited groceries available. A shoulder begins now.

59.4 Rogers Bay Family Campground on the left. In addition to the usual amenities, it offers groceries, a pool, and a laundromat.

Cyclists riding through Camp Lejeune Marine Base

Rogers Bay Family Campground to Salter Path Family Campground (50.7 miles)

Delightful as usual, today's path leads along Topsail Island, through the Camp Lejeune Marine Base where traffic is basically light, to Bogue Banks where traffic is also light except for weekends and holidays.

As you travel along Bogue Banks, a narrow 25-mile-long island surrounded by the Atlantic Ocean and Bogue Sound, you'll see everything from dense maritime forests to ocean-front hotels.

You'll find the Salter Path Family Campground a perfect place to end your day. Shady sites may make the heat a bit easier to bear.

MILEAGE LOG

0.0 From Rogers Bay Family Campground, go left on Hwy. 210.

1.6 Start heading inland, away from the ocean.

1.9 Cross the Atlantic Intracoastal Waterway. The bridge curves up at least 100 feet above the water.

2.4 End of bridge and paved shoulder. A grass shoulder now borders the two-lane road.

4.1 Grocery store and drug store on the left.

5.7 Turn right on Hwy. 172. There are several restaurants here.

7.8 Turnoff to Sneads Ferry, an old-time fishing village on the New

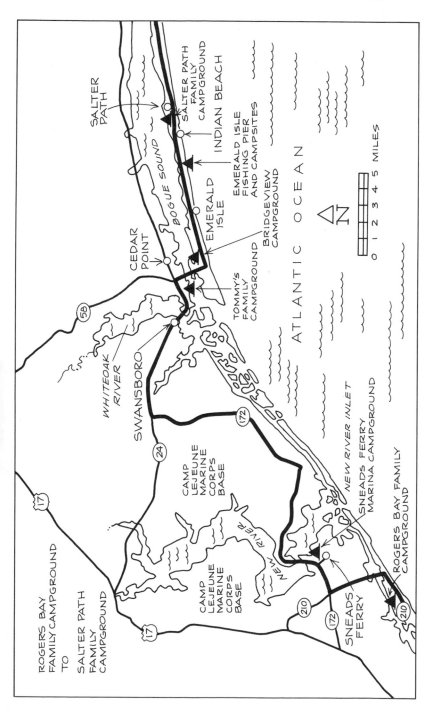

River; there are a couple of restaurants before this junction. Sneads Ferry is about 1 mile southeast of here.

9.0   Sneads Ferry Marina Campground on the right, just before crossing the New River. Shady sites and a limited supply of groceries are offered at this full-service campground that has reduced rates for bicyclists.

9.5   Camp Lejeune Marine Corps Base. Obtain a free entrance pass at the entry gate.

18.5   Hwy. 172 curves around to the right.

24.2   Exit Camp Lejeune.

28.3   Junction. Make a right on Hwy. 24. There are two convenience stores at the junction. The road is four lanes wide with a bumpy shoulder.

31.6   Convenience store on the right.

32.8   No shoulder now.

34.3   There are a couple more convenience stores before reaching Swansboro city limits. You'll find all amenities. If you're in town in May, be sure to stop for the annual Arts by the Sea Waterfront Festival. "The Friendly City by the Sea" also hosts the Mullet Festival, a coastal seafood celebration, the second weekend in October.

35.6   Cross the Whiteoak River.

36.1   Cedar Point city limits. Now there's a shoulder.

37.4   Tommy's Family Campground is located down the long dirt road to your right. You'll find all services, with opportunities for fishing in the Atlantic Intracoastal Waterway.

38.8   Turn right on Hwy. 58. There are restaurants and a grocery store here; the highway has a good shoulder.

39.0   Visitor center on the right.

39.4   B. Cameron Langston Bridge over the Atlantic Intracoastal Waterway.

40.3   Emerald Isle city limits, boundary of a sea turtle sanctuary, and part of North Carolina's Crystal Coast, which extends north to Cedar Island.

40.8   Bridgeview Campground on the left. In addition to all services, it offers shady sites, a swimming pool, and a laundromat.

41.5   Shopping center on the left; restaurants in the area. There's a motel as you continue.

46.5   Convenience store on the right.

46.9   Emerald Isle Fishing Pier. There are some campsites here, with all services and limited groceries.

50.0   Indian Beach city limits. To the right there's a fishing pier and campsites with all amenities. There's an eating establishment too.

50.7   Salter Path Family Campground's office and some campsites are on the left, with more sites on the right. You'll find all services, with a limited supply of groceries and a gift and candy shop next door. There is a grocery store and restaurants nearby.

Salter Path Family Campground to Teeter's Campground (55.4 miles)

A wide shoulder continues to escort you along Bogue Banks, past the North Carolina Aquarium and over to Beaufort, where the Maritime Museum will provide enough entertainment for a nice long rest.

Upon leaving Beaufort, the road narrows and should be traveled on weekdays if possible, as heavy traffic often plagues the roadway on summer weekends and holidays. I traveled US 70 to Cedar Island the day after Memorial Day and found the highway basically deserted. Hopefully you'll find the same.

You'll pedal past tiny fishing villages and traditional boat-building communities as you make your way to the Cedar Island National

Ocracoke Lighthouse, Ocracoke Island

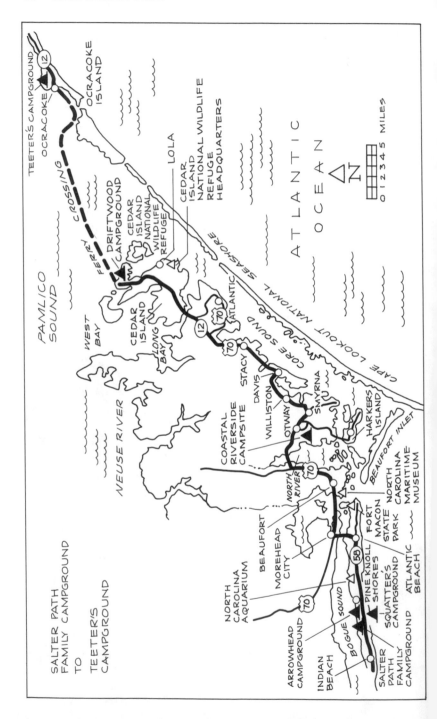

Wildlife Refuge en route to Cedar Island. Although you can camp at Cedar Island, activities are limited, so your best bet would be to take the ferry across to Ocracoke Island.

Ocracoke Island is the first of three narrow islands linked by both ferry and bridge to form the Cape Hatteras National Seashore. Typically called The Outer Banks, there the park has five campgrounds and there are several private campgrounds on the islands outside of the park boundary. Sport fishing is legendary in this area.

Unique, quaint, and thoroughly enjoyable, Ocracoke Village is a fishing hamlet resting near the southern side of the island closest to Pamlico Sound, the largest inland body of water on the Atlantic Coast. A popular retreat, the area was also a favorite haunt of the infamous pirate Edward Teach—better known as Blackbeard—who died here in 1718.

Ocracoke Village radiates the friendliness of a small, isolated town, rich in history. Nearly cut off from the rest of the world (even today access is only by ferry, private boat, or airplane), many native residents still speak in quasi-Elizabethan accents.

MILEAGE LOG

0.0 Continue north from the Salter Path Family Campground via Hwy. 58.

0.1 Arrowhead Campground on the left; all services.

0.3 Squatter's Campground on the right. This is a full-service campground with a laundromat. There are restaurants in the area.

1.0 Park on the right; picnic facilities, rest rooms.

1.9 Pine Knoll Shores city limits: a bird and sea turtle sanctuary.

4.3 Public library on the left.

4.4 Turnoff to the North Carolina Aquarium. **SIDE TRIP:** Follow signs to the left for 0.6 mile to the aquarium, one of three such aquariums dotting the North Carolina coast. Here you'll learn that North Carolina's barrier islands are the most extensive in the world. Barrier islands such as Bogue Banks endure the full force of the ocean's winds, waves, and storms, thus protecting the mainland wetlands by acting as buffer zones. Unlike most barrier islands, Bogue Banks lies in an east–west bearing instead of a north–south direction and is partially protected from the forces of the ocean by the extended tip of Cape Lookout. The Theodore Roosevelt Natural Area, a 297-acre maritime forest, surrounds the museum, where admission is free although a donation is always appreciated.

6.6 Atlantic Beach city limits; bird sanctuary; motels and all services.

8.8 Shoulder ends; the road is four lanes now.

9.3 Go left toward Morehead City via Morehead Ave. **SIDE TRIP:** Go to Fort Macon State Park, about 3 miles to the east, continue

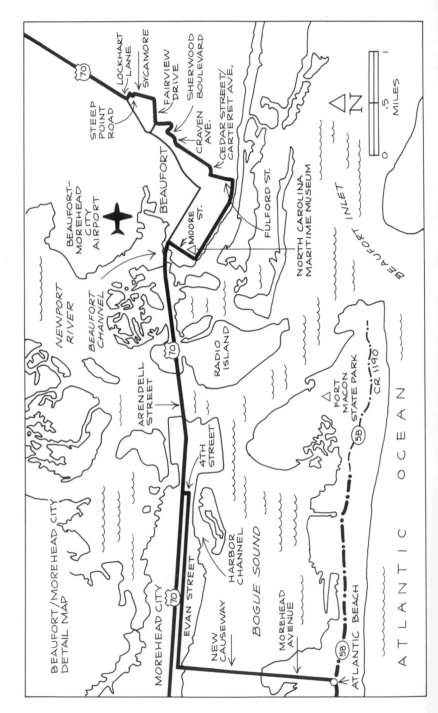

BEAUFORT/MOREHEAD CITY
DETAIL MAP

Bicycles leaning against a bridge over Bogue Sound

straight ahead on Hwy. 58, which dead ends at the park and turns into CR 1190. The park offers a beach, a picnic area, a bathhouse, a snack bar, a nature trail, and opportunities for fishing. And you won't want to miss a tour of Fort Macon, guardian over Beaufort Harbor during the Civil War.

10.3 Begin crossing the New Causeway, a bridge spanning the Atlantic Intracoastal Waterway (Bogue Sound). There's a wide shoulder on the bridge.

10.8 Hop over the curb to your right just before reaching the traffic light on Arendell St. in Morehead City, a town with all amenities. There's an opening in the fence that will enable you to roll your bike onto Evan St., a quiet residential lane. **SIDE TRIP:** If you need a bike shop, continue to the light, make a right, and the bike shop is 0.1 mile on your left.

12.0 Ride along the restored Morehead City waterfront district. Sportfishing is popular here, with charter fishing boats luring visitors out to sea. Those more inclined to stay on the mainland often opt for lunch or dinner at one of the world-famous seafood restaurants hanging over the pilings on Bogue Sound. Others shop to their hearts' content. If you're in town on the first weekend of

October, be sure to stop by the North Carolina Seafood Festival.
12.4 Make a left onto 4th St.
12.5 Go right on Arendell St. (US 70). Keep to the left just after turning. There's no shoulder here. Use caution.
13.0 Cross the Newport River. There's a small shoulder.
13.6 End of bridge. The road is four lanes, with no shoulder.
14.6 Cross the Grayden Paul Bridge over Beaufort channel.
14.7 Beaufort city limits; all services can be found in North Carolina's
third-oldest town. Situated in the center of town is the Beaufort
Historic Site, with numerous homes and buildings seen via a self-
guided walking tour. (Pick up a map at the welcome center at
Beaufort Historic Site, 138 Turner St.) Cycle around Beaufort and
see more than 100 buildings constructed before the Civil War.
14.8 Make a right on Moore St., a quiet residential street. There's a
convenience store on the corner.
15.1 Make a left on Front St. Follow this pleasant road along the restored waterfront area, where you're bound to see everything
from working skiffs to waterway luxury liners to racing yachts.
15.2 The North Carolina Maritime Museum on the left; open daily.
There's no admission charge to this fine museum with its impressive collection of ship models, ranging from sailing skiffs to
full-rigged ships. In addition to ship models, there are exhibits
boasting shells found here in North Carolina and around the
world. Also, there are coastal bird and mammal specimens, marine fossils, and maritime artifacts.
16.0 Cycle left on Fulford St. (The next few miles lead through residential areas.)
16.3 Turn right on Cedar St., which turns into Carteret Ave. Bike Route
signs point the way.
16.8 Bear to the right on Craven Ave.
16.9 Make a right on Sherwood Blvd. and follow it around to Fairview Dr.
17.2 Go right on Fairview Dr.
17.4 Head left on Sycamore.
17.7 Make a right on Steep Point Rd., then a left on Lockhart Lane in
100 yards or so. Cross through the Beaufort Square Shopping
Area en route to US 70. There's a grocery store/drug store here.
17.9 Go right on US 70, a busy two-lane highway without shoulders.
Be prepared for a lot of traffic on summer weekends and holidays.
19.1 Convenience store on the right.
21.9 Keep right on US 70.
22.9 Cross the North River; shoulder on bridge only.
24.0 Turnoff on left leads to Bettie; keep straight.
25.3 Bridge over inlet.
26.2 Coastal Riverside Campsite turnoff. **SIDE TRIP:** If you're interested, go right on Gillikin Rd. (CR 1331), then right again on CR

1329 for a total of about 1.5 miles. Located on 22 quiet and secluded acres, there's a pool, a laundry room, a campground store with limited groceries, a game room, and opportunities for fishing in addition to the usual facilities.

26.9 Harkers Island Rd. turnoff. Convenience store on right.

28.4 Keep left on US 70. There's a convenience store and market here in the town of Smyrna.

29.3 Ice cream/yogurt and pizza/sandwich shop on the left.

34.7 Davis. Keep left on US 70. There's a convenience store at the junction.

36.3 Cross another inlet.

38.1 Pedal over another inlet.

38.2 Stacy.

41.2 Convenience store on the left; grill with miscellaneous food items as well.

42.6 Daniel E. Taylor Memorial Bridge over Salters Creek.

43.0 Junction. Go north on Hwy. 12.

45.2 Market on the right.

46.3 Bridge. Enter Cedar Island National Wildlife Refuge. A resting and feeding area for migrant and wintering waterfowl, this vast refuge is inhabited by more than 270 species of birds. Comprised of approximately 12,526 acres, it has 10,000 acres of irregularly flooded salt marsh and 2,041 acres of woodlands. The endangered brown pelican can be viewed on occasion, with the refuge being the northernmost limit of its range. Permanent residents include the little blue heron, green heron, clapper and Virginia rails, and belted kingfisher.

51.5 Junction; continue on Hwy. 12. **SIDE TRIP:** Lola Rd. leads to the right to Cedar Island National Wildlife Refuge headquarters in about 2 miles.

55.0 Driftwood Campground on the right. It's a full-service camp located 100 yards or so from the ferry terminal. There's also a convenience store, motel, picnic area, and restaurant nearby. You can camp here or take the ferry across to Ocracoke Island. The 20-mile ferry ride takes 2¼ hours; bicycles are $2. There are four or five daily departures in the summer, two daily crossings from November through April. Call (919) 928-3841 for the current schedule. There are rest rooms and a snack stand on board. From the ferry landing in Ocracoke, head north on Hwy. 12, passing the visitor center as you ride along Silver Lake to the quaint village of Ocracoke.

55.2 Turn left on CR 1324. There's a sign pointing the way to Teeter's Campground.

55.4 Teeter's Campground; open from March 1 through November 15. This full-service camp offers both shady and sunny sites. There are no laundromats here or in town.

Teeter's Campground to Salvo Campground (45.7 miles)

The ride from Ocracoke Village to the free ferry is one of pure delight as you cross creek after creek, and parallel mile upon mile of windswept beaches. Wildflowers and wild ponies will undoubtedly add to the scene.

A shoulder is available for the first few miles and traffic is light if you travel before the massive crowds, which usually appear in July and August. Weekends and holidays in June and September are also quite congested. As always, be careful. A shoulder assists in and near towns, but is usually nonexistent between them.

As you travel along, be prepared for stiff winds, which often batter the islands along with angry waves. Fortunately, prevailing winds typically blow from the south, year-round, at about 12 mph.

Enter Hatteras Village after a 40-minute ferry ride, then continue on through tiny towns, where homes perch upon stilts, to Cape Hatteras Lighthouse. Stretching 208 feet into the heavens, the lighthouse was built in 1870 using an amazing total of 1,250,000 bricks.

The tallest lighthouse in the United States, it was recently rehabilitated (the project was due for completion in spring 1992), with

Cyclist boarding the ferry at Ocracoke Island

planning currently underway to move the entire complex—lighthouse, principal keepers' quarters, and double keepers' quarters (the Hatteras Island visitor center)—to an area about 2,500 feet southwest of its current location. The move is a result of continued erosion.

Thomas L. Hartman, superintendent with the National Park Service, reports that the move will probably be within the next three to five years. According to Hartman, "a lot will depend on the stress that shoreline erosion will place on the lighthouse over the next couple of years."

The segment ends at Salvo Campground, a Cape Hatteras National Seashore facility.

MILEAGE LOG

0.0 Teeter's Campground. Just beyond the campground is the British Cemetery, resting place for four British sailors who washed ashore from torpedoed HMS *Bedfordshire* on May 14, 1942. Head back to town.

0.2 Turn left on Hwy. 12. Before heading out of town, be sure to pedal up and down the various streets (there aren't many), admiring this delightful community where you'll find plenty of motels, restaurants, and a couple of small markets.

0.5 **SIDE TRIP:** A side road leads a short distance to the right to the Ocracoke Lighthouse. Standing reign over the tiny village since 1823, this 75-foot light is the oldest operating lighthouse on the North Carolina coast and the second-oldest continuously operating light in the United States. (A light in Sandy Hook, New Jersey, has the distinction of being the oldest.) There's a shoulder as you head out of town.

2.2 Beach access on the right; outhouses.

4.4 Ocracoke Campground on the right. Open from April through October, it is one of five Cape Hatteras National Seashore camps. It is located in the open, protected from the ocean and heavy winds by a ridge of dunes. You'll find all services, although showers here are cold, not hot.

4.5 Island Creek. There's a narrow shoulder now.

4.9 Shade Hole Creek.

5.4 Old Hammock Creek.

5.8 Molasses Creek.

6.4 Quorks Point Creek.

6.9 Parkers Creek.

7.3 Try Yard Creek.

7.7 Ocracoke Pony Pastures on the left. The ponies viewed here are descendants of a herd that once roamed free on the island. The Banker ponies, as they are called, are a special breed closely related to the Spanish mustang. The ponies were here before the first settlers came to Ocracoke, but no one knows how they got to the island.

14.1 Hatteras Inlet Free Ferry Terminal. There is a picnic area here with covered shelters, and rest rooms. The 40-minute ferry ride is free and runs on the hour year-round from 6:00 A.M. to 6:00 P.M. and at 8:00 P.M. and 10:00 P.M. (Hours fluctuate a bit if headed from north to south, with additional departures in the summer for both directions.)

14.2 Hatteras Ferry Terminal. There's a shoulder now.

14.3 Future site of the Graveyard of the Atlantic Museum, an idea that is still in the planning stages. Estimated opening date is sometime from 1995 through 1997.

14.7 Teach's Lair Marina and Campground is on the left. This full-service camp has limited grocery items.

14.8 Junction with Eagle Pass Rd. **SIDE TRIP:** The Hatteras Sands Campground is located 0.2 mile to the right. In addition to the usual services, you'll find a pool, a laundromat, and a recreation room.

15.3 Hatteras Village; motels, restaurants, markets in area.

16.8 End of town.

17.1 Beach access on the right; shoulder disappears.

18.6 Beach access and rest rooms.

18.7 Shoulder begins again.

19.0 Cape Hatteras Fishing Pier on the right.

19.2 Restaurant on the left.

19.8 Shopping center and the Frisco Native American Museum on the left.

20.3 Frisco Woods Campgrounds is on the left. Located on Pamlico Sound, a popular windsurfing site, shaded sites are offered at this full-service camp.

22.2 Laundromat on the right. Scotch Bonnet Marina on the left. There are some shaded sites, all services, a gift shop, and limited groceries.

25.4 Turn right on Buxton Back Rd. There's a church on the corner. This road is two lanes and uncrowded.

26.0 Cape Woods Campground on the right. There are many shaded sites; there's a pool, laundry, and freshwater fishing at the pond in this all-service campground.

26.6 Stowe-A-Way Campground, a full-service facility on the right.

26.7 Road curves back to Hwy. 12. Make a right. Now there's a shoulder again.

26.9 Turnoff to the right for signed Cape Hatteras Lighthouse and the Cape Point Campground. **SIDE TRIP:** Cape Hatteras Lighthouse, the tallest brick lighthouse in America, is 0.9 mile away. There's a visitor center/museum near the lighthouse. The full-service campground is another 2 miles or so to the south of the lighthouse. There are restaurants, motels, et cetera, as you continue on Hwy. 12.

27.3 Exit town; no shoulder now.

31.1 Beach access on the right; rest rooms.

31.2 Avon. There's a shoulder once again.

Cape Hatteras Lighthouse, Cape Hatteras National Seashore

32.0 Supermarket on the left.

33.4 Market on the left. Kinnakeet Campground is behind the market; you'll find open sites at a park catering mostly to RVs.

33.9 Restaurant.

34.6 End of shoulder.

37.1 Little Kinnakeet U.S. Life Saving Service Station on the left.

41.6 Beach access; no rest rooms.

45.7 Salvo Campground on the left; it's open from Memorial Day through Labor Day. One of five Cape Hatteras National Seashore campgrounds, Salvo Campground offers sunny sites and all services, although showers are unheated.

Salvo Campground to Joe and Kay's Campground (38.9 miles)

Today's ride is pleasant if traveled in the spring or fall, or early in the morning during the summer when traffic is less demanding. Uncrowded weekdays are also recommended. After crossing Oregon Inlet you'll encounter additional traffic, but a side road leads through a residential area where traffic is light.

En route to Nags Head you'll ride along the beach on a frequent basis, but don't expect to see much of the ocean, as it is often blocked by sand dunes. Keep your ears open, however, as you're bound to hear it.

Jockey's Ridge State Park is a place where you can learn to hang glide or watch others do the same. The park is the site of the largest natural sand dune on the Atlantic Coast, and many people enjoy the challenge of scaling the 100- to 125-foot-high dune. The view from atop the ridge is spectacular, particularly at sunset.

Hang gliders test their wings at Jockey's Ridge State Park.

The Wright Brothers were the first to make use of the area's prevailing winds, ranging from 10 to 15 mph. You'll ride by the Wright Brothers National Memorial during the next day's segment. If time permits, you could visit the site earlier. See the next segment, Joe and Kay's Campground to Barnes Campground, for more information.

This segment is short due to a lack of campgrounds north of Kill Devil Hills. No need to worry, however; there are plenty of things to see and do.

MILEAGE LOG

0.0 Continue north from Salvo Campground via Hwy. 12.

0.2 Beach access on the right; no rest rooms.

0.7 Shoulder again.

0.8 Salvo Beach and Bay Campground on the left; all services. There are a couple of small stores in town and a restaurant up the road in 1.5 miles.

3.0 Ocean Waves Campground: full services with some shady sites and a pool.

3.3 Cape Hatteras KOA. Open from March through December, it offers all the usual amenities plus a recreation hall, a swimming pool, and limited groceries.

3.7 Waterfall Park; a variety of rides and other amusements here. Motels and restaurants are in Rodanthe.

4.6 North Beach Campground and market on the right; all services in addition to a pool and laundromat.

4.9 End of business section of Rodanthe. Now travel through a residential area, passing the restored Chicamacomico U.S. Life Saving Service Station as you continue north. This free museum tells the story of twenty-four pre-Coast Guard lifesaving stations, which serve as reminders of the storms and shipwrecks of centuries past in an area that became known as "the Graveyard of the Atlantic." (On a special note, with 600 known shipwrecks off the coast, diving opportunities are virtually unlimited.) Summer visitors may enjoy the living history re-enactment/beach apparatus drills performed at the station as well.

5.6 End of shoulder; road is narrow.

10.5 Boat launch on the left; outhouse.

11.1 Beach access on the right, Pea Island National Wildlife Refuge Information Center on the left.

13.5 Rest rooms and a self-guided nature trail through the refuge, on the left.

15.2 Beach access on the right; no rest rooms.

17.6 Cross the Oregon Inlet via the Herbert C. Bonner Bridge; there's a shoulder over the bridge and a breathtaking view of Pamlico Sound and the Atlantic Ocean.

20.1 End of bridge and shoulder; road is narrow again. Just beyond is the Oregon Inlet Campground, another of the Cape Hatteras National Seashore campgrounds. As mentioned previously, these camps offer all services, but showers are not heated. It is open from April through October. To the left is a marina. Also you'll find a restaurant, groceries, and a gift shop. On display is a world-record Atlantic blue marlin that weighed 1,142 pounds when captured 37 miles from this area.

23.9 Turn right on Old Nags Head Rd.; two lanes, no shoulder, uncrowded.

24.0 Nags Head town limits. Road is now called Old Oregon Inlet Rd. and is also known as Hwy. 12 and US 158 Business. Later it's called Va. Dare Trail.

28.4 Beginning of motels and other services.

28.8 Junction with US 64 on the left. Now there's a shoulder.

33.2 E. Conch St.; turnoff for Jockey's Ridge State Park. **SIDE TRIP:** If you're interested, go left and then right in 0.1 mile on US 158 West Bypass, then left at signed Jockey's Ridge in 0.3 mile. Facilities include a natural history museum, picnic shelters with tables and grills, and rest rooms. Favorite activities include hiking, hang gliding, kite flying, nature study, and photography.

35.7 Kill Devil Hills; motels and services. Most of the restaurants, however, are nearby on the US 158 Bypass.

37.2 Head left on Ocean Bay Blvd. (CR 1217).

37.4 Pedal across the US 158 Bypass, continuing on the narrow, shoulderless road. Traffic may be heavy, so use caution.

38.9 Joe and Kay's Campground on the left. Sites are shaded at this full-service campground, which is open year-round.

Joe and Kay's Campground to Barnes Campground (44.3 miles)

With a low-mileage day in store, you can lounge around camp, waiting for the Wright Brothers National Memorial to open, before heading north. The 60-foot Wright Memorial Shaft crowns Big Kill Devil Hill, a 90-foot sand dune, its shifting sands now secured with grass and other vegetation. A nearby visitor center/museum welcomes guests and provides information. Also you'll see full-scale replicas of the Wrights' 1902 glider and the 1903 flying machine.

In addition, you can walk the grounds and stand on the exact spot where the two Ohio bicycle mechanics made four take-offs and landings.

Afterward, it's past more stilt-based houses, then over Currituck Sound via Wright Memorial Bridge for a pedal through rural North Carolina, a land of farms and open spaces. Along the way, notice the cemeteries sprouting up amid fields of corn and wheat.

This segment is quite pleasant, as shoulders usually exist when

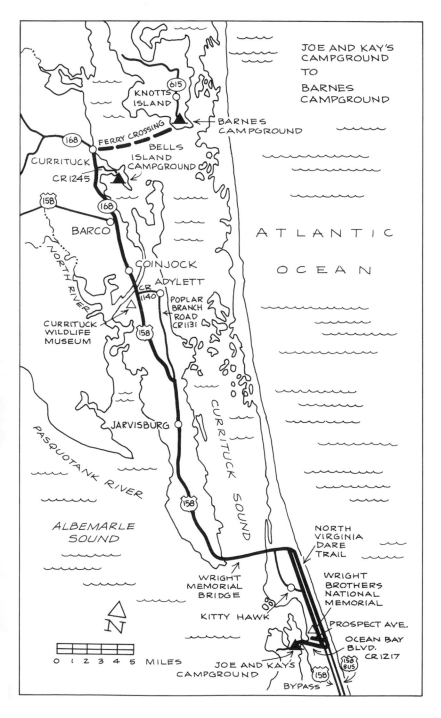

JOE AND KAY'S
CAMPGROUND
TO
BARNES
CAMPGROUND

615

KNOTTS
ISLAND

168

CURRITUCK

CR 1245

BARNES
CAMPGROUND

FERRY CROSSING

BELLS
ISLAND
CAMPGROUND

158

168

BARCO

COINJOCK

NORTH RIVER

CR
1140

CURRITUCK
WILDLIFE
MUSEUM

ADYLETT

POPLAR
BRANCH
ROAD
CR 1131

158

A T L A N T I C

O C E A N

JARVISBURG

PASQUOTANK RIVER

158

CURRITUCK SOUND

ALBEMARLE
SOUND

△
N

0 1 2 3 4 5 MILES

WRIGHT
MEMORIAL
BRIDGE

KITTY HAWK

158

NORTH
VIRGINIA
DARE
TRAIL

WRIGHT
BROTHERS
NATIONAL
MEMORIAL

PROSPECT AVE.

OCEAN BAY
BLVD.
CR 1217

JOE AND KAY'S
CAMPGROUND

BYPASS

158
BUS

168
BUS

Wright Brothers Memorial Shaft, Wright Brothers National Memorial

roads are heavily trafficked, and primarily uncrowded roads make riding a treat. Prior to day's end, you'll ferry across Currituck Sound to Knotts Island for an uncrowded afternoon of relaxation.

MILEAGE LOG

0.0 From Joe and Kay's Campground, head back to the US 158 Bypass.

1.5 Turn left on US 158. There's a shoulder now.

2.0 Turn left on Prospect Ave. A sign points the way to the Wright Brothers National Memorial. After visiting the museum, head back across US 158 and on to less-traveled US 158 Business.

2.2 Turn left on N. Va. Dare Trail (US 158 Business).

5.0 There are fewer motels and restaurants as you pedal through a mostly residential area.

9.1 Large shopping center on the right. The road is four lanes, then narrows to two lanes with a narrow shoulder.

10.3 Begin crossing the Wright Memorial Bridge over Currituck Sound. Notice the abundance of osprey nests balancing atop the posts paralleling the road.

13.4 Small store on the left; end of bridge just prior. There's a couple of restaurants in the area as well. The road is now four lanes with a good shoulder.

15.1 Restaurant on the right. The road passes through rural area, farmland, and a town now and then.

17.1 Convenience store on the left.

21.0 Motel on the left; a market just prior.

21.5 Restaurant and gifts to the left.

23.3 Jarvisburg; convenience store/deli/bakery on the right.

25.2 Road is four lanes, no shoulder now.

25.5 Markets, restaurants in area.

26.2 Junction with CR 1131/Poplar Branch Rd. **ALTERNATE ROUTE**: Turn right if you'd like to pedal along a quiet back road for about 8 miles. CR 1140 leads back to US 158 at the 32.8-mile mark.

26.9 Market on the left. There's a shoulder again.

29.2 Junction with Hwy. 3 to the right.

30.4 Motel/restaurant on the left.

31.6 Rest area on the left.

32.8 Junction with CR 1140 to Adylett. Those who opted for the 8-mile side road via CR 1131 will merge back here.

33.3 No shoulder; small convenience store on the left.

33.9 Shoulder again.

34.3 Joseph Palmer Knapp Bridge over the Atlantic Intracoastal Waterway.

34.8 End of bridge.

35.5 Coinjock; shoulder ends upon entering town. There are a couple of cafes and a convenience store.

36.5 Convenience store on the left.

36.8 Currituck County Library.

38.1 Junction with Hwy. 168; US 158 heads left to Elizabeth City; head straight on Hwy. 168. There's a convenience store at the junction. The road narrows to two lanes, with no shoulder.

38.5 Barco.

42.1 Junction with CR 1245, which leads right 3 miles to the Bells Island Campground, open year-round. You'll find all services, including a recreation hall and swimming and fishing opportunities.

43.4 Turn right on Courthouse Rd., which leads to the Currituck Sound ferry. There's a large convenience store at the junction.

43.8 Ferry terminal; rest rooms, picnic facilities, shade. The 40-minute ferry runs several times daily. Write the North Carolina Department of Transportation, Ferry Division, 113 Arendell St., Morehead City, NC 28557, for more information.

44.3 Once across Currituck Sound and on Knotts Island, go straight and then make a right on Hwy. 615. Barnes Campground is on the waterfront. It offers some shade and rest rooms, but no showers. Opening and closing dates not available.

Barnes Campground to Virginia Beach KOA (28.8 miles)

Begin today's ride on a peaceful note with rarely a car visible as you head north through rustic North Carolina and on into rural southeast Virginia. You'll enjoy a narrow but uncrowded pedal, where you're more apt to see cornfields than rows of condos.

Traffic increases on a dramatic note, however, upon entering Virginia Beach, and fast-food establishments replace cornfields. If you want to explore Virginia Beach, though, and crowds don't bother you,

Turtle found along Highway 615 in Virginia

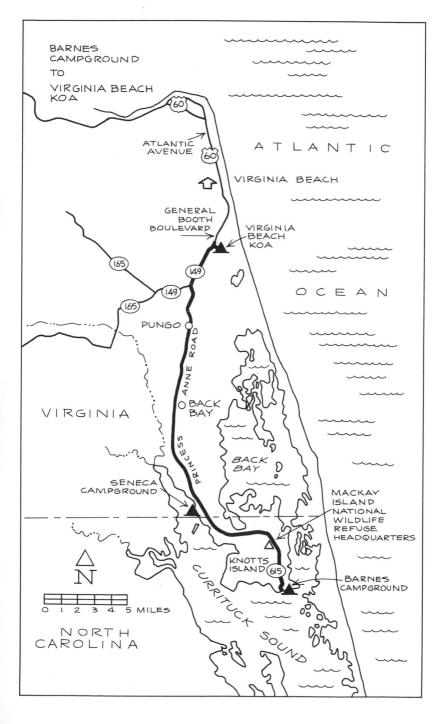

BARNES
CAMPGROUND
TO
VIRGINIA BEACH
KOA

60

ATLANTIC
AVENUE

60

A T L A N T I C

VIRGINIA BEACH

GENERAL
BOOTH
BOULEVARD

VIRGINIA
BEACH
KOA

165

149

149

O C E A N

165

PUNGO

PRINCESS ANNE ROAD

O BACK
BAY

VIRGINIA

BACK
BAY

SENECA
CAMPGROUND

MACKAY
ISLAND
NATIONAL
WILDLIFE
REFUGE
HEADQUARTERS

KNOTTS
ISLAND

615

BARNES
CAMPGROUND

N

0 1 2 3 4 5 MILES

NORTH
CAROLINA

CURRITUCK SOUND

you can take the free shuttle from the KOA to the beach. Or, if you'd prefer, there's a hostel in town, just one block from the beach. The hostel is closed from October through March. For more information, call or write Angie's Guest Cottage, Bed & Breakfast and AYH Hostel, 302 24th St., Virginia Beach, VA 23451; (804) 428-4690.

If you'd rather skip the beach, why not combine this segment with the next?—Virginia Beach KOA to Lake Butler Campground. Because the KOA is 3 miles off the main route, you'll cycle 25.8 miles of this segment, and 49.7 miles of the next, for a total of 75.5 miles.

MILEAGE LOG

0.0   From Barnes Campground, go back to the Hwy. 615 junction and go straight. The highway is narrow, but very uncrowded.

2.7   MacKay Island National Wildlife Refuge headquarters is on the left. There are rest rooms, foot trails, and species information.

3.6   Market on the right.

4.1   Hwy. 615 curves around to the west.

6.8   Cross a small bridge over the inlet that makes Knott Island an island.

9.0   Enter state of Virginia! Hwy. 165 is now called Princess Anne Rd.

9.5   Seneca Campground on the left. In addition to the usual services, there's a pool, a laundromat, a small store, cabins, and some shaded sites.

13.5 Supermarket on the right.

17.0 Back Bay. Traffic begins to pick up as you go north. Road conditions are the same—no shoulders.

17.4 Small supermarket on the left.

21.3 Natasha's Bistro on the right, with good food and prices.

22.5 Pungo. There are plenty of convenience stores and restaurants from here on through Virginia Beach. Motel accommodations are also plentiful in Virginia Beach.

25.8 Junction. Turn right on General Booth Blvd., which sports a bike lane. **ALTERNATE ROUTE**: Those choosing to forego camping at the KOA should skip to the Virginia Beach KOA to Lake Butler Campground segment at the 3-mile mark.

28.8 Virginia Beach KOA on the right. It's more than 2 miles to the beach, but a trolley will transport you there free of charge from Memorial Day through Labor Day. You may want to forego riding in heavy traffic and take advantage of this service. In addition to the usual amenities, you'll find two pools, free miniature golf, a grocery store (there's another grocery store 1 mile prior to the campground), and shaded sites. The campground is open from March through November.

Virginia Beach KOA to Lake Butler Campground (52.7 miles)

Although it would be nice and convenient to cross Chesapeake Bay via the Chesapeake Bay Bridge-Tunnel and continue up the coast, the bridge-tunnel is off limits to bicyclists. Bicycles are also not permitted on two other area bridges: the James River Bridge at Newport News, and the Hampton Roads Bridge-Tunnel.

Taking that into consideration, this guide takes you northwest to Williamsburg, then northeast to Smith Point. From there, you'll travel by boat to either Smith or Tangier Island, continuing on to the mainland at Crisfield, Maryland. The route again drops back into Virginia for a night at Assateague Island, famous for its wild ponies.

There's a bonus to heading inland, however, and it comes in the form of Jamestown, Williamsburg, and Yorktown. Those traveling straight up the coast would miss these fine historic towns. They'd also miss Virginia's Northern Neck, a land of natural waterways adorned with creeks and inlets. Unless you leave very early on a weekend morning, you're bound to experience a nerve-wracking ride along 8 miles of Princess Anne Road. The busy road is narrow and without shoulders for much of the way and during rush-hour traffic it's treacherous. Unfortunately, there aren't any other roads in the area heading west that sport bike lanes.

Providence Road and the Military Highway provide some relief, although they are congested too. Riding through Suffolk is a bit congested, but seems a breeze when compared to Virginia Beach.

Once out of town, however, you'll soon forget about the hustle and bustle of city riding. Along Virginia's quiet back roads you may see deer, a variety of birds, turtles, and lush forests. You'll rarely see a car.

Gentle, rolling hills, and some curves add personality to the ride. Fields of grains—corn and more—add spice. This segment ends at the Lake Butler Campground, a clean, quiet camp.

MILEAGE LOG

0.0 From the Virginia Beach KOA, go back the way you came. You can use the bike lane on the opposite side of the street if you like.

3.0 Junction with General Booth Blvd./Princess Anne Rd. Head straight on Princess Anne Rd., a four-lane shoulderless highway. As mentioned previously, ride out of town early on a weekend morning if possible.

3.2 Road is now two lanes, narrow, with no shoulder. Traffic is heavy.

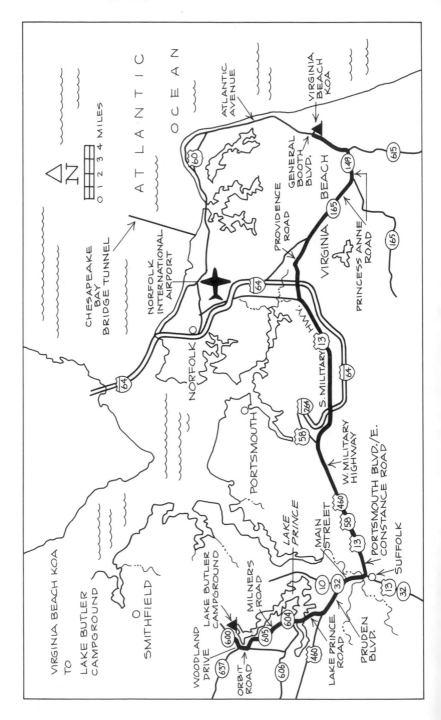

5.3   Stay on Princess Anne Rd. (Hwy. 165), which takes off to the right.

10.6   Road increases to four lanes; still no shoulder.

11.2   Turn left on Providence Rd., which begins as four lanes, but narrows to two almost immediately; no shoulder. **SIDE TRIP:** There's a bike shop another 0.5 mile up Princess Anne Rd. at the corner of Green Meadows Dr.

13.0   Road widens to four lanes; no shoulder. Travel through residential areas at first, then there are some markets, restaurants, et cetera. Traffic is a bit heavy, but not nearly as congested as on Princess Anne Rd.

14.9   Cross over I-64.

16.3   Turn left on S. Military Hwy. (US 13). There's a shoulder for the most part. Sometimes it disappears for a short time, however, or is very bumpy.

18.6   Road widens to six lanes; no shoulder.

19.3   Cross under Hwy. 168. The road is back to four lanes.

20.6   Cross under I-464.

21.5   Cross the southern branch of the Elizabeth River. After the crossing, there's a small shoulder.

21.9   Shoulder ends, but there's a side road to the right that bears little traffic. Motels and restaurants are available now. When this road ends, head back out on the main road, staying on US 13.

25.5   Cross under I-64.

28.6   Junction with West Military Hwy. Make a right, following US 13 South/US 58 West/US 460 West.

28.8   Turn left toward Suffolk on the above three highways. There's a wide shoulder now.

32.0   Suffolk city limits. This is Virginia's largest city (not in population but in land area) with a total of 430 square miles. Peanuts are the city's largest crop, with the headquarters of Planters Life-Savers Company established here in 1912.

35.2   Fork; go right on US 460 Business/US 58 Business/US 13 South to downtown Suffolk. Bikes are prohibited on the left fork.

36.3   Motels and restaurants begin. Once in town, this road is called Portsmouth Blvd., then E. Constance Rd.

39.3   Make a right on Main St., which is Hwys. 10 and 32 North. There's no shoulder.

40.8   Fork; go left on US 460 Business (Pruden Blvd.) and head out of town.

42.0   Pass under US 58.

43.9   Make a right on Lake Prince Rd. (CR 604). Now you'll travel secondary roads for the remainder of this segment, a welcome relief from the heavy traffic encountered in Virginia Beach. As you cycle along, you'll see Lake Prince, a 777-acre fishing dream with largemouth bass, striped bass, and blue-gill to name a few.

Fishing at Lake Prince, a 777-acre fishing dream

47.0 Make a left on CR 605 (Milners Rd. for now; later it becomes Murphy Hill Rd.)
50.5 Go right on CR 637 (Orbit Rd.). There's a small market on the left just past the junction: last chance for food until Jamestown.
51.0 Make a right on CR 600 (Woodland Dr.). Look for turtles in the pond along the way.
52.7 Lake Butler Campground, open March through November.
52.9 Reach the campground office via a hard-packed gravel road. You'll find a limited supply of groceries and all services, with both shady and open sites.

Lake Butler Campground to Jamestown Beach Campground (34.1 miles)

This ride is a real treat: it runs along narrow, uncrowded rural roads through tree-studded farmland with an occasional home here and there. A lack of cars will obviously delight all bikers, and with a short-mileage day you should have plenty of time for exploring Jamestown, a must-see.

The Jamestown Island portion of the Colonial National Historical Park (comprised of both Jamestown and Yorktown Battlefield) is lo-

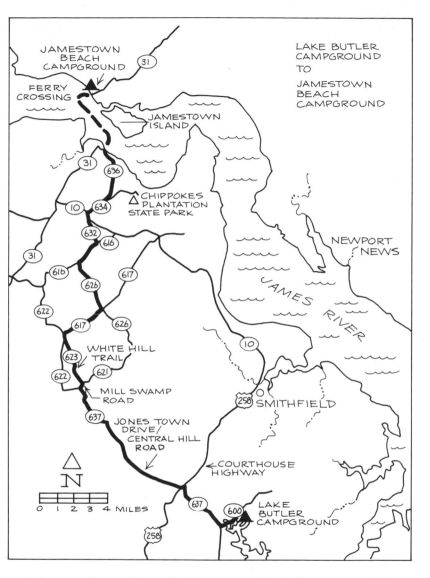

cated across the road from the Jamestown Beach Campground. Upon entering the park (open daily except Christmas), you can watch costumed craftsmen demonstrate the art of glassblowing at the reconstructed Jamestown Glasshouse of 1608. At the Dale House, artisans create pottery in the seventeenth-century style.

Although the town itself no longer exists, there's a visitor center at the edge of the original townsite. You'll find a theater, museum exhibits, a gift shop, and footpaths leading through the historic site. The

A costumed craftsman demonstrates the art of glassblowing at Jamestown.

Old Church Tower is all that remains of the original seventeenth-century structures.

Jamestown Festival Park boasts a re-creation of the original Jamestown, America's first permanent English settlement. A living-history museum located near the original town, it shows seventeenth-century Virginia as colonists and Powhatan Indians go about daily life. Real people, men and women alike, dressed in the costumes of the time, go about their daily chores, cooking food, repairing houses, mending clothes, and tanning deer hides, just like they did in those early days.

In addition, you'll view full-size reproductions of the tiny English ships—the *Susan Constant, Godspeed,* and *Discovery*—that departed from London, England, December 20, 1606, and arrived in Jamestown on May 13, 1607. Visitors may board the largest of the three, the 110-foot *Susan Constant,* for further inspection. The park is open daily except Christmas and New Years Day.

MILEAGE LOG

0.0   From Lake Butler Campground, go back the way you came.
1.7   Back at CR 637, turn right.
5.3   Junction; turn left on US 258, also called Courthouse Hwy.
5.6   Make a right, picking up CR 637 again (it's now called Central Hill Rd.).
11.3   CR 637 heads to the left and is now called Jones Town Dr.
14.8   Junction; turn right on CR 621 (Mill Swamp Rd.).
15.1   Go left on CR 623 (White Hill Trail).
17.6   Keep straight on CR 623, which merges into CR 622. (The roads aren't named now, only numbered.)
18.2   Turn right on CR 617.
21.0   Make a left on CR 626.
24.4   Go right on CR 616.
26.0   Turn left on CR 632.
27.5   Make another left on Hwy. 10. This shoulderless road may be busier than the others.
28.1   Make a right on CR 634. Again traffic is light.
29.5   Make a left on CR 636. This turn also leads to a **SIDE TRIP** to Chippokes Plantation State Park, a plantation established in 1619 by Captain William Powell of Jamestown. The plantation is to the right about 3 miles.
33.0   Turn right on CR 656, which leads to Hwy. 31 and a short ferry ride (there are numerous daily crossings) across the James River.
33.3   Ferry toll booth; fare is 15 cents. Automobile ferry service via the *Captain John Smith* began near this site on February 26, 1925, providing a significant link for Maine-to-Florida travelers.
33.8   Toll booth on the Jamestown side of the river.
34.1   Jamestown Beach Campground on the left; open all year. In addition to the usual services, there are shaded sites, groceries, and a small restaurant. Jamestown Island and Jamestown Festival Park are both across the street from the campground. Both charge an entrance fee.

Jamestown Beach Campground to Grey's Point Family Campground (56.9 miles)

You couldn't ask for a nicer ride from Williamsburg to Yorktown via the Colonial Parkway, as commercial trucks are prohibited. First, though, you'll ride from Jamestown to Williamsburg, pedaling directly through Colonial Williamsburg en route to the Colonial Parkway. Although this guide follows Highway 31, those who'd rather hop on the 23-mile Colonial Parkway can do so across the street at Jamestown. The parkway reaches downtown Williamsburg in about 8 or 9 miles.

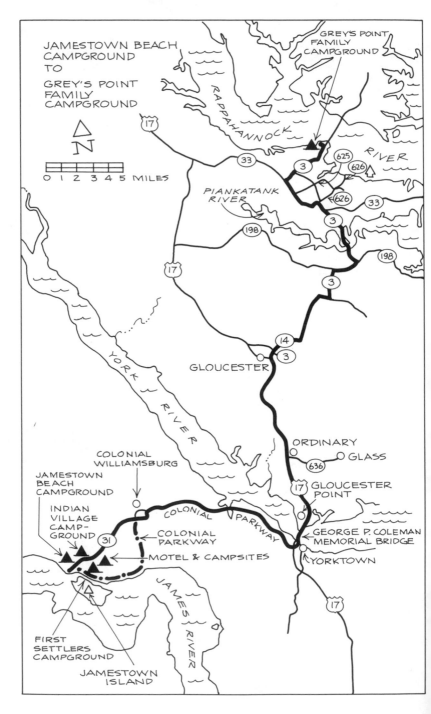

JAMESTOWN BEACH CAMPGROUND TO GREY'S POINT FAMILY CAMPGROUND

Costumed "colonists" at Colonial Williamsburg

Colonial Williamsburg is a definite must-see and a fun place to cycle, as there are many interesting streets to explore. The capital city of colonial Virginia has been restored to its eighteenth-century appearance, with many of the homes and buildings open to the public, although it will cost you: tickets are quite expensive. If you'd rather see the town for free, you can pedal up and down the various streets, just looking at the buildings and visiting some of the gift shops for an inside view. Colonial Williamsburg is open daily.

Yorktown is also an interesting stop, and it's free.

On October 19, 1781, the Yorktown Battlefield saw one-third of all British forces in North America surrender to colonial troops under the command of General George Washington. Today, visitors can see the historic buildings in Yorktown or take a ranger-guided tour of the

Yorktown Battlefield. Directions for a self-guided drive of the battle-field and a walking tour of Yorktown are also available. The Battlefield visitor center, open daily except Christmas, offers a free film, gift shop, museum, and rooftop overlook.

After visiting Yorktown, it's a hectic ride north on US 17, where traffic increases. Fortunately, you'll switch over to Highway 3 after about 12 miles, where you'll find a bit of a reprieve from the traffic.

The day ends at Grey's Point, a beautiful spot along the Rappahannock River where brilliant sunsets paint the sky, fishing is out of this world, and peace and quiet are yours for the asking.

MILEAGE LOG

0.0 From Jamestown Beach Campground, go north on Hwy. 31. This road is two lanes, narrow or with no shoulder.

0.5 First Settlers Campground, a full-service camp on the right.

1.3 Indian Village Campground on the left; all services and shady sites.

1.4 Convenience store on the left.

1.5 Motel and campsites on the right.

2.4 Matoaka Lake.

Cyclist camping at Jamestown Beach Campground

3.6 Market and other shops as you enter Williamsburg. Hwy. 31 is called Jamestown Rd. upon entering town, where you will find all services. This is a good route through town; streets are fairly wide.

5.4 College of William and Mary.

5.7 Fork; turn left at signed "Northern Boundary," then make a quick right on unsigned Duke of Gloucester Rd. This is the main road through historic Williamsburg. Though it is closed to motor vehicles, expect immense flocks of people during the summer, weekends, and holidays.

6.5 When you see the Capitol Building straight ahead, curve to the right, reaching a stop sign in 100 yards. Turn left on Francis.

6.8 Fork; head left on Hwy. 31 North, also called Page St.

7.4 Turn right on Hwy. 162 East (2nd St.).

7.5 Laundromat on the left.

7.6 Go left on Hwy. 163 North.

7.8 Hop on the on-ramp toward Yorktown, pedaling east on Colonial Pkwy., a wide two-lane road where commercial traffic is prohibited.

10.5 Cross the Jones Mill Pond.

11.4 Cross over Hwy. 199.

12.7 Cross Kings Creek.

13.9 Felgates Creek crossing. The road travels along the York River now. Look for the Ringfield Picnic Area on your left before crossing Felgates Creek.

15.5 Indian Field Creek.

17.0 Brackens Pond.

19.4 Junction with US 17; keep straight.

19.5 Cross Yorktown Creek.

19.8 Junction with Hwy. 238. Keep straight to the Yorktown Museum and visitor center.

20.1 Visitor center. There are rest rooms in addition to the film, exhibits, and gift shop. After visiting the area, cycle back the way you came.

20.4 Turn right on Zweybrücken Rd., toward Yorktown.

20.6 Pass the Victory Monument, now traveling Main St. through Yorktown. Be sure to pick up the Town Tour guide at the visitor center, which describes Yorktown and the buildings seen today.

20.9 Turn left on Ballard St. as you exit town.

21.1 Turn right on Alexander Hamilton Blvd.

21.3 Walk your bike over the barricade leading to US 17. Make a right on US 17 and go north. The road is four lanes, with no shoulder.

21.6 George P. Coleman Memorial Bridge over the York River. The Virginia Department of Transportation prohibits bicycling across the bridge, but you can walk across (fortunately, there's a narrow sidewalk). Be thankful you have to walk, as wide expansion joints near the top would undoubtedly swallow up bicycle tires.

22.3 Exit the bridge; enter Gloucester Point soon after. There are motels and other services for the next few miles. The road is four lanes, with a narrow shoulder.

27.5 Junction with Hwy. 636. **SIDE TRIP:** Gloucester Point Campground is located about 4 miles away and it offers a laundromat, groceries, a recreation room, a pool, and fishing opportunities in addition to the usual services. To reach the campground go east 0.5 mile on Hwy. 636, south 1.5 miles on Hwy. 656, south 1 mile on Hwy. 641, east 0.3 mile on Hwy. 655, and north 0.2 mile on Hwy. 714.

27.6 Enter Ordinary.

28.0 End of shoulder. Traffic may be quite heavy.

33.6 Fork; make a right on Hwy. 3 West and Hwy. 14 East.

34.8 Shopping center on the left.

34.9 Head right on Hwy. 3 West; historic Gloucester is to your left. The road is two lanes, with no shoulder. Traffic is usually not as heavy here.

37.5 Shoulder begins—not the smoothest, but it's there if you need it.

40.8 Market on the left.

41.4 Turn left on Hwy. 3 West. The road is two lanes, with no shoulder, but fairly uncrowded.

43.5 Hwy. 3 merges with Hwy. 198 East. Keep right on Hwy. 3.

Rappahannock River at sunset from Grey's Point Campground

45.1 Head left (north) on Hwy. 3 West.

46.0 Bridge over the Piankatank River. There's a shoulder on the bridge only.

49.7 Turn left on Hwy. 3 and Hwy. 33 West. There's a convenience store and restaurant nearby. There's a shoulder now.

50.2 Junction with Hwy. 626; keep straight. **SIDE TRIP:** Hwy. 626 leads to the Sangraal By-the-Sea AYH, located on Chesapeake Bay. It is open year-round. If you'd like to spend the night at the hostel, located on Mill Creek Landing Rd. in Wake, follow Hwy. 626 for about 3 miles. For further information, write or call P.O. Box 187, Urbanna, VA 23175; (804) 776-6500.

52.9 No shoulder now.

53.2 Keep right on Hwy. 3.

56.0 Motel/restaurant on the left.

56.9 Turnoff on the left to Grey's Point Family Campground, located on the shores of the Rappahannock River. This full-service camp is open from March 15 through November 15, and offers reasonably priced, shaded sites and a limited supply of snacks.

Grey's Point Family Campground to Janes Island State Park (34.2 miles)

Be sure to leave Grey's Point early in the morning if possible, as the bridge over the Rappahannock River is 2 miles long and quite narrow. An early-morning crossing would be much more relaxing.

Rolling hills and uncrowded roads are delightfully yours as you pedal through Virginia countryside where lush green vegetation predominates and farms speckle the land.

Visit historic Christ Church en route through several very small towns on your way to either Smith or Tangier Island. Both islands promise secluded, quaint fishing villages and both require a private cruise ship crossing from near Reedville, Virginia. Choose the island of your choice, then it's on to Crisfield, Maryland, and Janes Island State Park, a wonderful place to visit along Tangier Sound. In the summer, pontoon boats take campers across to Janes Island, an undeveloped haven with miles of isolated shoreline and sandy beaches.

There are two options to crossing Chesapeake Bay. You can go from the Buzzard's Point Marina to Tangier Island and then on to Crisfield, or you can pedal to the Chesapeake/Smith Island KOA, take the ship to Smith Island, and then on to Crisfield.

The ships operate several days a week or month in May, depending on the demand, and daily from Memorial Day to October. A three-day advance notice is requested, and highly recommended, for each boat operator, but it's not mandatory. Be prepared for delays at either

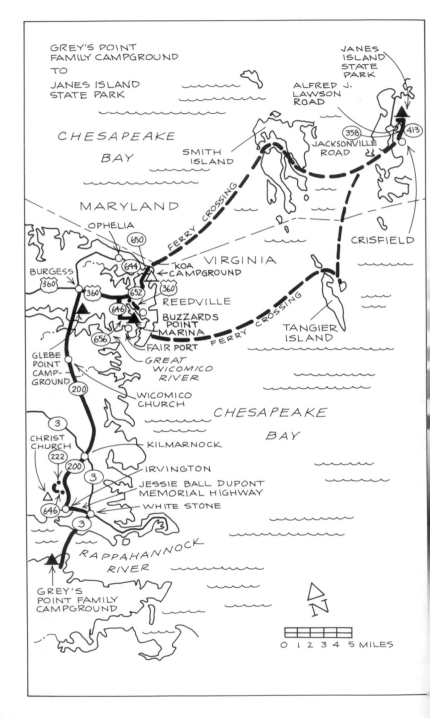

GREY'S POINT
FAMILY CAMPGROUND
TO
JANES ISLAND
STATE PARK

marina. Boats may be detained a day or so because of bad weather or due to a lack of customers.

Buzzard's Point offers free camping to bikers interested in going to Tangier Island via the *Chesapeake Breeze* (804-333-4656). It offers the usual services and some shade. Pop and snack machines are available. Rates are $10.75 (including bike) to Tangier Island. From Tangier Island to Crisfield, you'll have to employ the *Steven Thomas* (301-968-2338) for another $12. The *Chesapeake Breeze* leaves the marina at 10:00 A.M. and the *Steven Thomas* will have you in Crisfield about 5:00 P.M.

From the KOA, you'll board the *Captain Evans* (804-453-3430) for $10 and it'll deposit you at Smith Island in about 1½ hours. With several hours to spare, you'll have time to explore the island, eat lunch, et cetera. Several private boats will transport you to Crisfield, but the *Mail Boat* (301-968-3206) is the cheapest. Cost is $5 and the boat leaves at 4:00 P.M. You'll get to Crisfield by 5:00 P.M.

The total cost for boating over from the KOA to Crisfield via Smith Island is $15. It'll cost $22.75 for the same service via Tangier Island. (Prices quoted reflect 1991 rates.) If you decide to spend two days cycling this segment and you need a campsite, it's cheaper to go to Tangier Island and take advantage of the free site. If you don't need a campsite, opting instead to cycle straight through to Maryland, it's by far cheaper to go via the KOA and Smith Island.

MILEAGE LOG

0.0 Entrance at Grey's Point Family Campground. Continue north on Hwy. 3.

0.3 Begin crossing the narrow and shoulderless bridge over the Rappahannock River.

2.2 End of bridge. There's no toll, although the current state map shows it as a toll bridge. A shoulder escorts you into town.

3.2 White Stone corporate limits; store and cafe in town.

3.8 Turn left on Hwy. 200 (also called the Jessie Ball Dupont Memorial Hwy.) toward Irvington. This two-lane road, like others you'll be traveling today, is shoulderless (although sometimes there's a narrow shoulder), with little traffic.

4.9 Cross Carters Creek. Enter Irvington corporate limits just after the crossing. Stay to the right on Hwy. 200.

5.7 Services are limited here, although an inn is nearby.

6.7 Convenience store on the right.

6.9 Junction with CR 646. **SIDE TRIP:** Turn left to go to the historic Christ Church, 0.7 mile away. Completed in 1732 by Robert "King" Carter, the Christ Church is one of a very few colonial churches in America that have never been altered. Carter reserved one-quarter of the seats in the typical early eighteenth-century structure for his tenants and servants. Robert Carter is buried here. The church is open daily except for Christmas.

8.0 Junction with Hwy. 222; market on the left. Those visiting the Christ Church can loop back onto Hwy. 222 at this point.

9.6 Kilmarnock corporate limits and bird sanctuary.

10.4 Head left on Hwy. 3 West and Hwy. 200 North. Just before the junction, there's a supermarket on the right. Head through the downtown area.

10.5 Turn right on Hwy. 200 North. If you're in need of a restaurant, fast food, or supermarket, et cetera, continue on Hwy. 3 for 0.6 mile.

15.3 Small store on the left.

17.8 Enter the town of Wicomico Church.

18.3 Two small combination market/delis on the right.

20.5 Cross the Great Wicomico Bridge; narrow shoulder. Be careful crossing the steel deck. It's slippery when wet or dry.

21.5 Glebe Point Campground on the right near junction with Hwy. 753. You'll find shady sites, a pool, and a laundromat in addition to the usual amenities.

22.7 General store and restaurant on the left.

23.4 Junction. Turn right on US 360 East. There's a restaurant on the left as you enter Burgess.

23.5 Road is four lanes now, with no shoulder.

23.9 Road narrows to two lanes; narrow shoulder at times, none at others.

24.6 Market on the left; convenience store/deli next door.

26.5 Keep to the left on US 360. There's a restaurant in Lilian, at the junction with CR 646, which leads to Fair Port. **ALTERNATE ROUTE**: If you're heading to Tangier Island, turn right on CR 646 toward Fair Port. In 1.3 miles turn left on CR 656, pedaling to the Buzzard's Point Marina in another 0.5 mile. From here you can take the ship to Tangier Island. (If you need groceries, from the junction of CR 646 and CR 656, go 0.7 mile on CR 646. There's a market on the left.)

27.4 Motel on the right.

28.3 Fork; head left on CR 652 to Beveryville, and the signed Smith Island cruises. A short **SIDE TRIP** leads to the right 2.3 miles to historic Reedville via US 360. Reedville, one of the busiest fishing ports in the nation, offers several bed-and-breakfast inns in stunning Victorian mansions, and a convenience store/deli.

28.6 Country store on the left.

30.2 Junction with CR 644 and CR 651. Keep left on CR 644.

30.7 Junction. Go right on CR 650.

31.1 KOA entrance. A gravel road leads to the office. This full-service camp has a pool, a laundromat, limited groceries, and shaded sites. If it's hot, you might consider an air-conditioned Kamping Kabin, also available.

Elizabeth House bed-and-breakfast inn, Reedville

31.2 Arrive in Crisfield, Maryland, after ferrying over to Smith Island or Tangier Island en route. Cycle Main St. through the full-service town.

31.4 **SIDE TRIP:** At 9th St., turn right and go 0.1 mile if you'd like to go to the visitor center or the Governor J. Millard Tawes Historical Museum. Before heading out to camp, you may want to explore Crisfield, home of Maryland's largest marina, an annual crab and clam bake on the third Wednesday in July, and a three-day event on Labor Day weekend, including the famous Crab Derby. Crisfield's working waterfront is still the heart of the community, a town built primarily on a huge bed of oyster shells. Crabbing has replaced oystering in recent years, however, with crabs the foundation of the local seafood trade. In fact, John T. Handy Company of Crisfield is the largest soft-shell crab processor and shipper in the world.

31.6 Fork; head to the left on Hwy. 413. The highway is shoulderless through town; later, a parking lane provides plenty of room.

32.6 Cycle left onto CR 358 (Jacksonville Rd.). There's a shoulder now.

33.8 Turn left on Alfred J. Lawson Rd.

34.2 Janes Island State Park entrance booth. Located on Tangier Sound, this full-service, 3,600-acre park is popular for swimming, fishing, and crabbing. There are more than 100 shady sites. Four modern three-bedroom cabins are also available. The cabins have electric heat and fireplaces, and bed linens are furnished. There's a two-night minimum-stay requirement, with reservations and a deposit necessary. Although the campground is open year-round, the cabins are available only from March through November.

Janes Island State Park to Assateague State Park (66.7 miles)

Most of this ride is virtually free of traffic and passes through scenic farm- and ranchland, where chickens are raised for name-brand chicken suppliers. From Janes Island State Park you'll travel through rural Maryland, where shoulders are often available and convenience stores are few and scattered about.

Head northeast through the state, stopping at various small towns along the way. Snow Hill and Milburn Landing at Pocomoke State Park are particularly nice. A walk or ride through historic Berlin is also a real treat. Marvel at the many celebrated homes, including the preserved Calvin B. Taylor Home. It is open to the public, and knowledgeable hosts will answer your questions.

Then it's on to Assateague State Park, a barrier island fashioned by sand and chronic waves, where wild ponies roam the land. According to National Park Service literature, "Today's wild ponies on Assateague Island are descended from domesticated stock that was grazed on the island as early as the seventeenth century by Eastern Shore planters. The planters grazed their horses here to avoid mainland taxes and fencing requirements."

Although the ponies often appear docile, don't approach too closely as they are unpredictable and may bite. It is illegal to feed or pet the ponies.

MILEAGE LOG

0.0 Toll booth at Janes Island State Park campground. Head back out to the main road.

0.4 Turn left on CR 358 (Jacksonville Rd.). There's no shoulder, but the road is uncrowded.

1.4 Road turns into Plantation Rd. Continue straight.

1.9 Back at junction with Hwy. 413; turn left. There's a wide shoulder now.

4.6 Go right on Hwy. 667; no shoulder, but traffic is nil. There's a convenience store at the junction.

4.8 Marion; you're now riding what is known as the Beach to Bay Indian Trail, a self-guided driving tour of Maryland's Southern Eastern Shore, a low, flat, and sandy region comprised of tidal creeks, vast wetlands, evergreens, and fertile farmland.

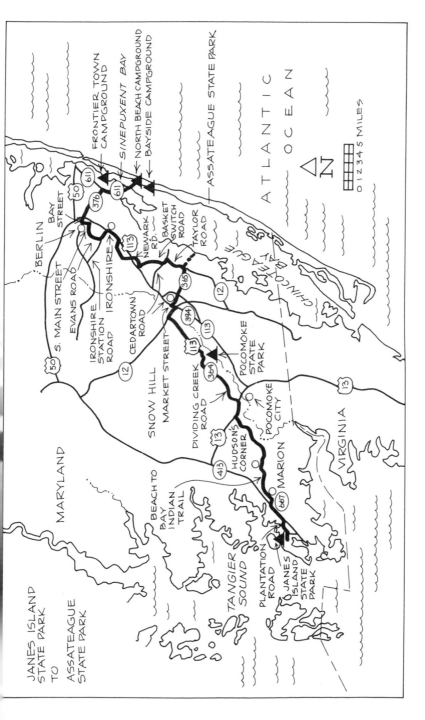

5.4 General store/cafe.

9.2 Hwy. 667 jogs to the right at Hudson's Corner. Old Country Store Museum is located at the junction, and open by appointment only.

11.7 Market on the left. There's a shoulder now.

16.5 Junction. Turn right on US 13 South; there's a wide shoulder.

18.4 Make a left on Hwy. 364, also called Dividing Creek Rd. There's a good shoulder. **SIDE TRIP:** If you need something to eat before making this turn, go straight on US 13 to Pocomoke City in about 2 miles.

18.7 Market on the left.

23.8 End of shoulder; however, road is uncrowded.

24.9 Milburn Landing at Pocomoke State Park. **SIDE TRIP:** It's 0.9 mile to the registration office, and the camp is just beyond. Shady and sunny sites are available at this all-service camp, which is open one week before Easter to the first week in December. The Pocomoke River stretches 73 miles, conceived in the Great Cypress Swamp on the Maryland–Delaware border, merging into Chesapeake Bay at Pocomoke Sound. A tidal river, with up to a 3-foot rise and fall, it is a popular spot for fishing, canoeing, hiking, biking, and wildlife-watching. Those with animal life on their minds should note that 27 species of mammals, 14 species of amphibians, and 172 species of birds have been observed in the wetlands hugging the river.

31.8 Junction. Turn right on Hwy. 12. There's a wide shoulder now.

31.5 Enter Snow Hill, a tiny town embraced by enormous sycamores and stately homes. Founded by English colonists in 1642, the town was named after a district in London. There are restaurants, markets, and three bed-and-breakfast inns.

32.9 Cross the Pocomoke River. The library is just ahead as you enter this historic town. Bikers are urged to take the time to cruise the various streets, marveling at some of the buildings that date back to early years.

33.0 Junction. Turn left on Hwy. 394 (Market St.). **SIDE TRIP:** If you're interested, there's a museum nearby. From the junction, go right for three blocks. The Julia A. Purnell Museum houses a collection of colonial and Indian lore.

33.2 Make a right on Hwy. 365 (Bay St.).

33.6 Wide shoulder now.

34.2 Cross US 113.

39.5 Turn left on Taylor Rd. There's no shoulder, like the roads to come, but it's uncrowded. **SIDE TRIP** to the water at Chincoteague Bay: before turning on Taylor Rd., continue straight on Hwy. 365 for 1.6 miles. There are outhouses and a shady picnic area.

42.0   Keep to the left at the fork.

42.3   Turn right on Basket Switch Rd.

45.9   Make another right on Newark Rd.

46.7   Cross US 113 and continue on Newark Rd.

47.5   Newark Post Office on the right. **SIDE TRIP:** If you need a snack or groceries, go right on the first street (Patey Woods Rd.) past the post office. A convenience store and laundromat are out on US 113 in 0.3 mile.

49.7   Junction. Make a left on US 113. There's a wide shoulder.

52.1   Country store on the right. Exit busy US 113 by turning left on Ironshire Station Rd. There are no shoulders, but the road is un-crowded. **ALTERNATE ROUTE**: If you'd rather take US 113, the direct route, head north for approximately 3 miles. You'll reach the junction of US 113 and Hwy. 376 in Berlin, the 58.0-mile mark for this segment.

53.6   Just beyond the railroad tracks, turn right on Evans Rd., which becomes Buckingham Lane in 2.8 miles.

56.9   Make a left on S. Main St., entering Berlin. There's a small market on the left.

57.6   Turn right on Bay St., which is just across from the Atlantic Hotel. Although a fine place to stay, understandably the hotel does not permit bikes in its rooms. There's a bed-and-breakfast inn in town as well. If you'd like to explore historic Berlin, go right ahead. Free maps of the newly restored downtown area make the trip much easier. Of special interest is the Calvin B. Taylor Museum, a restored "turn-of-the-century home" located 0.2 mile ahead on Main St. The museum is free, but a donation is requested.

58.0   Bay St. leads to the junction of US 113 and Hwy. 376 East at this point. Go straight on Hwy. 376. There's no shoulder; traffic may be heavy.

59.2   General store on the right. A wide shoulder begins just past the store.

61.4   Cross Ayres Creek.

62.2   Junction. Go right on Hwy. 611. The wide shoulder continues. There's a market and restaurant at the junction, and the Frontier Town Campground is just across the street and to the left. This full-service camp offers shady sites, a pool, and a laundromat.

62.3   Store on the right.

64.0   Restaurant/market on the right.

64.5   Fork; keep to the left on Hwy. 611.

65.0   Assateague State Park headquarters on the right.

65.2   Barrier Islands visitor center for the Assateague Island National Seashore on the right.

65.3   Boat landing/rest rooms on the left.

65.5 Verrazano Bridge crossing over Sinepuxent Bay.

66.4 **SIDE TRIP:** If you'd like to camp at the national seashore, detour right about 2 miles to North Beach and Bayside campgrounds. Open all summer, both camps offer primitive sites. There are chemical toilets and cold outdoor showers.

66.7 Registration office for Assateague State Park. The state park camp offers all services. Also, there's a small camp store and restaurant in the summer.

Wild ponies at Assateague State Park

MIDDLE ATLANTIC STATES

Cyclist riding along a deserted Atlantic Coast back road

Although you'll no doubt marvel at Delaware's lovely coastline, and certainly enjoy New Jersey's popular shore as well, you won't see much of the coast during this portion of your ride.

After corresponding with a number of New Jersey cyclists and the New Jersey Department of Transportation, I made the decision to head inland in Ocean City, bypassing Atlantic City and points north such as New York City. It was done for obvious reasons—to avoid the chaos associated with New York City and surrounding areas.

Fortunately, the trip does not suffer by riding inland. If anything, it is probably enhanced, for it provides a unique look at rural New Jersey, its Pine Barrens, and the lovely Delaware River, a liquid fence dividing New Jersey and Pennsylvania. Best of all, you'll see a part of New York totally unlike what most people think of when they hear "New York." This region is basically quiet with jaunts through farm country and quaint towns. (Traffic picks up some as you enter Poughkeepsie and cycle north along the Hudson River.)

You'll cycle 442.4 miles through the Middle Atlantic States. Delaware provides 29.2 miles, New Jersey boasts 277.4 miles, Pennsylvania offers a mere 15.5 miles, and you'll ride 120.3 miles through New York.

Terrain changes immensely upon entering the Middle Atlantic States, for it is not only flat in sections, but mountainous as well. Although you'll enjoy an easy ride in Delaware and on through much of New Jersey, you will come face to face with a number of steep climbs along the Delaware River and into New York as well. On a positive note, most of the climbs are not that long (although it may seem like it).

Roads in Delaware are substantial, with fairly wide lanes common. If the roads aren't perfect, their beaches are, and historical Lewes is a definite must-see en route to day's end at Cape Henlopen State Park.

A ferry transports you to Cape May, New Jersey, a restored town where it's possible to spend the whole day just cruising around town, admiring the wide array of elderly buildings. From there, toll bridges and fairly wide roads lead north along the New Jersey coast to Ocean City where you'll head inland through rural New Jersey, a place where traffic is nil and small towns dot the land.

Upon reaching Hightstown, another region void of campgrounds, you'll have to determine once again if you should splurge and get a motel room, or ask someone to use a speck of his or her lawn for the night.

Although road conditions in New Jersey don't pose a problem in most cases, you will encounter heavy traffic upon cycling out of Hightstown. Fortunately, you'll latch onto some quieter roads about 12 miles out of town.

The D & R Canal Towpath offers peaceful cycling along the Delaware River and when it ends, you'll travel uncrowded roads (most are secondary) on both sides of the Delaware, until reaching New York.

New York highways skirt through an abundance of tiny towns, the only portion of the entire ride where it was often difficult to find a rest room. In most Eastern towns, customers—paying or not—have access to rest rooms. Others allow use as long as some purchase is made. But in New York, many businesses refuse the simple request of paying customers as well.

Traffic increases upon entering New Paltz and remains so as you cross the Hudson River at Poughkeepsie, traveling north on Highway

9 past several fabulous mansions, including the former home of Franklin D. Roosevelt, now a historic site open to the public.

After entering Rhinebeck, you'll return to the serenity of back-road bicycling, with rural roads linking several small towns en route to the Connecticut border.

Cold winters and warm, humid summers are common in all the Middle Atlantic States. Highs are usually in the mid-80s during the summer, cooler in the spring and fall (around 70 degrees Fahrenheit in May and October), with snow falling on some areas from November through March. Prevailing winds usually blow from the south/southwest, May through September.

Rain gear is a necessity, as precipitation can be expected all year, with slightly heavier concentrations in the summer due to afternoon or evening thunderstorms.

For additional information in regards to road conditions and bicycling, contact:

Larry Klepner, bicycle coordinator
Delaware Department of Transportation
P.O. Box 778
Dover, DE 19903
(302) 739-3267

William Feldman, pedestrian/bicycle advocate
New Jersey Department of Transportation
1035 Parkway Ave. CN600
Trenton, NJ 08625
(609) 530-8062

Eric Eisenstein, bicycle safety coordinator
State of New York Governor's Traffic Safety Commission
Swan St. Bldg., Core 1, 4th Floor, Rm. 414
Albany, NY 12228

Gerald R. Fritz, director
Center for Program Development and Management
Pennsylvania Department of Transportation
Rm. 917, Transportation and Safety Bldg.
Harrisburg, PA 17120
(717) 787-2862

Assateague State Park to Cape Henlopen State Park (47.1 miles)

Wild ponies may bid you farewell as you leave Assateague State Park en route to Ocean City, Maryland. A long, extended beach city, Ocean City offers 10 miles of white, sandy, public beaches, numerous accommodations, and fine dining. In addition, there is a variety of shops and eating establishments along the 3-mile boardwalk. You can pedal along the boardwalk, home of one of the nation's oldest operating handcarved wooden merry-go-rounds, until 10:00 A.M. in the summer.

Enter Delaware, a small state (forty-ninth in size among the fifty states) with a ladybug reigning as state insect. Things quiet down as you move through a patchwork of residential and commercial districts, plus state parks. The three state parks limit the amount of man-made products seen here. Pedal along and you'll be awed by the natural beauty encompassing Delaware's 25-mile coastline.

Delaware Seashore State Park is particularly nice, with its campground located on the beautiful Indian River Inlet. This area makes for rainbow sunsets, spectacular fishing, and a great place to relax.

Lewes, just west of Cape Henlopen, is one town you won't want to miss. A seafaring town, Lewes is blessed with an excellent harbor and is home to a large fleet of charter fishing boats. It is also home to many

The boardwalk at Ocean City, Maryland

historic buildings, some built as early as the 1700s. Pick up a free "Historic Lewes, Delaware, Visitors Guide and Walking Tour" map at the visitor center.

The day ends at Cape Henlopen, with more than 4 miles of open shoreline where the Atlantic Ocean greets Delaware Bay. Be sure to look for Great Dune, which rises 80 feet above the shore at Cape Henlopen. It is the highest sand dune between Cape Hatteras and Cape Cod.

Nearly nonstop shoulders and pretty scenes make this ride a treat.

MILEAGE LOG

0.0 From the entrance at Assateague State Park Campground, go back the way you came.

4.5 Back at the junction of Hwys. 611 and 376, go straight on Hwy. 611, past the Frontier Campground mentioned in the Janes Island State Park to Assateague State Park segment, and a convenience store. There's a wide shoulder.

6.2 Junction with Eagle Nest Rd. The Eagle Nest Campground is located 1.6 miles down this road. You'll find all services and little shade.

8.1 Junction with Hwy. 701.

8.5 Make a right on US 50. You'll find all services from here to points miles and miles beyond. Traffic is heavy now, but there's a wide shoulder.

9.3 Begin crossing Assawoman Bay en route to Ocean City. The bridge is shoulderless, but there's a sidewalk.

9.9 Fork; go left on Division St.

10.0 Junction of Division and Baltimore. Go left on Baltimore, a one-way three-lane street with no shoulders. From 6:00 A.M. to 10:00 A.M. you can ride the 3-mile boardwalk if you'd rather. The boardwalk is about 100 yards straight up Division. **SIDE TRIP:** The Ocean City Life-Saving Museum is down the boardwalk to the right about 0.5 mile. Built in 1891, the building is one of the oldest structures in town. There are two large aquariums, many prized possessions, and a gift shop. A fee is charged.

11.1 Make a left on 15th St.

11.2 Go right on Philadelphia Ave., also called Hwy. 528. There's a special lane for bikes and buses, but bicyclists must yield to buses. The ride through the famous city itself would be a real nightmare if it weren't for this restricted lane.

11.8 Bike shop.

12.7 Ocean City visitor and convention center on the left.

13.8 Bike lane ends at 59th St. The road, now six lanes, is very busy.

14.0 Junction with Hwy. 90; continue straight on Hwy. 528, now called Coastal Hwy.

14.1 Bike/bus lane begins again.

14.6 Bike shop on the left.

18.8 Enter Delaware at a junction with Hwy. 54 West. The bike/bus lane ends, but there's a wide shoulder. You are now traveling Hwy. 1.

19.9 Visitor center on the right; last of the motels and restaurants for a while.

20.0 Fenwick Island State Park.

20.2 Entrance to the park on the right. There's a bathhouse with warm showers, rest rooms, and a snack stand. Access to the beach and facilities is free for cyclists. The 208-acre 3-mile-long park is a favorite with surf fishermen, beachcombers, swimmers, and surfers.

22.8 South Bethany; several shops in the area.

23.7 Restaurant, convenience stores.

24.5 Bethany Beach marker. Jog on over to the right a couple of blocks if you want to explore the town and boardwalk.

24.9 Junction with Hwy. 26.

28.6 Motel on the left as you enter Delaware Seashore State Park.

28.8 Beach access via a sandy road to the right.

29.6 Paved entrance leads to Delaware Seashore State Park Campground, open March 15 through November 15, and day-use area. Once you've completed your visit, return to the park entrance and begin crossing the bridge over the Indian River Inlet. The

Sunset along the Indian River, Delaware Seashore State Park

day-use area at the park is free for bicyclists. There are showers, rest rooms, and a concession stand. This is a popular surfing beach, although surfing is not allowed from 10:00 A.M. to 6:00 P.M. during the summer. The campground is reached by riding under the bridge, along the Indian River Inlet, to the registration booth. You'll find open sites at the full-service camp where grand sunsets abound. Watch at sunset as hordes of fishermen throw in their lines, sometimes hooking fish as fast as they can lure them in.

30.2 Turn left if you need state park information or permits, or if you'd like to go to the marina.

30.6 Day-use area on the right.

31.8 Small market/bait shop on the left.

34.6 Day-use areas on both the Atlantic Ocean and Rehoboth Bay.

35.5 Dewey Beach city limits; services begin.

36.2 Turn right on Hwy. 1A; shoulder continues.

37.0 Cross Silver Lake and enter Rehoboth Beach.

37.6 Make a left on Rehoboth Beach Rd. **SIDE TRIP:** If you'd like to explore the town, ride the boardwalk (before 10:00 A.M. in the summer), or shop in some of the numerous stores, head to the right. Please note: Rehoboth, a biblical word meaning "room enough," has become known as the Nation's Summer Capital due to the invasion of Washington-area visitors. Plan your visit accordingly.

37.7 Public library on the left.

37.9 Bike shop on the left. Just past this point, keep left at the fork.

38.1 Visitor center on the right.

38.7 Hwy. 1A merges with Hwy. 1, taking off to the right. Ride the service road (Hebron Rd.) for a short distance.

39.1 Hebron Rd. merges with Hwy. 1. Go right (north).

40.9 Junction with Hwy. 24. CR 270, located just before this junction, leads to the right to the Big Oaks Campground, a full-service camp located 0.5 mile away. You'll find all services in this area.

42.1 Take the right fork (US 9) toward Cape Henlopen State Park. The shoulder continues.

43.5 Lewes (pronounced "Lewis").

43.8 Turn left to go to historic Lewes, now driving the Kings Hwy.; no shoulder. **ALTERNATE ROUTE:** If you'd rather bypass the town, you can keep to the right at the fork, meeting up with this segment at the 45.5-mile mark.

44.5 Visitor center on the left. Just ahead is a junction. Turn right on Savannah Rd.

44.7 Cross the bridge over the Lewes-Rehoboth Canal. A shoulder begins at the end of the bridge. There's a bike shop on the left just past the bridge.

45.1 Make a right on Henlopen Dr.

45.5 Junction with US 9. This is where those who decided to bypass the historic area will meet up with the route.

45.9 Ferry entrance on the left; the ferry runs daily all year, with additional departures scheduled in the summer. The 70-minute (one-way) cruise lands at Cape May, New Jersey. In 1991 the price for a bicycle, including passenger, was $8. You'll come back to this same point upon riding the next segment, Cape Henlopen State Park to Winding River Campground.

46.8 Entrance to 3,020-acre Cape Henlopen State Park. Follow the signs to the campground entrance.

47.1 Make a right to the full-service campground, which is semi-shaded. In addition, there are hiking trails, tennis and basketball courts, a softball field, a hockey field, and a nine-hole disc golf course. The campground is open from April 1 through October 3. If you want to climb the nearby tower, do not turn into the campground, but instead continue past the campground entrance for another 0.4 mile. There's a grand view from the tower, which was designed for Fort Miles. It is open April 1 through October 31, from 8:00 A.M. to sunset.

Cape Henlopen State Park to Winding River Campground (67.8 miles)

You'll begin your day with a ferry crossing of Delaware Bay, a liquid line dividing New Jersey and Delaware. A significant link in the Atlantic Intracoastal Waterway, it services Philadelphia to the north by means of a channel in the Delaware River.

The 70-minute ferry ride ends at popular Cape May, New Jersey. While you may have seen towns with a historic building or two, or maybe several of them, Cape May is one place where the entire town makes the list. Designated a National Historic Landmark, it is one of the nation's oldest seaside resorts, boasting more than 600 Victorian-era homes, buildings, and hotels. In addition, there are quaint shops and wonderful beaches. This segment travels through a portion of downtown Cape May, a must-see, before heading over to Wildwood and more of the Atlantic Coast.

The route passes through a number of tourist towns linked together by five toll bridges (50 cents each). Like ghost towns in winter, these cities prosper in the summer when Easterners flock to the shore for sun, fun, and relaxation. There are boardwalks, fun zones, and foods galore. Also, in sharp contrast, pass through several wildlife management areas where animal life thrives.

Many of the roads throughout this segment are rough and bumpy,

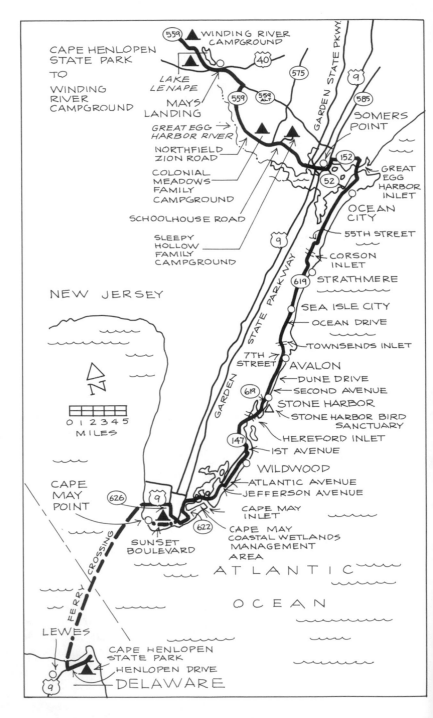

CAPE HENLOPEN
STATE PARK
TO
WINDING
RIVER
CAMPGROUND

559 ▲ WINDING RIVER
        CAMPGROUND
40
575
9
585
LAKE
LENAPE
559
559 ALT
SOMERS
POINT
MAYS
LANDING
GREAT EGG →
HARBOR RIVER
152
52
GREAT
EGG
HARBOR
INLET
NORTHFIELD
ZION ROAD
OCEAN
CITY
COLONIAL
MEADOWS
FAMILY
CAMPGROUND
55TH STREET
SCHOOLHOUSE ROAD
9
CORSON
INLET
SLEEPY
HOLLOW
FAMILY
CAMPGROUND
619 STRATHMERE
SEA ISLE CITY
OCEAN DRIVE
NEW   JERSEY
TOWNSENDS INLET
7TH
STREET
AVALON
N
DUNE DRIVE
619 ← SECOND AVENUE
STONE HARBOR
STONE HARBOR BIRD
SANCTUARY
0 1 2 3 4 5
MILES
147
HEREFORD INLET
1ST AVENUE
WILDWOOD
ATLANTIC AVENUE
JEFFERSON AVENUE
CAPE
MAY
POINT
626
9
CAPE MAY
INLET
622
CAPE MAY
COASTAL WETLANDS
MANAGEMENT
AREA
SUNSET
BOULEVARD
A T L A N T I C
O C E A N
FERRY CROSSING
LEWES
CAPE HENLOPEN
STATE PARK
HENLOPEN DRIVE
9
DELAWARE

GARDEN STATE PKWY.

STATE PARKWAY

GARDEN

Victorian-era home in Cape May

but smooth, resurfaced roads exist wherever new road construction has taken place. As you pedal along, watch out for turtles crossing the road.

Expect high densities of people during most of this segment. Thousands of people head for the New Jersey coast, especially on the holidays and weekends. Because of the masses in New York City and the busy New Jersey coast north of Atlantic City, this route heads inland. Everyone I contacted, from the New Jersey Department of Transportation to local bicyclists to bike shop owners, thought cycling through the Pine Barrens and along the Delaware River a far superior idea to pedaling directly along the Atlantic Coast.

In total contrast is the ride from Somers Point to the Winding River Campground, where you'll enjoy nearly 20 miles of uncrowded roads through rural New Jersey. Cranberry farms dot the landscape in some areas where homes, businesses, and cars are few for the most part.

Those wanting to spend more time at the coast may want to rent a motel room for the night, dividing this segment in half. There are no campgrounds along this portion of the Garden State coast.

MILEAGE LOG

0.0 Cape Henlopen State Park entrance. Head back toward Lewes.

0.9 Ferry terminal on the right. Bikes must be walked on and off the ferry; there are racks to hold the bikes in place while crossing. There's a passenger terminal with food, information, et cetera, while you wait.

1.1 Enter New Jersey as you cross Delaware Bay en route to the ferry terminal at Cape May. The terminal offers the same services as in Lewes. Head out from the ferry on US 9 North. There's a wide shoulder.

2.2 Restaurants, markets, et cetera, in this area.

3.5 Make a right on Seashore Rd., which is also CR 626; shoulder.

4.0 Cross the Cape May Canal.

5.2 Shoulder ends.

5.3 Road on the right leads to Depot Travel Park. This all-service camp offers some shady sites. There's a small shoulder now.

5.5 Fork; stay right on Broadway; no shoulder. Roads are narrow and bumpy.

5.9 Turn left on W. Perry; Sunset Blvd. takes off to the right. There's a convenience store on the corner. **SIDE TRIP:** Head to the right on Sunset Blvd. to reach Cape May Point State Park, Cape May Bird Observatory, and the Cape May Lighthouse in about 2 miles. The park offers nature trails, picnic areas, tall dunes, sandy beaches, and a small wildlife museum. A mecca for birders in the Northeast, Cape May has been called one of the top dozen birding "hot spots" in North America by famed birder Roger Tory Peterson. More than 200 species have been recorded on the cape in a single day, and more than 400 species have been recorded to date. Although spring and fall are the best times for viewing, many species live here year-round.

6.2 Fork; keep to the left on Jackson St. and continue to the beach. Before heading to the beach, be sure to cruise around town. There are beautifully restored homes, many of which are now bed-and-breakfast inns. The library is at the corner of Ocean and Hughes.

6.5 Turn left on Beach Ave. This is a lovely drive along the ocean, and a popular promenade.

7.7 Junction. Turn left on Pittsburgh Ave. (Hwy. 622). The lane is wide.

8.7 Road curves around a couple of times; follow the signs to the Garden State Pkwy., pedaling north on Hwy. 109.

9.1 Begin crossing the bridge over Cape May Harbor. The road narrows, with no shoulder.

9.5 Keep right on Ocean Dr., which leads to Wildwood. There's a shoulder again.

10.3 Bridge crossing/Mill Creek Marina on the right. Enter the Cape May Coastal Wetlands Management Area.

11.1 Narrow toll bridge—Middle Thorofare Bridge—over Cape May Inlet. Fee is 50 cents per cyclist.

12.3 Shoulder ends, but the road is wide as you travel through a mostly residential area.

12.5 Turn right on Jefferson Ave.; enter Wildwood Crest.

12.9 Turn left on Atlantic Ave. There are numerous motels and other services now as you pass near the Atlantic Ocean, one block east.

14.8 Wildwood. There's a boardwalk in town, stretching from Cresse Ave. to 16th Ave.

15.7 Fun zone off to the right. The road narrows to two lanes soon after.

16.3 Residential area again. Motels are scattered about.

17.4 Atlantic Ave. ends. Turn left on 1st Ave. The Hereford Inlet Lighthouse is off to the right.

17.5 Turn right on Central Ave.

17.9 Keep to the right, now riding Angelsea Dr. There's a restaurant near here.

18.5 Junction. Make a right on CR 147 West. There's a shoulder now.

18.8 Cross a wooden plank bridge that offers one heck of a bumpy ride. There's no shoulder on the bridge. Use caution.

19.2 Junction. Keep to the right on CR 619.

19.6 Cross narrow, shoulderless toll bridge—Grassy Sound Bridge—over Hereford Inlet. Fee is the usual 50 cents per cyclist.

21.0 Cross a *free* narrow bridge.

21.3 End of bridge.

21.6 At the first street you come to, turn right on 3rd Ave., then make a quick left on 118th St.

21.7 Turn left on Second Ave. There's a wide lane for riding.

22.9 Pass Stone Harbor Bird Sanctuary prior to reaching this area, which is rich in shops, et cetera. Nationally known for its thousands of nesting pairs of egrets, herons, and glossy ibises, Stone Harbor Bird Sanctuary encompasses 21 acres.

26.2 Road name changes to Dune Dr. as you reach Avalon; all services.

26.7 Bicycle shop on the left.

27.7 Make a left on 7th St. just before Dune Dr. ends.

27.9 Go right on Ocean Dr. The road narrows as you approach the bridge.

28.3 Cross a toll bridge over Townsends Inlet. As you may have guessed, the Townsends Inlet Bridge is shoulderless and there's a 50-cent fee for cyclists.

30.7 Sea Isle City; all services available. The road is narrow through town, but it's not too nerve-wracking, as traffic is usually just slugging along. There's a boardwalk with limited bike hours nearby. Expect wall-to-wall people on the boardwalk during

"Skimmer," a festival held on Father's Day weekend in June. There's an open flea market, a food court, and live music.

32.4 Back through residential areas now. There's a parking lane to ride in if it's not filled with cars.

33.7 Strathmere. Unlike many New Jersey beaches, this is a free beach.

34.5 Restaurant on the right.

34.7 Motel/market on the right.

35.0 Keep to the left on CR 619; shoulder now.

35.1 Toll bridge over Corson Inlet. As usual, there's no shoulder on Corson Inlet Bridge and the toll is 50 cents.

36.3 Bridge crossing; wide shoulder this time.

37.3 Ocean City sign. Go straight on 55th St.

37.5 Turn left on Central Ave.; no shoulder, but the road is wide.

41.8 Junction with 15th St. Continue straight on Central. **SIDE TRIP:** To see the remains of the ship *Sandia,* go two blocks to the right and up to the boardwalk. (The boardwalk runs from 23rd St. to St. James Pl. Hours are limited for bikers.) There are a few motels and bed-and-breakfast inns in the area.

42.5 Turn right on 9th St. **SIDE TRIP:** If you're hungry, go left a few blocks toward Hwy. 52, which is closed to bikers. There are many restaurants in the area.

42.6 Make a left on Wesley Ave., a wide road. It changes to Gardens Pkwy. farther along.

44.5 Tollgate for the Ocean City–Longport Bridge over Great Egg Inlet. This is now Hwy. 152 East. There's no shoulder and the toll is 50 cents for bikers.

45.2 End of bridge; shoulder now.

45.8 Turn left on Hwy. 152 West and cross another bridge. This one is free and sports a wide shoulder.

47.9 Shoulder ends but the road is wide. Hwy. 152 ends and becomes Maryland Ave. as you continue to Somers Point, a full-service town.

48.1 Turn left on Shore Rd.; no shoulder; convenience store at the junction.

48.7 Library on the right as you head through downtown historical Somers Point.

48.9 Atlantic County Historical Society on the right. Open Wednesday through Saturday, the museum houses genealogical records and a museum.

49.0 Somers Mansion on the right as you enter a traffic circle. Open every day except Monday, this is Atlantic County's oldest home. Keep to the right.

49.1 Begin riding CR 559 North. There's an intermittent shoulder along this fairly uncrowded road, with a shoulder more often than not.

50.1 Convenience store/restaurant on the right as you leave town.

50.7 Cross a small bridge.

53.2 Junction with Schoolhouse Rd.; go straight, continuing on CR 559. **SIDE TRIP:** Go right to reach the Sleepy Hollow Family Campground in less than 1 mile. Make another right on Bevis Mill Rd. in 0.1 mile. Go left at the sign in another 0.5 mile. Follow a soft dirt road for 0.3 mile to this shady full-service campground.

54.4 Junction with CR 575; keep straight on CR 559. Trucks are not allowed on this section of road.

55.4 Colonial Meadows Family Campground on the right. Access is easy to this shadeless all-service camp with a laundromat and limited groceries.

55.9 Junction with Northfield Zion Rd.; keep left on CR 559; wide shoulder now.

59.0 You'll pedal along the Great Egg Harbor River for a short time.

61.3 Alt. CR 559 merges with CR 559. Keep to the left.

63.0 Store on the left.

63.4 Junction with US 40. Go right, then left, on US 40/CR 559 North. Enter Mays Landing, a quaint town with cafes, markets, and shops.

64.1 Road curves to the left. In 0.1 mile, keep right on CR 559.

64.5 Atlantic County Park at Lake Lenape. Shady sites are offered at this scenic camp offering all amenities.

67.8 Winding River Campground on the right. Open May through September, it has shady sites in addition to all the usual services. Also, there's a pool, a laundromat, and limited groceries. Popular activities include tubing and canoeing the river; tubes and canoes are available for rent.

Winding River Campground to Wading Pines Campground (25.5 miles)

Rural New Jersey is at its best as you travel through the Pine Barrens. Hardly barren, the New Jersey Pinelands, as they are also known, teem with plant and animal life. Officially designated by the National Parks and Recreation Act in 1978, the 1 million-acre Pinelands National Reserve boasts 850 plant species (including twenty-one types of wild orchids) and more than 350 species of birds, mammals, reptiles, and amphibians. Comprised of relatively level forests of oak, pine, and cedar, with slow-moving streams, extensive bogs, and swamps strewn about, it is the largest tract of wilderness on the Middle Atlantic Coast.

Once thought barren by the original settlers who tried and couldn't farm its sandy soil (thus the name), the Pinelands yield some of the

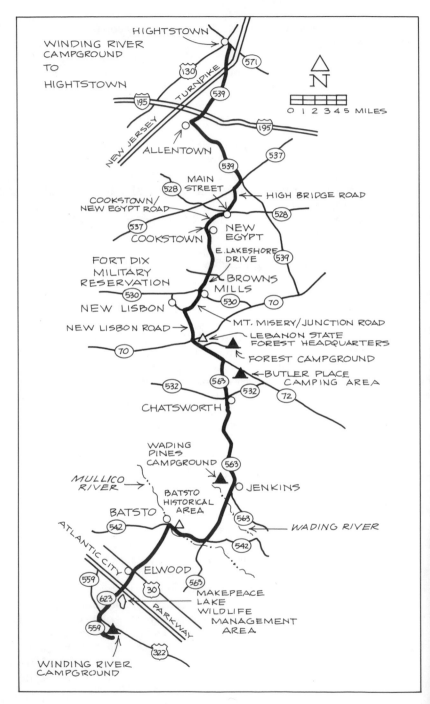

biggest crops of blueberries and cranberries in the nation.

Along the way you'll want to stop off at Batsto, a historic village. Batsto is the kind of place where one can spend hours viewing the ancient buildings, trying to imagine life in such a setting.

If you feel like playing instead of riding, canoeing and wading are popular along the many rivers flowing through the area. In fact, this segment is only 25 miles, allowing plenty of time for leisure activities. A short day is planned due to the lack of campgrounds farther ahead.

Special note: Those who'd rather continue on, skipping the upcoming motel-stop in Hightstown, will find two off-route campgrounds about 20 miles ahead. You'd combine part of the next segment, Wading Pines Campground to Hightstown, with today's ride for a total of about 45 miles. Combine the remaining portion of the next segment with all of the Hightstown to Bulls Island State Park segment, and you'd ride about 82 miles to the next campground. If you'd rather camp, it's your best bet. See the next segment, Wading Pines Campground to Hightstown, for more information on this alternate route.

MILEAGE LOG

0.0 From Winding River Campground, continue on CR 559.

1.9 Cross US 322; continue north on CR 559. Shoulders continue to be narrow or nonexistent, but roads are uncrowded.

2.1 Weymouth Park on the right. There's cold artesian well water just past the entrance. Pedal into the park and you'll see it on your left. You'll also see the Weymouth Furnace ruins, an early nineteenth-century South Jersey iron furnace. Here, iron was produced from "bog ore" mined in surrounding swamps. Transported to the furnace by barges towed along small canals, the iron spawned pots, pans, and stoves. This furnace was also responsible for the first iron pipe for the city of Philadelphia. The furnace closed in 1862, a paper mill starting up operations shortly thereafter and closing in 1887.

2.3 Junction. Go straight on CR 623 North to Elwood.

3.8 Pass through Makepeace Lake Wildlife Management Area.

5.5 Cross over eastbound traffic on the Atlantic City Pkwy.

5.6 Cross over westbound traffic on the Atlantic City Pkwy.

7.6 Cross US 30 in Elwood. There's a deli on the left with huge, delicious sandwiches and groceries too.

8.1 Junction with CR 561. Keep straight on CR 623.

8.4 Junction with CR 612 to the right. Keep straight. A junction with CR 658 is just beyond. Again, keep straight.

12.5 End of road. Go left on CR 623.

13.0 Bridge over a creek.

13.2 Make a right on CR 542 to Batsto. There's a shoulder now. Enter the Wharton State Forest.

14.1 **SIDE TRIP:** The Batsto Historical Area is on the left—a definite must-see. Proceed 0.5 mile to the Wharton National Forest office, the Batsto visitor center, exhibits, and restored village. Batsto is open daily except Thanksgiving, Christmas, and New Years Day.

15.7 Pass the Mullico River on the right. This is a popular water sport area. Traffic may increase now.

16.1 Crowley Landing picnic area on the right.

17.4 Bellhaven Lake on the left; campground is for lease sites (seasonal) only.

17.8 Grocery store/restaurant on the right.

18.5 Make a left on CR 563; no shoulder; traffic may be heavy.

24.0 Keep left on CR 563. Prior to this point, you will cross the Wading River.

Batsto Historical Area

24.6 Turnoff on the left to Wading Pines Campground.

25.5 Located along the Wading River, the full-service campground offers a pool, a laundromat, and a store. It is open April through October.

Wading Pines Campground to Hightstown (58.4 miles)

Cranberry fields, forest, and rural New Jersey accompany you along today's route, which continues through nearly flat terrain with some rolling hills popping up now and again. Although portions of the ride require riding heavily trafficked roads, most of the ride is easy going, with jaunts through the woods and looks at expansive farms.

Campgrounds are numerous in some parts of New Jersey, but not in the central part of the state where this route leads. For this reason the previous segment, Winding River Campground to Wading Pines Campground, was cut short, stopping at the last camp for more than 95 miles. You'll find the next campground at Bulls Island State Park, a wonderful site along the Delaware River, the destination for the segment after this segment.

This segment ends at Hightstown, however, where you'll find a couple of low-budget motels. In addition, you'll find grocery stores, restaurants, and other services. If motels aren't your style, perhaps there's a church or landowner who would allow you—with permission—to camp on their property.

Special note: There are two campgrounds off the route, however, one near the Highway 72 and Highway 70 junction, the other near the junction of Highways 563 and 72. If you extended the previous segment, Winding River Campground to Wading Pines Campground, you could stay at one of the two off-route sites, adding the remainder of this segment to the next segment, Hightstown to Bulls Island State Park, and skipping the motel stop in Hightstown. It's about an 82-mile ride from the off-route sites to Bulls Island State Park.

MILEAGE LOG

0.0 From Wading Pines Campground, go back to the main road and continue on CR 563 to the north.

1.2 There are snacks and a canoe rental place on the left.

9.8 Shoulder now.

10.1 Chatsworth; general store/grill on the left. If visiting in October, be sure to attend the annual Chatsworth Cranberry Festival, where you can taste everything from cranberry breads and jams to cranberry ice cream.

10.8 Shoulder ends.

14.1 End of CR 563. Go left on Hwy. 72; wide shoulder. Now there are

Immature blue jay

scattered restaurants as you pedal along the busy road. **SIDE TRIP:** If you're interested, there's a group campsite about 2 miles to the right (southeast) off Hwy. 72. Signs point the way to Butler Place group camping area, which offers a water spigot only, but there's a reduced fee due to lack of amenities. It is open all year.

16.6 Turnoff on the right to the Lebanon State Forest headquarters, located about 0.5 mile away. **SIDE TRIP:** There's a forest campground about 3 miles farther, with all services. The wooded camp also offers lake swimming and fishing. It is open from March through November. Pay for your campsite at the headquarters.

17.5 Market on the left.

17.6 Traffic circle. Curve right, then left, on Hwy. 70 West, then it's another quick right on New Lisbon Rd. This road offers some shoulder, but very little. Traffic is moderate.

22.4 Turn right on Mount Misery. There's no shoulder for the first mile; traffic is moderate.

24.5 Road curves to the left and becomes Junction Rd.

26.1 Turn left on Lakehurst Rd. Now you're in Browns Mills, a town with all services.

26.3 Make a right on Clubhouse Rd. There's a shoulder for part of the road, which leads through residential areas and along Mirror Lake.

26.8 Road curves around to the right and becomes N. Lakeshore Dr.

27.2 Cross over Turtle Log Bridge just before making a left on E. Lakeshore Dr.

33.1 Junction. Keep straight on unsigned Cookstown Rd. through the Fort Dix Military Reservation. There's a narrow shoulder for most of the road, which passes through the trees. Traffic is fairly light.

37.0 Cookstown. There's a small motel and other services as you pass through town.

37.4 Fork; keep to the right and follow the Cookstown/New Egypt Rd. There's a diner on the right.

38.8 New Egypt. There's a wide parking lane for riding. There are a store and restaurants in town.

39.7 Junction with CR 528 just ahead; keep straight on Main St.

40.4 Left on High Bridge Rd., a farm country road with a shoulder.

41.7 Make a right on CR 537 to the east.

42.6 Go left on CR 539 North; shoulder continues.

43.5 Top of small hill.

45.8 Deli on the left. The continuous shoulder ends, although you'll find intermittent patches here and there. The road continues through rural New Jersey.

49.4 Enter the quaint town of Allentown, where there are numerous shops, cafes, and groceries. There's no shoulder.

49.6 Turn right on CR 539. Later there's an intermittent shoulder.

50.6 Deli/groceries on the left.

50.8 Cross over I-195.

55.5 Cross over the New Jersey Turnpike.

56.8 Hightstown and an array of beautiful old homes.

57.2 CR 571 merges with CR 539. Continue straight on CR 571.

57.6 Turn left on Stockton Rd. (CR 571); there's no shoulder, but the road is wide.

58.4 Junction of CR 571 and US 130. Two motels are located on US 130. One is to the right, the other to the left. There are plenty of restaurants and markets in between.

Hightstown to Bulls Island State Park (36.7 miles)

Today's ride is different from those traveled north from Florida, as you'll have a couple of hills to contend with. Although they're nothing serious, the days of nearly flat riding are over for the time being.

The ride begins in heavy traffic, but travels through some wide-open places as well. You'll pedal through industrial areas, residential tracts, and some farm country, too, while heading to Washington Crossing State Park. Shoulders are nil for the first portion of the ride, then there's a shoulder and later a scenic tow path along the Delaware River, the dividing line between New Jersey and Pennsylvania.

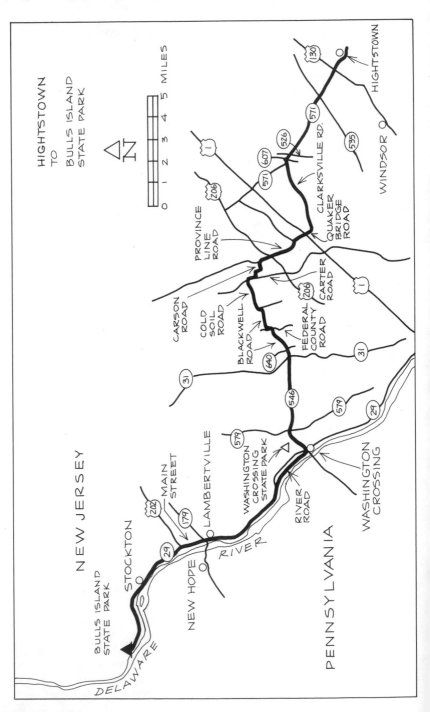

Cyclist walking the bridge between Lambertville, New Jersey and New Hope, Pennsylvania

The D & R Canal Tow Path leads directly to Lambertville, a quaint little town with many fine shops. Across the river, you'll find New Hope, Pennsylvania, and several motels and a bike shop.

Whether by tow path or Highway 29, the trail to beautiful Bulls Island is a pleasant one. Lush green vegetation decorates both the mostly flat tow path and Highway 29, which sports a shoulder from Prallsville, north of Stockton. Prior to Prallsville, Highway 29 is narrow and congested.

In the early summer, orange day-lilies decorate much of the roadway. Garnishing the roadway from Florida to Maine, these orange lilies are not true lilies at all, they just resemble them. They are a hybrid of plants native to Europe and Asia that escaped from cultivation.

MILEAGE LOG

0.0 Junction of CR 571 and US 130. Head straight (west) on CR 571. There's a shoulder and heavy traffic.

1.1 End of shoulder, but there's a middle turning lane now and plenty of room for riding, if motorists will cooperate.

1.5 Junction with CR 535. Remain straight on CR 571. The road narrows to four lanes, with no shoulder.

3.5   Lane narrows considerably.

4.4   Cross CR 526; cross CR 607 soon after. Stay on CR 571.

5.0   Turn left on Clarksville Rd. There's an intermittent shoulder.

5.9   Library on the right.

6.9   Road is narrow over a bridge spanning a set of railroad tracks. Use caution. A narrow shoulder begins after crossing.

8.5   Turn right on Quaker Bridge Rd., which is four lanes, with no shoulder.

9.0   Keep left toward US 1 South and then continue straight.

9.6   T-junction; go left on Province Line Rd.; narrow. Watch for heavy traffic, especially in the afternoon during rush hour.

11.4   Unsigned junction to US 206. Keep straight.

11.8   Turn left on Carson Rd., a narrow road, but the first quiet path of the day. Pass through a rural area with little traffic.

12.8   Make a right on Carter Rd. There's a shoulder now.

13.2   Make a left on Cold Soil Rd., which is narrow but uncrowded.

14.3   As you continue, you're finally high enough to see some nearby mountains, the first mountains of the entire trip.

14.6   Go right on Blackwell Rd.

15.6   Go left on unsigned Federal County Rd., then right on the first road (in about 200 feet), which is Blackwell Rd.

16.8   Shoulder now.

17.0   Cross CR 640. Keep straight.

17.5   Enter traffic circle at Hwy. 31. Use caution. Go past two exits, going halfway around the circle, to the third exit, which goes to CR 546, in 0.1 mile. There's a wide shoulder now as you ride a series of rolling hills.

21.0   Junction with CR 579. Headquarters for Washington Crossing State Park is on the right; information, rest rooms. Go straight on CR 546.

21.5   Park entrance on the right. Located on 800 lovely acres, Washington Crossing State Park provides a unique blend of historic features, a natural area, and recreational facilities. Established in 1912, its activities include picnicking, camping (for groups only), fishing, and hiking. Stop at the visitor center for more information. It's open daily in the summer, Wednesday through Sunday the rest of the year.

22.3   Junction with Hwy. 29. There's a store and deli on the corner. Keep straight and go toward the bridge leading over the Delaware River. **SIDE TRIP:** Before crossing the bridge, however, turn right on unsigned River Rd., a narrow road passing the approximate area where General George Washington and about 2,400 of his soldiers landed after their historic crossing of the Delaware River on Christmas night 1776. If you want to visit Pennsylvania and its Washington Crossing State Park, walk your bike across the footpath on the bridge to the other side, where you'll find a bike shop, a pizza shop, and more.

24.2 Road curves to the right to the canal. Take the D & R Canal Tow Path on the left. This is a wonderful ride on compacted quarry grit, a surface rigid enough for those with narrow tires. In contrast, nearby Hwy. 29 is narrow and fraught with truck traffic. The tow path parallels the Delaware and Raritan "feeder" Canal, opened in 1834 and built to provide a safe and short waterway between Philadelphia and New York City. One of the nation's busiest navigation canals for a century, the 60-mile canal, and a narrow band of state-owned land hugging its banks, now serve as a state park where people come to canoe and fish, jog, walk, or bicycle.

27.6 Parking area for the D & R Canal.

29.2 Parking area for the Inn at Lambertville Station. The tow path merges onto an old road just prior to this point. Pedal through the parking area.

29.3 Junction with Hwy. 179. The tow path peters out here. Actually it does continue someplace in Lambertville, but it's not recommended, as it is very bumpy. It's easier to catch the tow path farther north. Turn right on Hwy. 179, passing a visitor center as you head through this quaint town with all services. You'll find all amenities in New Hope, located across the Delaware River in Pennsylvania, as well.

29.5 Turn left on Main St./Hwy. 29. The road is narrow, with no shoulder, but increases to four lanes in less than 1 mile.

30.5 Junction with US 202 on the right. Continue on Hwy. 29.

30.7 Shoulder begins as you pass Holcombe River View Cemetery.

30.9 Shoulder ends; road is two lanes now.

31.2 D & R Canal Tow Path begins on the left.

32.8 Stockton; all services; no motels, but there's a bed-and-breakfast inn. Catch the tow path in another 0.2 mile.

33.0 Hop on the tow path near here; turn left and ride 150 feet to the canal. Remember, if you'd rather ride Hwy. 29, a wide shoulder begins in Prallsville, just west of Stockton.

36.4 Bulls Island State Park entrance; turn left.

36.7 Registration office and information. You'll find beautiful campsites along the Delaware River, all of which are in a lush setting. You'll find all amenities, including a laundromat. The campground remains open all year. Special note: If you chose to skip the overnight stay in Hightstown in the previous segment, redividing and combining segments and overnighting instead in one of two off-route campgrounds, as described in the two previous segments, you will end this segment here at Bulls Island State Park, along with those who rode all the segments as they're described.

Bulls Island State Park to Driftstone Campground (50.7 miles)

Except for a few areas of heavy traffic, the roads paralleling the Delaware River are fun to ride and the scenery is breathtaking. Cliffs line part of the roadway, and dense vegetation makes a formidable barrier, allowing for occasional views of the Delaware. Along the way, you'll ride both the Pennsylvania and New Jersey sides of the river, the dividing line between the two states.

You'll climb the steepest grades to date on your Atlantic Coast journey (if you're cycling south to north), but you'll pass through farm country and lovely country homes en route. Except for the steep grades, this is touring at its finest. Best of all, the day ends at a wonderful campground offering discounts for bikers.

MILEAGE LOG

0.0 Entrance to Bulls Island State Park. You can ride the tow path or Hwy. 29, which offers a wide shoulder now.

1.1 Cross CR 651.

8.7 End of shoulder. Enter Frenchtown just beyond; all services except motels. Instead there's a bed-and-breakfast inn.

9.1 Road ends. Turn left on Bridge St., then make a quick right on Harrison St. (CR 619).

9.9 Shoulder now.

10.6 Market on the left.

11.5 Road narrows considerably; shoulder is present at times, but usually nonexistent.

12.6 Library on the left as you enter Milford.

12.7 Turn left on unsigned Bridge St.

12.9 Turn right on Church St. The road curves to the left, then to the right, and becomes Spring Garden Rd. (CR 627). The road is narrow but uncrowded.

14.5 The road narrows to one lane for 0.8 mile; fortunately the speed limit is 25 mph.

16.6 Top of the first big hill on the entire Atlantic Coast ride. There's a grand view from here.

17.1 Top of another hill.

19.5 Cross a creek. There's a shoulder now.

19.7 T-junction; turn left on unsigned road as CR 627 heads off to the right.

19.9 Cross some nasty railroad tracks and curve around to the right. The town of Riegelsville, Pennsylvania, is off to the left.

22.7 T-junction; make a left on Creek Rd. and go under the railroad tracks.

A foggy sunrise on the Delaware River, Delaware Water Gap National Recreation Area

23.5 Pass through Carpentersville, a very small town.

24.1 Road is called River Rd. again, but changes to Carpentersville Rd. in about 0.8 mile.

25.7 A couple of short, steep grades lead to the top of another hill, where there's a good view.

26.4 Shoulder now.

26.6 Cross over I-78.

26.7 T-junction again; go left on Carpentersville Rd. It's downhill from here.

27.5 Turn left on S. Main St. in Phillipsburg. Just before the light, you'll descend under an old bridge. The road is quite rough as you descend. Be careful!

28.1 Road is two lanes; no shoulder. Traffic may be a bit heavy.

29.6 Junction of Union Square and N. Main St.; stay straight on N. Main (CR 621), which later becomes River Rd. **SIDE TRIP:** Go left on Union Square and over the bridge if you want to go to Easton, Pennsylvania, where there's a bike shop, motels, and other services. Services are limited in Phillipsburg.

29.9 Cross under US 22, staying straight on Broad St.

30.2 Turn right on 4th St.

30.3 Turn left, back onto N. Main St., which turns to River Rd., a narrow road with no shoulders.

35.0 Begin very steep climb for 0.3 mile. Roads are narrow, but uncrowded.

36.1 Back to fairly level ground.
36.7 T-junction at Brainards. No services; go right on Brainards Rd. (CR 621).
37.0 Turn left on Garrison Rd.
37.6 Make a left on River Rd.
37.8 Reach the top of another hill and begin descending.
38.4 Begin climbing again.
39.0 T-junction; make a left and go under the railroad tracks, then curve right and continue along the river.
39.5 Pub and grill on the left.
40.5 Road curves to the right and under the railroad tracks. Turn left on Foul Rift Rd.
42.1 T-junction; make a left and go under another set of railroad tracks. Follow the river.
44.0 T-junction; make a left on unsigned Greenwich St. There's a laundromat across the street. There's a shoulder now.
44.3 Belvidere. There's no shoulder, but the road is wide.
44.6 Junction with Front St. Continue through town. There's all services here. **SIDE TRIP:** There's a bike shop to the right 0.2 mile.
44.7 Turn left on Water St. There's a laundromat on the right before the turn.
45.0 Walk bikes on the footpath across the Delaware River.
45.2 Enter Pennsylvania. Turn right on the first road to the right (CR 1037) and pedal along the river. There's a hotel/restaurant at the corner.
46.2 Make a sharp right on an unsigned road after climbing a steep hill, and continue to climb. Roads are narrow again, but uncrowded.
46.4 Grade lessens.
46.5 Head downhill, then begin pedaling along a series of rolling hills.
47.4 Junction with Hemlock Dr. Bear right and continue on toward Portland.
50.7 Driftstone Campground on the right; open May 8 through September 20. It offers reduced rates for bicyclists. This is an excellent full-service camp with some shade, delicious well water, a pool, a game room, and a laundromat. Also, there's a store with limited groceries.

Driftstone Campground to Shippekonk Campground (53.5 miles)

From the campground you'll enjoy a relatively traffic-free ride for 4 miles. Upon entering the small town of Portland, Pennsylvania, however, you'll find more traffic, enough to make the narrow roads seem even narrower.

Cross from Pennsylvania back into New Jersey at Delaware Water Gap, and enjoy the many sights of Delaware Water Gap National Recreation Area. Shoulders are nonexistent, but it doesn't matter—traffic is nil. In talking with local residents, it seems this stretch of highway remains uncrowded (except for the area around the Delaware Water Gap NRA visitor center), even in summer.

Hugging a 40-mile stretch of the Delaware River—one of the cleanest and most scenic rivers in the East and, as mentioned previously, the dividing line between Pennsylvania and New Jersey—this 70,000-acre preserve is a wildlife- and birdwatcher's dream. It also offers fishing, swimming, and picnicking opportunities. In addition, the Appalachian Trail traverses 25 miles of the park. Those interested in canoeing, tubing, or rafting will find vendors willing to rent equipment and provide transportation.

You'll ride in roller-coaster fashion along River Road, CR 615, and Old Mine Road, with some steep climbs challenging those with fully loaded bikes. Fortunately, most of the climbs are short, but it's well worth the effort, as the scenery is the best imagined and there's the opportunity to see beavers, deer, marmots, squirrels, and much more.

Built in 1659, Old Mine Road was once used by Dutch settlers to transport copper ore from the Pahaquarry Mines to Esopus (now Kingston, New York).

Flowers line portions of the roadway, a creek parallels the road for miles, and rural homes occasionally dot the landscape. This area is so remote that markets are rare, so carry plenty to eat.

MILEAGE LOG

0.0 Entrance to Driftstone Campground. Continue north on the same unsigned road that you cycled in on. The road may be narrow, but it's uncrowded.

3.2 Picnic area/outhouses on the Delaware River.

3.8 Cross under Hwy. 611, merging onto Hwy. 611 North. Enter Portland just after; you'll find all services here.

4.1 Turnoff to Shady Acres Campground on the left. Hwy. 611 is two lanes, with no shoulder. **SIDE TRIP:** Go 0.7 mile to Turkey Ridge Rd., then west 0.5 mile, to reach the campground; hot showers, limited groceries, pond fishing, game room.

5.2 Steep road on the left leads to a motel; restaurant/food stand just before.

6.0 Entrance to Slateford Farm on the left. Costumed rangers lead tours of the 1800s farm, one of several historic sites at Delaware Gap NRA. It's open Wednesday through Sunday (during the summer), where you'll learn about the early slate industry.

7.0 Arrow Island Overlook on the right. The road narrows.

7.6 Point of Gap Overlook on the left; outhouses.

9.2 Reach the top of a hill, then descend a steep grade, entering the town of Delaware Water Gap.

9.7 Turn right on Broad St., following the signs to I-80.

10.0 Just past a cafe and convenience store, go left onto the on-ramp for I-80 East. There's a motel on the right. The on-ramp is narrow, but there's a rough shoulder for part of the ride. In 0.2 mile there's two lanes, with no shoulder.

10.5 I-80 sports a shoulder from this point.

11.0 Toll bridge over the Delaware River. You won't have to pay a toll if you're cycling from south to north. **ALTERNATE ROUTE:** There's a sidewalk if you'd like to walk your bike. Please note: If you walk, you'll end up using a different exit than those riding across. Both exits reach land back in New Jersey, however.

11.5 End of toll bridge.

11.7 Exit I-80. Delaware Water Gap NRA parking area and Kittatinny visitor center is just ahead. To continue, go right here to signed Worthington State Forest via unsigned River Rd. The center is open daily in the summer, May through October; weekends in the winter. There's a book store and information, and various hikes begin here.

12.0 Those walking over the bridge will exit the bridge at this point, and rejoin the route.

12.2 Cross under I-80. The road narrows to one lane in sections, but it is uncrowded. Just the same, you'll want to use caution. Enter Worthington State Forest, and begin climbing and descending, staying above the river.

15.1 Entrance to Worthington State Forest Campground on the left; open April through December. The registration booth is in 0.2 mile. This is a wonderful camp with shaded sites on the wooded banks along the Delaware River. There are picnic tables and out-houses, with modern rest rooms and hot showers planned for the late summer of 1991. (From this point to Shippekonk Camp-ground, there are continual ups and downs, with some steep grades. Fortunately, most are short ups. The grade remains fairly level upon nearing Shippekonk Campground.)

18.0 Leave Worthington State Forest; enter Delaware Water Gap NRA.

19.6 Copper Mine hiking area.

21.6 Turnoff to Depew Recreation Site, a picnic area.

21.8 Dirt road leads to Van Campens Glen Recreation Site, another picnic area.

24.0 Fork; cycle left, bracing for a steep climb that is 0.6 mile long. At the fork, just before the steep climb, you'll see Millbrook Village, a re-creation of a late nineteenth-century crossroads hamlet. With a brochure in hand, you can enjoy a self-guided walking tour of the village, thus learning about the buildings and life as it was 100 years ago. Watch as workers demonstrate traditional crafts such as woodworking and blacksmithing. Visit the first weekend of October and watch the village "come to life" when the Millbrook Days celebration occurs.

24.7 Small pond on the left. Look for beavers.

25.0 Steep descent for 1.2 miles. Please note: There's a stop sign at the bottom of the hill.

Vancampen Barn, Millbrook Village

26.2   Stop sign. Turn right on CR 615. The road follows along Flat Brook.

29.8   Walpack Wildlife Management Area.

32.3   Walpack Valley Inn (limited hours at this restaurant).

32.6   Ranger station on the left.

36.1   Peters Valley Craft Village. This town literally bursts with artists specializing in wood, fiber, pottery, fine metals, blacksmithing, and photography. The artists live here year-round, selling their wares in the craft store, open daily.

36.8   Bear left on CR 640.

38.1   Turn left on CR 560 West; shoulder now. This is the town of Layton. There's a general store/grill on the corner.

40.7   You'll climb out of Layton, then descend a steep grade to this point. While en route downhill, turn right on unsigned Old Mine Rd., a path leading across gentle rolling hills (except for a few short, steep pitches) to Montague and Hainesville. There's no shoulder, but the road is uncrowded. **SIDE TRIP:** If you're in need of a campground, go straight across the Delaware River, then south on US 209. Dingman's Campground, a full-service camp, is about 2 miles from here.

43.0   Turnoff to Old Mine Road AYH, P.O. Box 172, Layton, NJ 07851; (201) 948-6750. The hostel is closed for the Thanksgiving and Christmas holidays, including Christmas Eve Day.

47.5   Junction with US 206. Make a left on US 206, then an immediate right on CR 521 North, continuing on Old Mine Rd. There's a shoulder now.

50.5   Short, steep paved road leads to Cedar Ridge Campground. Open year-round, it has hot showers, a pool, a laundromat, and a small store.

53.5   Entrance to Shippekonk Campground. Open May through October, this is a nice clean camp with some shady sites and reduced rates for bicyclists. In addition to hot showers, there's a pool, and snacks are also available. If you feel like stretching your legs after cycling all day, try hiking the trail to the top of nearby Shippekonk Mountain, where you'll see into New York, New Jersey, and Pennsylvania.

Shippekonk Campground to Ganahgote Campground (51.2 miles)

Today's ride leads directly into New York, the largest of the Middle Atlantic States. Again the ride is pleasant and not too crowded, although you will encounter heavy traffic on US 209. Be sure to stock up on fresh spring water just north of Port Jervis, the first New York city you'll come to, before catching the heavily trafficked road north.

Today you'll pedal up and down gentle rolling hills for the most

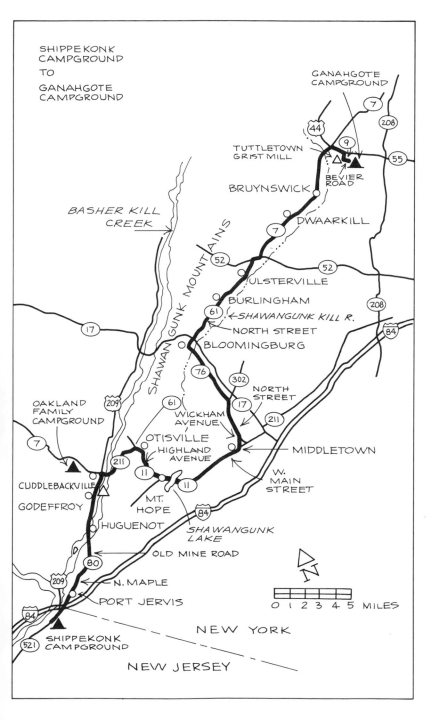

part. Highway 211 guides you into the Shawangunk Mountains and the small town of Otisville. Descend in roller-coaster fashion, with more downs than ups, to Middletown, a busy small town.

As CR 11 did, CR 76 and CR 7 lead through the back roads of New York where towns are small, services nearly nonexistent, and rest rooms often difficult to find.

End the day along the Walkill River at the Ganahgote Campground. If your budget permits, you might want to pig-out at a well-known lobster restaurant located nearby.

MILEAGE LOG

0.0 Shippekonk Campground entrance. Continue on CR 521 North, which still sports a shoulder.

1.2 Cross under I-84 and enter the state of New York.

1.3 Road changes to S. Maple as you enter Port Jervis. There's no shoulder now.

1.7 Junction. Cross E. Main St., staying straight on N. Maple/CR 80. You'll find all services to both the right and left of the junction.

6.0 Fowler's Spring on the right. Be sure to fill up with some delicious, ice-cold spring water.

6.2 Bridge leads over the Delaware River, which has decreased dramatically in size.

6.5 Turn right on US 209, a continuation of the Old Mine Rd., which ends in Kingston, nearly 60 miles to the northeast. This section of Old Mine Rd. possesses considerably more traffic than the New Jersey section; use caution. There's no shoulder; the road is quite busy. Enter Huguenot.

7.3 Country market/deli on the left.

9.0 Godeffroy; no services.

9.2 Turnoff on the right to the American Family Campground; hot showers, laundromat, pool, store.

10.3 Cross narrow bridge.

10.4 Cuddlebackville.

10.9 Deli/market on the left.

11.0 Junction. Go right on Hwy. 211. There's a shoulder now. **SIDE TRIP:** The nearest campground is straight ahead on US 209 for 0.1 mile, then left on CR 7. A steep grade leads 1.8 miles to the Oakland Family Campground, where you'll find all shady sites, hot showers, and a laundromat.

11.1 Pass the post office, then begin climbing over the Shawangunk Mountains.

11.5 Cross Basher Kill Creek.

13.6 Junction with CR 61 to the left. Continue up Hwy. 211.

13.8 The village of Otisville marks your high point, then you head downhill.

14.7 Turn right on Highland Ave. (CR 11); no shoulder, some traffic. **SIDE TRIP:** If you need a convenience store, continue straight on Hwy. 211 for 0.2 mile.

15.3 CR 11 is now called Mount Hope Ave.

17.0 Mount Hope. There's a country store here. Bear left on CR 11.

17.8 Shawangunk Lake crossing.

21.8 Middletown. Route becomes W. Main St.

22.3 Cross Monhagen Ave. Continue straight on W. Main St. A nearby market/grill has excellent food and prices. There's a laundromat here, too.

22.6 Fork; keep left on Wickham Ave.

23.1 Turn left on North St./CR 76. The road is wide for the most part. **SIDE TRIP:** There are two bike shops in town. From the junction, head right a few blocks for one, or go straight on Wickham 0.4 mile for the other.

24.4 Shoulder now. The terrain is comprised of rolling hills.

24.9 Library.

26.0 Junction with Hwy. 302. There's a pizza shop on the right.

26.8 Junction with Hwy. 17 North on the right.

28.1 Junction with Brown Rd. **SIDE TRIP:** If you head right across Hwy. 17, you'll find a motel, and a restaurant and market nearby.

30.8 Cross Shawangunk Kill River and enter the village of Bloomingburg; restaurant, groceries.

31.1 Turn right on North St./CR 61; shoulder.

32.0 Cross over Hwy. 17; no shoulder, but road is uncrowded.

34.9 Burlingham; general store.

36.4 Road name changes to CR 7.

37.4 Deli/snacks on the right.

39.0 Merge right on Hwy. 52. Caution: Traffic may be heavy now.

39.5 Pedal left, riding CR 7 again, at the New Prospect Church.

43.3 Dwaarkill; deli/grocery store.

43.5 Bear right as the road curves, now following a "Winery Tour" sign.

45.6 Bruynswick.

49.4 Short climb before reaching a junction; go right on Hwy. 55/US 44. There's an Italian restaurant on the corner; the road has a shoulder.

50.5 Turn right on CR 9 toward Tuttletown Grist Mill. Pass the mill (a nice place to explore) and ride over a bridge.

50.8 Make a left on Bevier Rd., a dead-end road.

51.0 Lobster Pound Restaurant offers reasonable prices.

51.2 Ganahgote Campground; shady and open sites along the Walkill River. Open May through October, this camp offers hot showers, some groceries, and a laundromat.

Ganahgote Campground to Interlake Campground (43.0 miles)

The road from here to popular New Paltz is uncrowded for the most part and scenic, and gentle rolling hills are usually the norm.

Historic New Paltz is popular with many folks. It's an artsy community, and you may want to spend time exploring the many shops in the area. From New Paltz, it's a nice ride to Poughkeepsie via several back roads, all with fairly gentle grades.

Crossing the Hudson River is simple as long as the bridge sidewalks are open. When they're closed at times due to various bridge improvement projects, you'll have to check with the New York State Bridge Authority for current conditions: Bridge Plaza, Highland, NY 12528; (914) 691-7245.

You'll find riding along the Hudson River, New York's longest (it flows from the Adirondacks to New York Bay), both pleasant and history-filled. Although the road is heavily trafficked, you'll enjoy a shoulder for the most part, with gentle rolling grades. Visit the Home of Franklin D. Roosevelt National Historic Site, the Vanderbilt Mansion National Historic Site, and the Mills Mansion along the way.

After passing through Rhinebeck, another popular spot, you'll travel east over hilly terrain, where some hills are wrought with steep, albeit

Franklin D. Roosevelt National Historic Site

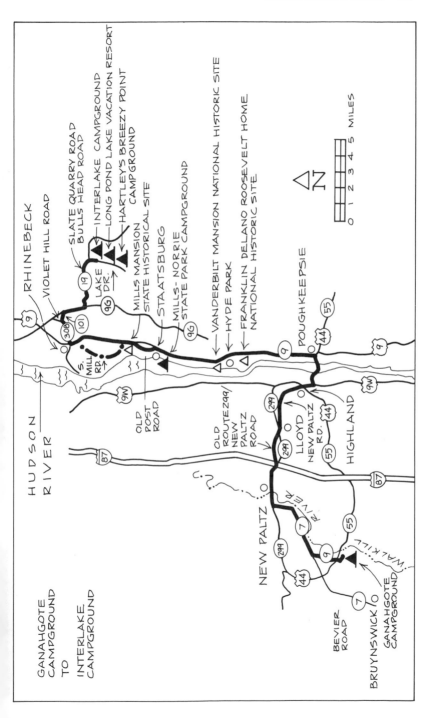

GANAHGOTE
CAMPGROUND
TO
INTERLAKE
CAMPGROUND

short, pitches. Cycling through rural New York, you'll end the day at the Interlake Campground, or one of two other nearby facilities.

MILEAGE LOG

0.0 Ganahgote Campground entrance; head back the way you came.

0.7 Back to Hwy. 55. Keep straight on CR 9. There's no shoulder, but the road is uncrowded.

1.1 Climb to this point, then head downhill.

2.1 Turn right on unsigned CR 7. The path continues along the same kind of terrain as yesterday's ride—mostly ups and down, with more downs than ups, and some flat riding as well.

4.5 Walkill River on the right.

7.1 Turn right on Hwy. 299; busy road; no shoulder.

7.9 Enter New Paltz as you cross a bridge over the Walkill River. Climb to downtown, where you'll find all services.

8.3 Junction with Front St. Two bike shops are located one and two blocks to the left, respectively.

8.8 Shoulder begins.

9.1 Visitor information center on the left.

9.4 Cross over I-87.

9.9 At the second light after crossing I-87, turn left on Ohioville Rd. and make an immediate right on Old Route 299. Old Route 299 becomes New Paltz Rd. in 1 mile or so.

12.1 Head left on unsigned Hwy. 299 and make a right in about 50 yards on New Paltz Rd.

12.8 Pass through the town of Lloyd.

15.6 Highland; New Paltz Rd. changes to Main St. All services can be found here.

15.8 Pass a post office and turn right on Vineyard (Hwy. 55/US 44).

16.2 Turn left on Tillison Ave. Go uphill for 0.2 mile, then down.

16.7 Make a right on Hwy. 55/US 44. Stay to the right, following signs to Mid-Hudson Bridge. There's a shoulder now.

17.5 Toll booth. Be sure to check here for current bridge conditions. I approached the bridge without calling in advance and found the sidewalks closed. After a quick phone call, however, the toll booth person agreed to let me cross the bridge because it was a Sunday morning and traffic was light.

18.4 Top of the Mid-Hudson Bridge, completed in 1930 and generally recognized as one of the most beautiful steel suspension bridges in the world. Cross US 9 and climb up Church St. The road is six lanes, with no shoulder.

19.4 Turn left on Market St., a one-way street. Head through downtown Poughkeepsie. Market turns to Civic Center Pl. and ends at the old post office.

19.7 Turn left, then make a right in 0.1 mile on Washington St. (Hwy.

9G), the first street you'll come to. It sports two wide lanes.

20.8 Junction; turn right on US 9 North. It's a two-lane shoulderless highway, but the lanes are wide.

21.5 Shoulder begins.

22.8 Notice the beautiful buildings on the left at the Culinary Institute of America. Once the site of the St. Andrew-on-Hudson Jesuit Seminary, the school boasts of four restaurants—reservations are necessary.

23.6 Climb to this point. This is Hyde Park now, an all-service town.

24.3 Turnoff on the left leads to the Home of Franklin D. Roosevelt National Historic Site, open daily from April through October, and Thursday through Monday, November through March (except for Thanksgiving, Christmas, and New Years). There's an admission charge. This is also the site of the Franklin D. Roosevelt Library and Museum, which houses documents, manuscripts, photographs, and other artifacts relating to the lives of both Franklin and Eleanor Roosevelt.

24.7 Tourist information center on the right.

25.3 No shoulder, but the road is fairly wide. At this point, you'll see a small fieldstone house (across from the D-5 historic marker). It is one of only two remaining mid-eighteenth-century homes in Hyde Park.

26.0 Junction with CR 41; shoulder resumes. Keep straight on US 9.

26.2 Vanderbilt Mansion Historic Site on the left. Enter here, then cycle to the mansion and out to US 9 on a one-way road. Built between 1896 and 1898, this was the spring and fall home of Frederick and Louise Vanderbilt. Whether you pay to enter the mansion or not, you'll want to cycle the grounds, where there's a grand view of the Hudson River. The mansion is open the same hours as at the FDR site.

26.8 Exit the Vanderbilt Mansion grounds.

27.6 Reach the top of another hill, most of which have been gentle grades.

28.8 Small market on the right.

29.4 Sign for Staatsburg and Mills Mansion State Historic Site. Bear left on Old Post Rd. There's no shoulder. **SIDE TRIP:** If you're interested in Mills-Norrie State Park, bear left again before heading north. Actually two connecting parks—the Margaret Lewis Norrie and the Ogden and Ruth Livingston Mills Memorial State Parks—they comprise more than 1,000 acres, bounded on the west by the Hudson River. There's a campground with hot showers, cabins, an environmental museum, hiking trails, two golf courses, and, of course, the Mills Mansion. The campground opens about May 10 and closes on or before October 31.

29.8 Staatsburg, thought to be the earliest settlement in Hyde Park.

30.2 St. Margarets Episcopal Church, a mid-nineteenth-century English Gothic adaptation renowned for its French medieval stained glass windows. There's a library on the right just beyond.

30.7 Turnoff to Mills Mansion State Historic Site, the country home of Ogden and Ruth Livingston Mills, built in 1895–96. It's closed Mondays and Tuesdays, and there's an admission fee.

31.6 Back on US 9; four lanes, with a shoulder. Go left.

32.0 No shoulder.

32.4 Junction with S. Mill Rd. on the left. **ALTERNATE ROUTE**: If US 9 is crowded, you may want to turn left here. S. Mill Rd. and CR 85 are one and the same for a while, but when CR 85 takes off to the left, continue on S. Mill Rd. and back to US 9. S. Mill Rd. is about 4.5 miles long and merges with US 9 at the 35.7-mile mark.

34.5 Lane narrows to two lanes.

35.4 Shoulder again as you enter the historic town of Rhinebeck, where all services are available.

35.7 John Benner Stone House, built in 1740.

36.1 Information center on the right as you pedal through town.

36.2 Turn right on Hwy. 308.

36.7 Shoulder now.

37.5 Turn right on CR 101 (Violet Hill Rd.); no shoulder; steep climb.

38.3 Road ends (after climbing); make a right on unsigned Hwy. 9G. There's a shoulder, though at times it's narrow and bumpy.

39.4 Turn left on CR 19; no shoulder. It's also called Slate Quarry Rd. and Bulls Head Rd.

40.6 Top of short, but very steep hill. Although the grade lessens in intensity, it climbs another 0.2 mile.

42.3 Begin downhill.

43.0 Lake Dr. on the right. Three private campgrounds—Interlake, Long Pond Lake Vacation Resort, and Hartley's Breezy Point—are located within 2 miles of this junction. The first, Interlake Campground, is less than 0.5 mile away. All offer hot showers and lake swimming, and all but Hartley's has a laundromat. Although they have different opening and closing dates, at least one of the three is open from April 15 through November 31.

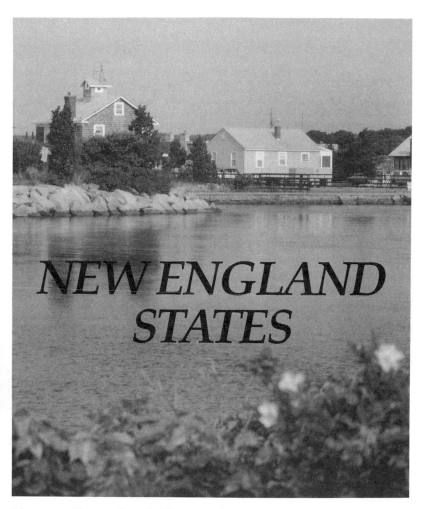

NEW ENGLAND STATES

Flowers and homes along Weekapaug Inlet

Mention New England and most people think of fall colors, cold winters, Cape Cod, the mansions of Newport, Rhode Island, and Maine's magnificent coastline. Cycle New England and you'll find all of this and more.

More is New Hampshire's 18-mile coastline. Slight but stunning, it's a place where Rye Harbor begs you to spend the day and whales blow offshore, inviting you to enjoy a day or evening of whale watching. It's Manchester, Massachusetts, and its lovely harbor; downtown Boston where the old blends with the new; it's a maze of steep hills linking one Connecticut valley with another.

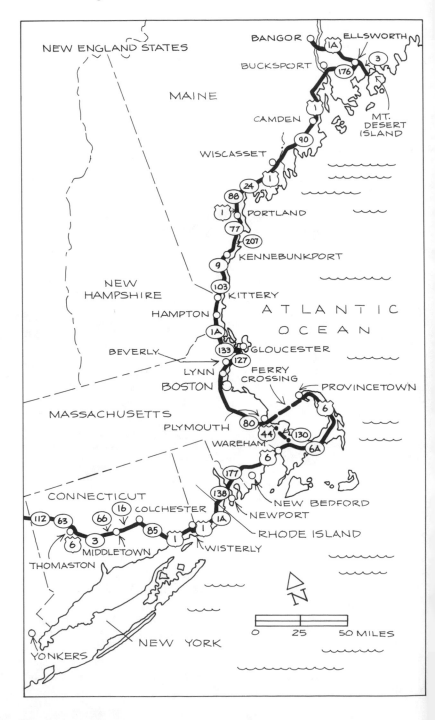

This route leads 755.9 miles through five of the six New England states, excluding only Vermont in its path back to the sea. State miles include Connecticut, 135.3 miles; Rhode Island, 63.3 miles; Massachusetts, 250.6 miles; New Hampshire, 19.9 miles; and Maine, 286.8 miles. Mileage listed for Maine includes an ending segment of 39.3 miles that extends from Mount Desert Island to the Bangor International Airport.

Although a series of steep climbs makes the Connecticut portion of the route the most difficult of the New England states, you'll enjoy some easier Connecticut riding too. The highway flattens out some upon entering Rhode Island, Massachusetts, and New Hampshire, although you will encounter a few short, steep climbs. Maine offers both flatlands and hills, several of which warrant a granny gear. Connecticut road conditions are superb, with the route following uncrowded roads, or highways with a shoulder, for its entirety. The only heavy-traffic area is in Middletown and New London (where you'll reach the Atlantic again), which really poses no problem.

The award for the state with the bumpiest roads has to go to Rhode Island. In its defense, it has managed to build smooth roads wherever new construction warrants it. Although bumpy, at least most roads sport a shoulder or they are free of heavy traffic.

Bumpy or not, you won't be able to ride your bike over the Newport Bridge leading into Newport, Rhode Island, as bikes are prohibited. Unsafe, too, as there are wide expansion slots just waiting to gobble up bike tires, it is the only site on the entire coast where you won't be able to ride or walk to your next destination (except for ferry crossings).

Hitching a ride shouldn't pose a problem, however, as motorists are often willing to give bikers a lift. As you can imagine, waiting bikers are a familiar sight, thus the sympathetic motorists. Offering to pay the toll is a nice way of showing your appreciation.

Once across the bridge, you'll encounter heavy traffic for a short distance, then it's a mostly pleasant ride into Massachusetts, where you'll continue pedaling a series of back roads.

Traffic increases upon reaching Wareham, but not for long, as you'll cycle the Cape Cod Canal path where motor vehicles are prohibited. Riding is a real pleasure throughout most of Cape Cod, with a bike path available in many areas; secondary roads are traveled in others.

Upon reaching Provincetown, you'll ferry over to Plymouth, continuing into, through, and out of Boston via a chain of back roads that pass through a number of small towns. Although you'll encounter heavy traffic in Boston, it's a pleasant city in which to cycle. Those who'd like to explore further will find a youth hostel in downtown Boston. Motels and hotels are abundant but very expensive.

You'll want to spend some time exploring the 18-mile New Hampshire coastline, easy to do considering its size. As you ride close to the ocean at all times, it is a true cycling delight.

Maine is enchanting as well. Highways lead along the coast and inland, traveling either narrow, uncrowded roads or busy roads with wide lanes or shoulders. Watch for heavy traffic in Portland and north of Camden on US 1. If you want to avoid the area north of Camden, an alternate route is listed.

The ride ends at Mount Desert Island, where there's a side trip circling the island, a definite must-see. Numerous campgrounds dot this natural wonder, home of popular Acadia National Park.

From here you'll have to decide how to end your ride. Does it end here or are you busing or riding to Bangor to catch a plane or bus? A final segment provides detailed instructions on reaching both the Bangor International Airport and the Greyhound bus station. Please be forewarned: Highway 1A leading to Bangor is often narrow, with motorists blowing by at high speeds. Although occasional shoulders provide some relief, there are shoulderless sections to contend with.

As you might have guessed, summer is the best time for cycling, although some may prefer the quieter times of spring and fall. However, be prepared for cold, wet weather if riding early or late in the season. Portland, Maine, for example, averages a high of 52 degrees Fahrenheit and a low of 32 in April.

In this region, temperatures often differ from day to day. Connecticut offers summer highs in the mid 80s, with temperatures of 100 degrees quite rare. Lows drop to about 63 in the summer. Typical highs in April reach 60 degrees, September averages about 75 degrees.

Once along the coast, you'll experience pleasant temperatures, with highs near 80 in midsummer and lows near 60. Watch for heavy fog on the coast during the summer.

Unlike the South Atlantic States where heavy rains douse the region in summer, precipitation is fairly constant, with an average of three inches per month falling each year.

Campgrounds are usually open from sometime in May through October. The majority close for the winter. Although plentiful in many areas, campgrounds are nonexistent in the section leading through Boston, where you must ride 92.5 miles from one campsite to the next. Options include staying in a motel in the town of your choice, staying at the youth hostel in Boston, or camping out on someone's lawn—with permission, of course.

If you need additional information on roads or biking conditions, call or write:

Bicycle Coordinator
Connecticut Department of Transportation
P.O. Drawer A, 24 Wolcott Hill Rd.
Wethersfield, CT 06109
(203) 566-6450

Roland Roy, bicycle coordinator
Department of Transportation
State Office Bldg., Station 16
Augusta, ME 04333
(207) 289-2954

David M. Luce, bicycle coordinator
Bureau of Transportation
10 Park Plaza
Boston, MA 02116
(617) 973-7473

New Hampshire Office of Vacation Travel
P.O. Box 856
Concord, NH 03301
(603) 271-2666

Planning Division
R.I. Department of Transportation
Two Capitol Hill
Providence, RI 02903
(401) 277-2694

Interlake Campground to Black Rock State Park (66.5 miles)

After a fun downhill (with one big uphill and several small ones thrown in for good measure), you'll enter Stanfordville, where you'll enjoy a ride across gentle rolling terrain. Farm fields and rural homes dot the beautiful mountains and valleys, linking this small town with another—Pine Plains.

Spend some extra time in Pine Plains if you can. There are small shops, a couple of restaurants, and delicious treats at a well-known bakery/deli.

Head out of town for a series of rolling hills and some steep pitches, too. Services are few as you cross from New York into Connecticut. Nicknamed the Constitution State, but also known as the Nutmeg State, Connecticut offers magnificent scenes with lush green valleys, enormous farms, and lovely homes. Traffic isn't too hectic either.

There are some steep climbs, however, and the day may seem longer than 66 miles. Towns are spaced some distance apart and when there is a town, don't expect a market. Many don't offer any services. Plan to ride with snacks in tow.

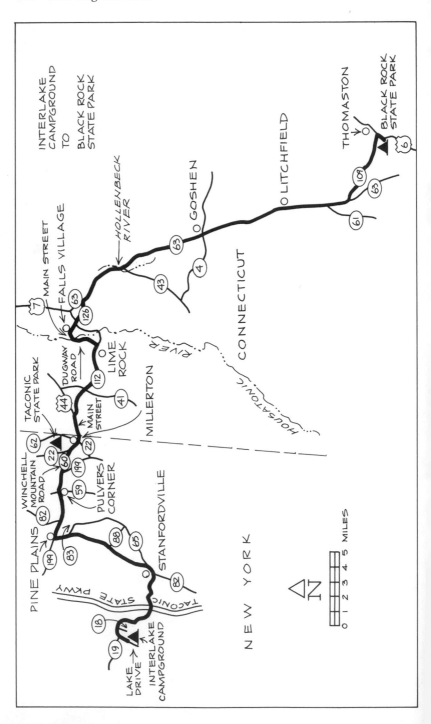

MILEAGE LOG

0.0 Junction of Lake Dr. and CR 19. Head right on CR 19, passing scattered homes and lush farmland en route.

0.4 Junction with CR 18.

1.0 Junction with CR 15.

2.7 Cross the Taconic State Pkwy.

7.8 CR 19 ends at the junction with Hwy. 82. This is now Stanfordville. Make a left on Hwy. 82, a wide road, pleasant for cycling. Pass a couple of restaurants and markets along the way. There's a bed-and-breakfast inn in town as well.

8.6 Junction with CR 65. Keep to the left on Hwy. 82.

9.4 Junction with CR 87.

9.7 Junction with CR 53.

12.5 Junction with CR 88.

16.6 Junction with CR 83. There's a restaurant here. Enter Pine Plains (elevation 474 feet) just past the junction. You'll find all amenities sans motels. Instead there's a bed-and-breakfast inn.

17.2 Junction. Turn right on Hwy. 82/Hwy. 199. Pass a well-known bakery/deli as you head east. There's a shoulder now.

18.6 Hwy. 82 leaves the route; keep straight on Hwy. 199 East.

19.2 Shoulder disappears now and again.

21.2 Pulvers Corner; no services. This is a high point—you'll descend from this point.

21.3 Junction with CR 59.

21.9 Begin climbing again.

23.1 Turn left on CR 60 (Winchell Mountain Rd.), an uncrowded, shoulderless road. Keep climbing, looking back every so often, as there are wonderful views of the surrounding mountains and valleys.

24.1 Top of hill; begin descending.

24.8 Irondale. No services.

25.4 Merge onto Hwy. 22. Keep to the right.

25.5 Village of Millerton. Shoulder is nonexistent.

26.1 Turn left on US 44 East, which is also Main St. Head through town, where you'll find all facilities, except motels.

26.4 Millerton Free Library on the left. Just ahead is the CR 62 junction. **SIDE TRIP:** To visit Taconic State Park, go left and up for 2 miles on CR 62 North to the park, where there's camping, hot showers, et cetera.

27.1 Shoulder now; supermarket, restaurants as you leave town.

27.3 Enter Connecticut, one of five New England states on this route. Begin pedaling uphill again.

28.1 Top of hill.

28.3 Turn right on Hwy. 112. There's a shoulder. Continue cycling numerous ups and downs in roller-coaster fashion.

Cyclist pedaling Highway 60, west of Irondale

29.7 Interlaken Inn on the right.

30.4 Junction with Hwy. 41. Continue straight on Hwy. 112.

33.7 Descend to Lime Rock; no services. The shoulder ends as you exit town.

33.9 The terrain levels off some; shoulder again.

34.3 Turn left before the cemetery on Dugway Rd.

35.8 Cycle along the Housatonic River.

36.4 To the right, there's a park (with rest rooms) overlooking the river.

36.5 Keep to the right and cross the river, then head up toward town.

36.9 Go under the bridge, staying on Water St. Turn right, then left on Main St., entering Falls Village. There are no markets here, just a post office and an inn that has limited hours.

37.3 Main St. merges with Hwy. 126; keep to the right. There's a shoulder. The terrain is rolling hills for the most part.

37.6 Junction with US 7. Continue straight.

39.5 Road ends; turn right on Hwy. 63 South. There's a shoulder, sometimes very wide. The hills continue.

40.6 Cross Hollenbeck River. You'll cross the river twice again in the next few miles.

43.2 Junction with Hwy. 43 South. Keep straight on Hwy. 63 and begin a long climb. The grade isn't tough at all in the beginning, but it increases in intensity as you continue on.

45.8 Top of hill (thank God!) although relief is short-lived.
47.3 Begin uphill again; a bit steep for 0.5 mile, then you'll descend.
49.2 Goshen; no markets on route. The road finally traverses rolling hills again.
49.5 Library on the left.
49.7 Junction with Hwy. 4. Keep straight on Hwy. 63.
52.0 Picnic area.
55.2 Descend into Litchfield, a wonderfully quaint town with a market, several restaurants, and a motel that is actually out of downtown 1.5 miles on US 202.
56.1 Reach a stoplight. Go left, then right, following the signs to US 63 South.
58.4 Continue in roller-coaster fashion to this point, then it's up a short, steep hill. There's a picnic area on the right.
58.8 Top of hill.
58.9 Junction with Hwy. 61 on the right. Climb again.
59.2 Level off some, then begin a steep downhill.
60.2 At the bottom of the hill, go left on Hwy. 109 East. There's a good shoulder. There's a convenience store and a pizza shop.
63.1 Highway follows along the Wigwam Reservoir.
65.3 Black Rock Dam overlook on the right.
66.1 Junction with US 6. Go right.
66.5 Entrance to Black Rock State Park. Comprised of more than 400 acres, it has shady and sunny sites with full facilities. It is open April 15 through September 30. This is a prime spot for swimming, fishing, and hiking. In fact, hikers often enjoy the Mattatuck Trail, which connects the park to the Mattatuck State Forest. In case you were wondering, the name "Black Rock" originates from local graphite deposits, mined by early settlers of the Naugatuck Valley.

Black Rock State Park to Markham Meadows Campground (47.0 miles)

Begin today with a quick warm-up and then it's a steep climb up to Plymouth. Fortunately, the hills lessen in intensity after this tough climb.

You'll pass through a variety of towns on your way to East Hampton and the last campground for the day. Good shoulders help make the ride as pleasant as city rides can be. Where shoulders are nonexistent, congestion usually isn't a problem. Traffic is heavy, however, on Highways 72, 3, and 66. Pedaling through Middletown is hectic, especially when crossing the bridge spanning the Connecticut River. Walk the sidewalk for a safer and less stressful ride.

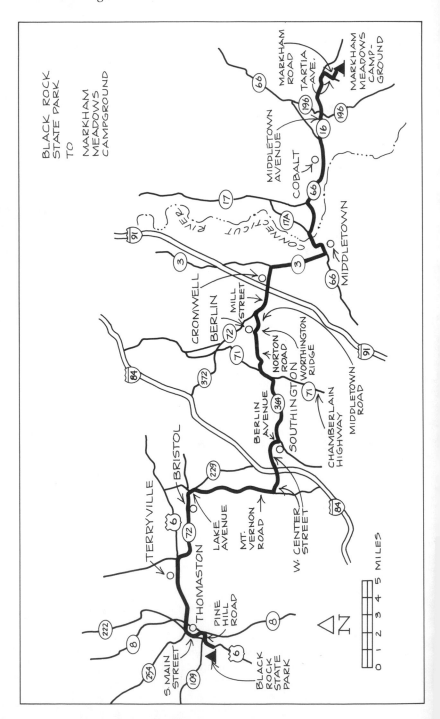

BLACK ROCK STATE PARK TO MARKHAM MEADOWS CAMPGROUND

Grades increase toward the end of the day, with Markham Meadows a pleasant stop for those who do not mind climbing hills early in the morning.

MILEAGE LOG

0.0 Entrance to Black Rock State Park. Head left on US 6.

0.4 Junction Hwy. 109 and US 6. Keep straight on US 6 and make a right on the first street, which is Pine Hill Rd. There's a shoulder. Look for a coffee shop, which is actually a diner with excellent food and prices, at the junction.

0.9 Junction with Hwy. 8. Turn left on unsigned Hwy. 254. There's no shoulder, but the road is wide.

1.6 Road becomes S. Main St. as you head through the town of Thomaston.

2.0 Opera House on the left. This unique old building is now a police station and city hall.

2.2 Turn right on E. Main St. toward US 6 and Hwy. 8.

Opera House (now a police station and city hall), Thomaston

2.5 Cross under Hwy. 8 and continue on US 6 East. There's a shoulder as you head up the very steep grade, probably the steepest or one of the steepest on the entire Atlantic Coast route.

2.9 Plymouth. The grade lessens in intensity, but is still steep.

3.6 Top of the hill. Now there's a series of roller-coaster hills for you to cycle, although you'll spend most of your time descending.

4.6 Terryville, an all-services town. Terryville is home to the Lock Museum of America, 130 Main St. (US 6). This museum boasts the largest collection of locks, keys, and ornate hardware in the United States, with some 22,000 items. It's open Tuesday through Sunday, May 1 through October 31.

6.3 Junction. Turn right on Hwy. 72; wide shoulder.

7.2 Bristol town line.

8.4 Cross the Pequabuck River. Although you'll lose the shoulder upon entering the town of Bristol, the road is fairly wide. Terrain is nearly flat or rolling now. You'll find all amenities in town.

9.3 Bear to the left on Hwy. 72.

9.6 Turn left on N. Main St. There are three bike shops in town. One is on N. Main St., a few blocks ahead.

9.7 Turn right on Riverside Ave. (Hwy. 72).

10.7 Road curves to the left.

10.9 Turn right on Hwy. 229 South.

11.2 Just past Mountain Rd., make a right on unsigned Lake Ave.; wide road and shoulder.

12.9 Lake Compounce Festival Park on the right. Call for schedule and rates: (203) 583-6000. Both the road and the shoulder are narrow now.

13.5 Road becomes Mount Vernon Rd.

13.8 Beginning of rolling hills. Although there's no shoulder, the road is uncrowded.

16.1 Turn left on W. Center St.

17.3 Cross under I-84.

17.5 Climb to West St., making a right and then an immediate left and continuing on W. Center.

17.8 Top of the hill.

18.5 Downtown Southington; all services.

18.6 Road changes to Columbus Ave.

18.7 Junction Maine St. (Hwy. 10). Keep straight on Berlin Ave.

19.4 Turn left on Berlin St. (also called Hwy. 364), not to be confused with Berlin Ave. There's a shoulder now.

20.8 Hwy. 364 makes a right on East St.

21.0 Hwy. 364 goes left on Kensington Rd.

21.2 See Sloper's Pond on the right through the trees.

22.0 Berlin town line.

23.1 Timberlin Park entrance on the left. The road becomes Southington Rd.

23.6 Make a left on Chamberlain Hwy. (Hwy. 71 North); shoulder.

24.3 Make a right on Norton Rd.; no shoulder, but road is uncrowded.

25.6 Follow Kensington Rd. to the north (left), if you need supplies or any other services in Berlin.

26.4 Norton Rd. changes to Hudson St. Continue straight. Cycle up a steep hill.

26.9 Cycle right on Worthington Ridge. Go about 200 feet or so and make a left on Middletown Rd. Descend, then cross US 5 and Hwy. 15, continuing straight.

27.9 Make a right on Mill St., which is also Hwy. 372 (formerly Hwy. 72). There's a bike shop on the left as you turn. Fortunately, this heavily trafficked road sports a shoulder as you pedal across gentle rolling terrain.

28.9 Cromwell town limits; all services.

29.2 There's a variety of motels, restaurants, and stores in this area.

29.5 Cross under I-91.

30.0 Junction with Hwy. 217. Keep straight.

31.0 Turn right on Hwy. 3 (also formerly Hwy. 72); no shoulder.

31.4 Shoulder reappears as you enter Middletown town limits, where you'll find all amenities. Traffic continually increases now.

34.5 Turn left on Hwy. 66 East. The road is four lanes, with a narrow shoulder.

34.8 No shoulder now as you enter downtown Middletown.

35.1 Turn left on Hwy. 66 East. Head through the center of town.

35.3 Keep following the signs to Hwy. 66 East, Hwy. 17 North.

35.7 Top of Arrigoni Bridge, which spans the Connecticut River, New England's longest river. The river flows for a total of 407 miles, 69 miles of which lie in Connecticut. The Arrigoni Bridge is three lanes, with two lanes heading one way, one the other. Under major construction that is scheduled for completion in October 1993, the bridge has sidewalks lining both sides, one of which is always open, even during the construction period.

36.3 Bear to the right on Hwy. 66 East and Hwy. 17 North; narrow shoulder, heavy traffic.

37.2 Wide shoulder begins just after passing a supermarket and other shops. Begin climbing.

38.3 Hwy. 17 leaves the route. Keep straight on Hwy. 66.

38.6 Reach this high point, then begin a series of ups and downs, mostly climbing to a point near East Hampton, then descending to the campground.

38.8 Road narrows to two lanes; shoulder narrows as well.

39.8 Motel on the right.

41.3 Enter Cobalt.

41.4 Junction with Hwy. 151; market on the right.

42.2 Take the right fork to Hwy. 16 (also called Middletown Ave.). This road isn't nearly as crowded as Hwy. 66.

42.4 Top of the hill. The town of East Hampton is 1 mile to the north on Hwy. 196. Stay straight on Hwy. 16. The route descends or remains on the level, then climbs again.

44.7 Convenience store on the left.

45.2 Top of the last big hill of the day.

46.0 Turn right on Tartia Ave. Rolling hills now, some steep (but short).

46.7 Turn left on Markham Rd., a packed dirt (and level) road leading to Markham Meadows Campground.

47.0 Campground office. In addition to the usual amenities, you'll find a small grocery store, a laundromat, shaded and open sites, a pond, and, best of all, reduced rates for bicyclists. The campground is open May 15 through October 1.

Markham Meadows Campground to Burlingame State Park (61.7 miles)

Today will be a memorable day for many as the route dips down to the south, paralleling the Atlantic Ocean once again.

The segment begins with a couple of miles of downhill, then a steep climb. The rest of the ride is mostly rolling hills with an occasional short, steep hill thrown in to keep those climbing muscles in good shape.

Traffic isn't too bad until you reach the junction of Highways 85 and 82, then it continually increases as you reach New London, Groton, and Mystic. Prior to New London, you'll travel through rural areas and small towns.

In New London you'll view an abundance of historic buildings, and in Mystic, the old and new. Mystic Marinelife Aquarium and Mystic Seaport are two of Connecticut's most popular attractions. In fact, more people visit Mystic Marinelife Aquarium than any other attraction in Connecticut, according to the folks there.

The trip from Mystic is a pleasant combination of rolling hills with an occasional steep one, and there are shoulders for the most part.

Enter Rhode Island, the smallest of the fifty states, at Westerly, heading back to the Atlantic just out of town. Be sure to visit popular Misquamicut State Beach en route to Burlingame, a well-liked Rhode Island state park.

MILEAGE LOG

0.0 Entrance to Markham Meadows Campground. Cycle back the same way you came.

0.3 Back to Tartia Ave. Turn right.

1.0 Back on Colchester Ave. (Hwy. 16). Cycle right.

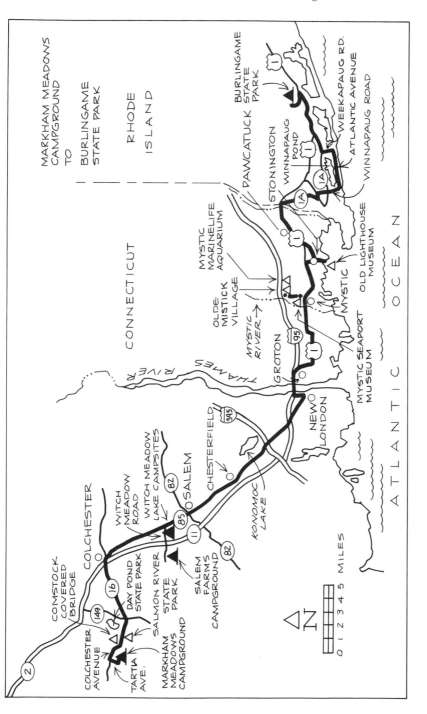

MARKHAM MEADOWS CAMPGROUND
TO
BURLINGAME STATE PARK

RHODE ISLAND

CONNECTICUT

BURLINGAME STATE PARK

WEEKAPAUG RD.

ATLANTIC AVENUE

WINNAPAUG ROAD

PAWCATUCK

STONINGTON

WINNAPAUG POND

MYSTIC MARINELIFE AQUARIUM

OLDE MISTICK VILLAGE

MYSTIC RIVER →

MYSTIC

OLD LIGHTHOUSE MUSEUM

MYSTIC SEAPORT MUSEUM

GROTON

THAMES RIVER

NEW LONDON

CHESTERFIELD

WITCH MEADOW ROAD

WITCH MEADOW LAKE CAMPSITES

SALEM

KONOMOC LAKE

SALEM FARMS CAMPGROUND

SALMON RIVER STATE PARK

DAY POND STATE PARK

COLCHESTER

COMSTOCK COVERED BRIDGE

COLCHESTER AVENUE

TARTIA AVE.

MARKHAM MEADOWS CAMPGROUND

ATLANTIC OCEAN

N

0 1 2 3 4 5 MILES

2.7   Comstock Covered Bridge, one of the five remaining covered bridges in the state, is on the left as you cross the Salmon River.

2.8   Entrance on the right to Salmon River State Park. An excellent trout fishing and fly fishing area, this is a popular spot in early spring for whitewater kayakers and canoers. Picnicking, hiking, horseback riding, and cross-country skiing are also favorite activities, here among the hemlocks. Begin climbing upon passing the park.

2.9   Colchester town line.

4.7   Junction with Hwy. 149; market at the top of the hill. The road leads to Day Pond State Park. Originally constructed by a pioneer family named Day, Day Pond produced more than just fish for supper. Water from the pond turned a large waterwheel, which served to power the family sawmill. Visitors won't see the waterwheel, for only stone foundations remain. The fishing is reportedly good, however, as the lake is regularly stocked with trout. Also, there are picnic facilities, hiking trails, and swimming opportunities.

6.0   Cross Pine Brook. Begin a series of easy ups and downs.

7.5   Cross Gillette Brook.

8.8   Cross Meadow Brook.

9.1   Junction with Hwy. 2. Bikes prohibited.

9.6   Junction with Hwy. 85 in downtown Colchester, where you'll find all services. At the junction, go right; there's a shoulder now. Motels aren't available, but there is a bed-and-breakfast inn. There's a library just before the junction.

10.4   Bike shop on the left. Fork; keep right on Hwy. 85 South. Rolling hills accompany you as you travel through an uncrowded rural area.

10.7   Cross under Hwy. 2.

13.8   Salem town line.

15.2   Cross Big Brook.

15.4   Small market on the left.

15.6   Junction with Witch Meadow Rd. **SIDE TRIP:** If you need a campground, head right to Witch Meadow Lake Campsites in about 1 mile. Salem Farms Campground is 2 to 3 miles down the same road. Both camps offer all amenities; they have laundromats and limited groceries as well. Also, there are swimming, fishing, and hiking opportunities. Cross Little Brook just past this junction.

16.5   Salem Free Public Library on the left.

17.5   Junction with Hwy. 82; market, restaurants here. Now traffic is heavier.

17.9   Fraser Brook crossing.

18.3   Fairy Lake on the left.

18.8 Horse Lake.

19.3 Highway picnic area on the right. No rest rooms.

20.4 Montville town limits.

21.5 Chesterfield; restaurants, motels, et cetera.

21.9 Junction with Hwy. 161. Bear to the left on Hwy. 85.

23.5 Waterford town line.

23.8 Konomoc Lake visible on the left.

25.4 Cross under I-395.

25.5 Hwy. 85 is now four lanes, with a narrow shoulder and heavy traffic.

26.0 Motel on the left.

27.2 Crystal Mall on the right; plenty of stores, services from now on.

27.9 Cross under I-95. The road narrows back to two wide lanes as you enter New London, a town with all amenities. Hwy. 85 is now called Broad St.

29.0 Junction with US 1. Continue on Broad St. for 1 mile to its end at the following junction.

30.0 Huntington St. and Governor Winthrop Blvd. Take the left fork, following Governor Winthrop Blvd. Before heading over to Groton, cycle around the downtown area, where eighteenth-century history abounds. You'll see the New London County Courthouse, built in 1784, and much more.

30.3 Road ends. Take a left on Water St. The road is now six lanes, with no shoulder.

30.6 Turn right on unsigned Crystal Ave. Follow "Bicycle Route" sign.

30.7 Go left on State Pier Rd.

31.0 Cross under I-95. Keep straight on Williams St.

31.2 Make a left on Bailey Circle. (Restaurant here.) Follow signs to the bike route and up the walkway onto the bridge. Bikes can be ridden across the walkway, which runs alongside I-95.

32.5 End of bridge over the Thames River. Exit on the walkway, descend, and circle back around under the bridge in 0.2 mile.

33.0 Walkway leads to junction of Bridge St. in Groton. Make a left on Bridge St.; there's a shoulder.

33.8 Turn right on US 1 North. Pass a variety of businesses (all services here) as you cycle along.

34.1 Four-lane shoulderless road now, but highway narrows to two lanes with a shoulder in another mile.

35.6 Bicycle shop on the right.

36.2 Junction with Hwy. 117.

36.7 Begin steep uphill; road is four lanes, no shoulder. Use the sidewalk if you like.

37.2 Junction with Hwy. 215. Bear left on US 1; there's a shoulder now. At the top of the hill, descend, climb another, then descend again as you travel on.

Mystic River, Mystic

39.6 Welcome to historic Mystic, originally a shipbuilding community in the 1600s. One of the smallest early seaports, Mystic produced a greater tonnage of select ships than any port of its size in the country. Today this busy all-service town caters to tourism with charming shops, a pretty harbor, and many attractions.

39.8 Junction: Hwy. 215 meets US 1 again.

39.9 Cross the Mystic River, then proceed a few hundred feet or so to Willow St. This road leads to Olde Mistick Village and visitor center, Mystic Marinelife Aquarium, and Mystic Seaport Museum. For more information, see "Mystic Side Trips."

40.5 Junction with Hwy. 27. There are rolling hills and a shoulder now.

41.4 View of the Atlantic Ocean.

41.5 Old Stonington Rd. 1B turnoff. **ALTERNATE ROUTE**: Take this for a short trip off US 1.

41.9 Old Stonington Rd. 1B merges with US 1.

42.0 Quambaug Cove.

43.3 Bear right on US 1A. The road is bumpy, with no shoulder, but uncrowded.

44.0 Left on Trumbull Ave.

44.2 Junction. Go left on US 1A East. **SIDE TRIP:** Road leads 1 mile to Stonington Point where there's a grand view. Pass through Stonington Village en route to the Old Lighthouse Museum. The first government lighthouse in Connecticut, the museum boasts of nineteenth-century portraits, Stonington-made stoneware, and whaling and fishing gear.

45.2 Junction with US 1. Go right.

45.6 Motel on the right; deli on the left; more motels as you continue for the next 0.5 mile. The shoulder continues.

46.4 Wequetequock Cove.

46.6 Pawcatuck.

47.4 Family restaurant; laundry on the left; several other shops.

48.3 Shopping center on the left.

48.5 Junction with Hwy. 234.

49.0 Junction with Hwy. 2. Continue straight.

49.1 Cross the Pawcatuck River and enter Rhode Island at Westerly. Bear right on US 1; there's no shoulder.

49.4 Leave US 1, staying straight on Main St.

49.7 Bear left, following signs to scenic US 1A North.

50.1 Tourist information center on the right.

50.2 Shoulder begins.

51.7 Sign to Misquamicut Beach and Westerly Airport. Bear left.

51.9 Road curves to the right. Follow signs to Westerly beaches.

52.8 Junction of Winnapaug Rd. and Shore Rd. Keep straight on Winnapaug Rd. and pass motels and restaurants en route to the beach.

53.5 Turn left on Atlantic Ave. As you pedal, notice all the wonderful spots for relaxing in the sun.

56.0 Market on the left.

56.1 Just past the Weekapaug Breachway, go left on Weekapaug Rd.; no shoulder.

57.0 Merge right on scenic US 1A; shoulder.

57.7 Bear right on US 1.

59.9 Junction with Hwy. 216; market at junction.

60.3 Road off to the right leads to Quonochontaug Beach.

60.5 Convenience store on the right.

61.1 Turn left at sign for Burlingame State Park. Make an acute left upon turning.

61.3 Make a right at sign to state park.

61.5 Entrance to park; turn right.

61.7   Burlingame State Park office and registration. An enormous full-service campground with 755 sites on the shore of Watchaug Pond, it also has a camp store. Two sites are always held open for late-arriving cyclists. Shady sites occupy the 2,100-acre park, open April 15 through October. Most of the park is graced with tall spruce trees. If hardwoods are more your thing, you'll find a variety of these growing in the park as well. Hiking, fishing, and swimming are the most popular activities, as well as swimming in the Atlantic, located 1 mile away.

Mystic Side Trips

To reach Olde Mistick Village/visitor center, go left on Willow, then left again on Hwy. 27, for a total of 1.7 miles. The Mystic Marinelife Aquarium is next door. En route to these sites, you'll pass Mystic Seaport Museum on Hwy. 27 in 0.6 mile.

Olde Mistick Village is a eighteenth-centurylike colonial shopping center open year-round. There's a theater, restaurants, and numerous shops. A visitor center offers a variety of brochures and information for those in need.

Mystic Marinelife Aquarium is open daily, except for Thanksgiving, Christmas, New Years Day, and the last week in January. A fee allows you to view seals and sea lions in habitats simulating natural ones. You'll see penguins and gaze at more than 6,000 marine creatures displayed in fifty exhibits.

Mystic Seaport is the nation's largest maritime museum, with seventeen riverfront acres. Stroll the cobblestone streets of a re-created nineteenth-century maritime village, explore three clipper ships that once sailed the seven seas, and watch craftsmen going about their daily work. Open year-round, it has an admission charge.

Burlingame State Park to Melville Ponds Campground (37.2 miles)

Rhode Island is not exactly biker-friendly, as roads are often bumpy and narrow, but you'll travel the best route possible. Of course, no route is traffic-free.

Unlike the hilly days of segments past, this segment consists of some flat terrain mixed with rolling hills, and a few short, steep grades. Although traffic is heavy on US 1, it sports a wide shoulder for the portions included in this segment. On a brighter note, whenever possible the route follows Scenic US 1A, a much nicer choice.

Upon reaching the top of the hill at the Jamestown Bridge exit, you'll probably encounter a lot of traffic. Although cyclists are allowed on the bridge, you'll want to use the narrow walkway to walk your bike.

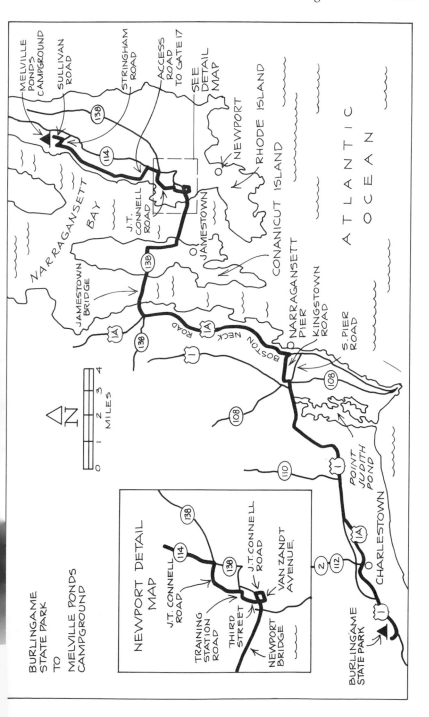

Crossing at rush hour or on a holiday is treacherous, so you'd be better off to walk. Walking is probably the best bet anytime.

A new, wider bridge—the Jamestown–Verrazzano Bridge—is currently under construction, with completion scheduled for fall 1992.

Upon exiting the Jamestown Bridge, you can ride to the Newport Bridge, where you'll have to hitch a ride as bikes are prohibited. And with good reason—expansion slots are wide and dangerous—not conducive to good biking.

Motorists in this region are used to seeing cyclists waiting for a ride and it usually doesn't take long to hitch one. Most cyclists offer to pay the toll. Hitching a ride over the Newport Bridge is much better than the alternative—riding to Providence. US 1 leading north to the state capitol is narrow, congested, and treacherous. Local bike shop owners all recommended hitching a ride over to Newport rather than cycling through Providence.

Upon entering Newport, you'll head north but, time permitting, you'll want to explore the elegant mansions of Newport to the south. These include The Breakers, a sixteenth-century Italian palacelike estate built in 1895 for Cornelius Vanderbilt.

Pedal 10-mile Ocean Drive, home to dozens of summer mansions and villas, walk along world-famous Cliff Walk, a 4-mile path along the Atlantic, visit Fort Adams State Park, and explore tourist-oriented Newport, where you can shop and eat to your heart's content.

From Newport you'll ride along Narragansett Bay, through Navy territory, to Melville Ponds Campground, a comfortable spot for the night or a base camp for Newport-bound explorers.

MILEAGE LOG

0.0 Burlingame State Park campground registration office. Return the way you came back to the main highway.

0.6 Back at US 1, cycle left (northeast). The shoulder continues.

1.3 Motels/restaurants in the area.

2.2 Head right on Scenic US 1A. There's a tourist information center at the junction. There's a shoulder for a portion of the ride, although the highway is not crowded.

3.5 Back on US 1.

3.6 Exit on Scenic US 1A (Old Post Rd.) to the right.

4.2 Pass Mills Public Library. There are motels along this route through Charlestown. If visiting in August, why not attend the annual Seafood Festival? Some of the area's best seafood is accompanied by live entertainment.

6.8 Merge back onto US 1.

9.0 Junction with Hwy. 110.

13.4 Cross bridge over Point Judith Pond.

14.1 Turnoff to Narragansett Pier. Go right.

14.2 Bear right on unsigned S. Pier Rd.; no shoulder.

Cyclist cruising past the Salve Regina University, Newport

14.4 Junction with Hwy. 108. Go left on unsigned Kingstown Rd., following signs to Scenic US 1A. There's a shopping center near the junction.

16.0 Bear left on US 1A; shoulder. Narragansett Pier is off to the right at the junction.

16.6 Wide shoulder.

17.2 Cross Narrow River Inlet. Scenic US 1A is also called Boston Neck Rd.

19.5 Bike shop on the left, restaurants in the area too.

19.9 Junction with Bonnet Shores Rd., which leads to Bonnet Shores. There's a market also.

20.2 Motel on the left.

23.5   Road leading to Hwy. 138 and Jamestown. Although the high-way wasn't signed in 1991 (probably due to construction of the new bridge), at the top of the hill, just past a convenience store, look for a steep road descending to Narragansett Bay. Cycle right; no shoulder.

24.1   Begin crossing Jamestown Bridge. The bridge is very crowded and narrow, thus the new bridge scheduled for a fall 1992 completion date. Walk bikes up the narrow walkway that parallels the eastbound side.

25.5   End of bridge; shoulder now.

26.7   Bear right, continuing on Hwy. 138.

27.7   Keep left to Newport toll bridge. Park off to the side of the road to hitch a ride. You may want to offer to pay the toll; cars and pickups were $2 in 1991. From the drop-off point (gas station) on J. T. Connell Rd., go right 100 feet or so to unsigned Van Zandt Ave. Make a right. There's no shoulder, but the road is fairly uncrowded.

27.8   Go right on unsigned Third St.

27.9   Head back under bridge.

28.4   Make a right on unsigned Training Station Rd.

28.5   You'll reach a traffic circle at this point. Go three-quarters of the way around the circle and ride straight on unsigned J. T. Connell Rd. (Although this is the same road you were dropped off on, this route is much more pleasant and less crowded.)

28.7   Shoulder now; mall on the right.

29.3   Road is narrow; no shoulder.

29.5   Road widens again.

30.2   Turn left on Hwy. 114, a busy road with no shoulders. Ride the sidewalks and parking lots if desired.

30.8   Bike shop on the right. There are many services in the area such as motels, restaurants, and supermarkets.

30.9   Turn left on unsigned road at the traffic light (access road to Gate 17). There's a large motel and a convenience store at the junction. There's a wide shoulder now.

31.7   Road curves to the right.

32.0   Merge right on an unsigned road, a road totally ignored on area maps. This is a fortunate error for cyclists, however, as the road harbors light traffic. There's a narrow shoulder for most of the road as it follows along Narragansett Bay.

36.2   Stop sign. Turn right on unsigned Stringham Rd. and head up the hill.

36.6   Top of hill. Turn left on unsigned Sullivan Rd. to the Melville Recreation Area. (It's signed from the opposite direction.)

37.2   Melville Ponds Campground office and entrance. You'll find both shady and open sites at this all-service facility—open April through October—with a few snacks for sale as well.

Melville Ponds Campground to Shawme-Crowell State Forest (60.7 miles)

Most of this course wanders along uncrowded roads, but you will find heavier traffic as you head through a small section of Portsmouth and on into Wareham, Massachusetts.

Lovely Massachusetts is the largest and most populous of the New England states visited on this ride, and you'll spend several days cycling through this land, where the ladybug is the state insect and the right whale is the state marine mammal.

View from the bridge between Portsmouth and Tiverton

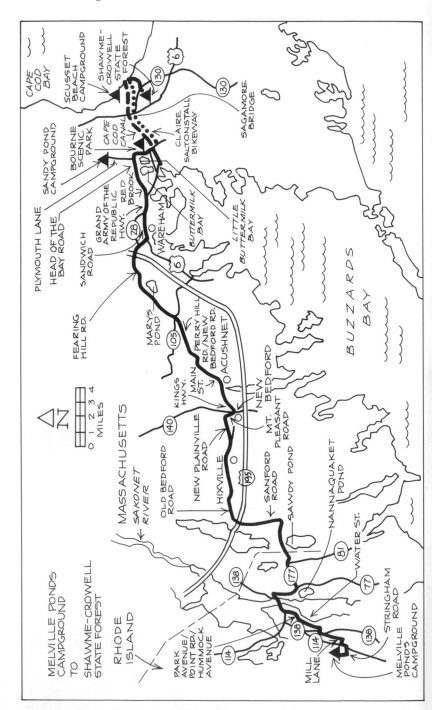

Upon leaving Rhode Island, you'll encounter rolling hills, some with intense grades—all a breeze, though, when compared to pedaling the Delaware River.

Pedal through a maze of rural areas in Massachusetts, where an occasional home and wonderful country scenes are the norm. This rural network is linked together by the busy communities of New Bedford, Acushnet, and Wareham.

For the last leg of the journey, ride along the nearly flat Cape Cod Canal bike path en route to the campground at Shawme-Crowell State Forest.

About 3 miles prior to reaching the campground, you'll cross under the Sagamore Bridge, where you'll have the option of heading north instead of out to Cape Cod. If you'd rather skip riding to the tip of the cape at Provincetown, and the ferry ride to Plymouth, see the alternate route at the 57.0-mile mark.

MILEAGE LOG

0.0 From Melville Ponds Campground entrance, head back the way you came.

0.6 Turn left on Stringham Rd.

0.9 Road ends. Turn left on Hwy. 114. There's a diner across the road with good no-frills food and excellent prices. Hwy. 114 is four lanes, no shoulder; use caution.

1.0 Turn right on Mill Lane. Climb. There's no shoulder, but it's an uncrowded two-lane road.

1.6 Road ends; make a left on Middle Rd.

1.8 Descend to a fork; keep left on Middle Rd.

2.6 Merge onto Hwy. 138 (E. Main). The road is four lanes, with no shoulder. Watch for heavy traffic and potholes as you descend.

3.4 Go right, staying on Hwy. 138. Just before turning, there's a market on the right.

3.5 Turn right on Church Lane; head through a residential area with no shoulder and little traffic.

3.7 Go left as road curves around and becomes unsigned Water St.

4.6 Road curves to the right, then left along the Sakonnet River and becomes unsigned Atlantic Ave.

4.8 Turn left on Tall Man Ave. and make an immediate right on unsigned Aquidneck Ave.

5.0 Road ends; make a right on unsigned Park Ave. and head past Island Park Beach and Grinnell's Beach. Park Ave. becomes Point Rd., then Hummock Ave., along the way to Hwy. 138. The road is fairly wide.

6.2 Shoulder now.

6.5 Cross bridge from Almy Point to Hummock Point.

7.1 Make a right on Hwy. 138. Cross the Sakonet Bridge; narrow shoulder.

7.7 Bear right at the first exit to Hwys. 77 and 177. There are restaurants and a market along the way.

9.9 As you pass Nannaquaket Pond, turn left on Hwy. 177 and begin climbing. There's a good shoulder.

12.9 Junction with Hwy. 81; top of the hill. (You'll encounter several other "summits" en route to this point.) There's a market/grill here and a bakery. Keep straight on Hwy. 177, also known as the American Legion Hwy.

13.5 Enter Massachusetts. Sawdy Pond is on the right. There's no shoulder now, but the road is fairly wide.

14.7 Market on the right.

15.3 At the first light, turn left on Sanford Rd., a fairly flat road without shoulders, but it's uncrowded.

17.1 Country store on the right.

17.3 A doughnut shop on the left. You'll find good prices and excellent donuts.

18.3 Road narrows.

18.8 Junction with US 6. Keep straight.

19.1 Cross under I-195.

19.2 Road curves around to the right and becomes unsigned Old Bedford Rd. It has no shoulder, but it's uncrowded. Terrain is rolling hills, some steep, for the continuation to Wareham.

20.9 Road changes to Old Fall River Rd.

23.4 Hixville General Store on the right. At the junction (road's end) with Hixville Rd., make a right, then an immediate left, continuing on Old Fall River Rd.

24.3 Cross Shingle Mountain Rd.

26.6 Fork; go left on unsigned New Plainville Rd. Old Plainville Rd. is to the right, but it dead ends.

28.5 Keep straight at junction leading to I-195. This is Mount Pleasant Rd., a wide highway.

28.6 Turn left on unsigned Kings Hwy. Sign reads "Hwy. 140 North to Taunton and Boston." Don't merge onto Hwy. 140, however; stay straight, riding past a variety of shops and restaurants.

29.1 Road is now signed Tarkiln Hill Rd. (Please note: You passed Tarkiln Hill Rd. 1 mile prior to this point. They don't tie in—the previous is a dead-end road.)

30.2 Keep straight through the town of New Bedford, where you'll find all amenities. The highway becomes Main St. and enters the town of Acushnet just after. There are no motels here, but there are restaurants and markets.

30.5 Russell Memorial Library on the right. Road narrows.

31.3 Small market on the right.

32.8 Market/grill on the right. Rolling hills continue.

33.0 Turn right on Perry Hill Rd., which is later called New Bedford Rd. There's a shoulder for a portion of the journey.

35.4   Ice cream/food stand on the right.

37.3   Head right on Hwy. 105, then make an immediate left on Marys Pond Rd. There's a market off to the right as you turn. There's no shoulder, but the road is fairly uncrowded.

38.7   Pond on the left.

39.5   Popular Marys Pond on the right. Often congested, it has a beach for tanning and pond swimming.

40.6   Junction with Country Rd. Continue straight on what is now called Fearing Hill Rd.

42.2   Road ends; bear right on Main St.

42.7   Cross under I-195. Keep bearing right on Main St. as you continue through Wareham.

44.6   Fork; turn left on Sandwich Rd. (US 6) and ride over the inlet. Continue straight. US 6 sports a nice shoulder. US 6 is also known as the Grand Army of the Republic Hwy.

45.9   Cross the Agawam River.

46.5   Junction; road curves to the right. Bear right on US 6 and Hwy. 28. The road is four lanes, with no shoulder. There's a sidewalk, however.

46.8   Keep straight on US 6 East, Hwy. 28 South to Buzzards Bay. The speed limit slows to 35 mph.

47.1   Shopping centers, restaurants, motels begin.

48.5   Turn left on Red Brook, heading out of town.

49.7   Road turns into Head of the Bay Rd. and hugs Buttermilk Bay for a small portion of the ride.

50.8   Junction with Plymouth Lane; stay straight on Head of the Bay Rd. **SIDE TRIP:** Reach Sandy Pond Campground by cycling left (north) 1.8 miles. It offers all amenities, including limited groceries, and fishing and swimming in Sandy Pond.

52.2   Junction with US 6. Pedal straight, then go left on US 6 East and Hwy. 28 South toward Hyannis and Provincetown. Go around a large traffic circle (rotary), following the signs to Hwy. 28 South to Falmouth.

52.4   Just after turning, see signs for the Bourne Bridge. A bike and pedestrian sidewalk leads to the bridge walkway.

52.6   Just past the Ramada Inn, begin riding across the bridge.

52.9   There's a good view from the top of the bridge. You'll also see a large campground on the north side of the canal. Bourne Scenic Park offers all the usual services, as well as a grocery store and a saltwater swimming pool. **SIDE TRIP:** If you're interested, head on over to the campground before crossing the bridge.

53.3   End of bridge; motels and restaurants near here. Keep right at the traffic circle, then make another right on Veterans Way. There's a shoulder.

53.5   Stop sign. Make a right.

53.6   Make a left at signed Bourne Bridge Canal area.

53.8 Go under the bridge to the canal and bike and pedestrian path; picnic facilities, rest rooms. You're now riding a portion of the Claire Saltonstall Bikeway, a designated route dedicated to the memory of a young woman who died while bicycling to Cape Cod. The bikeway extends from Boston to the Cape Cod Canal, and from the Cape Cod Canal to both Provincetown and Woods Hole. Please note: The bikeway is not a separate path. While it does include some bike paths and less-traveled roads, it follows some heavily trafficked roads as well. Use caution.

57.0 Cross under the Sagamore Bridge. Those riders interested in the **ALTERNATE ROUTE** to Plymouth should hop onto the Sagamore Bridge. After crossing, pedal north on the Claire Saltonstall Bikeway via State St., Hedges Pond Rd., Long Pond Rd., South St., and Sandwich St. (Hwy. 3A). You'll meet up with the main route at the 39.3-mile mark on the segment after next, Nickerson State Park to Pinewood Lake Campground, in Plymouth. This alternate route is approximately 18 miles long, with camping at Scusset Beach (nearest to the bridge and open all year) and Myles Standish State Forest (also open all year). For a copy of the Claire Saltonstall Bikeway map, write or call Boston–Cape Cod Bikeway, Central Transportation Planning Staff, 10 Park Plaza, Suite 2150, Boston, MA 02116; (617) 973-7100.

59.3 Cape Cod Canal Service Rd. ends; rest rooms. Ride out through the parking area to unsigned Tupper Road; make a right.

60.3 Junction with Hwy. 6A. Go straight across the road to Hwy. 130. Make a left.

60.6 Turnoff to the Shawme-Crowell State Forest, which is open year-round.

60.7 Entrance booth. There are shady sites at this 642-acre full-facility park. Camping fee includes use of Scusset Beach, which is to the north and across the canal.

Shawme-Crowell State Forest to Nickerson State Park (37.1 miles)

This segment and the next skirt the narrow spit of basically flat land known as Cape Cod. Shaped like an arm bent at the elbow, its hand pointed toward the heavens and its fingers curved back toward the torso, the cape is surrounded by salt water. In fact, there's no point on the peninsula where you can stand more than 6 miles from salt water.

From the mainland, where the Cape Cod Canal separates the peninsula, it is about 35 miles east to the elbow and another 35 miles north before hooking west at its tip.

Pedal from the shoulder to the curved elbow today, riding the 20-mile

Cycling the Cape Cod Rail Trail

Cape Cod Rail Trail path, a long stream of asphalt enjoyed by bikers, skaters, joggers, and walkers. And when the route isn't following the Cape Cod Rail Trail, it traces the Claire Saltonstall Bikeway mentioned in the previous segment.

From the campground you'll travel east, completing your ride through the scenic town of Sandwich, Cape Cod's oldest town. Rich in historic sites, Sandwich is the home of Hoxie House, the oldest house on the peninsula—a classic saltbox built in 1637. Also of interest is Dexter Grist Mill, a restored seventeenth-century mill where you can buy ground corn meal.

Next, you'll ride roller-coaster fashion along Service Road, a quiet, no-shoulder road paralleling US 6. Eventually you'll reach Highway 6A, known as the Old Kings Highway, a historic, scenic roadway winding through towns lined with traditional New England–style summer homes. It's a narrow road; beware of heavy traffic. Fortunately, traffic may be traveling at a slow pace due to congestion.

The tree-lined Cape Cod Rail Trail leads directly to Nickerson State Park, an enormous campground comprised of more than 1,700 acres. Along the way you'll pass through a potpourri of varying terrains— salt marshes, pine woods, cranberry bogs, and freshwater ponds. The ponds, common throughout Cape Cod, are called "kettle ponds," formed by glaciers many thousands of years ago. At the campground, trees tumble to the banks of eight such ponds, nourished by groundwater and annual precipitation.

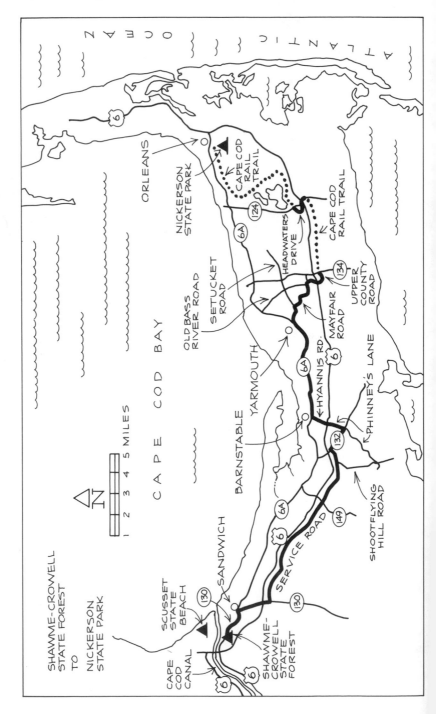

MILEAGE LOG

0.0 Shawme-Crowell State Forest entrance booth. Head back to Hwy. 130. Make a right. The highway is shoulderless as you pass through the picturesque town of Sandwich, where there are all services.

2.1 Shoulder now.

2.6 Cross under US 6. Keep straight.

2.8 Turn left on Service Rd., a quiet shoulderless road paralleling US 6.

9.6 Junction with Hwy. 149. Make a left, then an immediate right, continuing on Service Rd.

12.3 Junction. Merge left onto Shootflying Hill Rd.

12.4 Motel on the right.

12.5 Tourist information center on the left.

12.6 Turn right on Hwy. 132 South. There's heavier traffic now, and still no shoulder.

13.9 Junction to Barnstable. Head left on Phinney's Lane. (There are motels and restaurants prior to the junction.)

14.5 Shoulder begins.

14.8 Cross under US 6; road is now called Hyannis Rd.

15.7 Junction with Hwy. 6A. Turn right. There's no shoulder on this heavily trafficked roadway.

17.9 Yarmouth, the second oldest town on the cape; several shops in area; all services available in surrounding areas.

19.2 Market on the left.

21.2 Make a right on Setucket Rd., then a quick left. There's a bike lane on the opposite side of the road.

22.3 Turn right on Mayfair Rd.; no shoulder, but road is uncrowded.

23.8 Turn right on Old Bass River Rd.; bike lane on the left.

24.1 Johnny A. Kelley Recreation Area on the left; picnic facilities, rest rooms.

24.2 Bike lane ends.

24.4 Cross US 6. Enter South Dennis historic area.

25.1 Make a left on Upper County Rd. At the stop sign, bear left.

25.4 Junction with Hwy. 134. Head left. There's a bike lane on the right, and restaurants are in the area.

25.6 Cape Cod Rail Trail begins here. Go through the parking area to the trail. The path crosses several roads en route; bicyclists must stop at each street crossing.

30.4 Hwy. 124. Head left, riding the highway again. There's a narrow shoulder.

30.6 Cross over US 6.

30.7 Head left on Headwaters Dr.

31.1 Turn right and continue via the Cape Cod Rail Trail.

31.5 Pass a number of ponds en route to a general store, which is on the left.

34.9 Pizza shop/bike rental on the right.
35.0 Ice cream shop on the left.
37.0 Bicycle supplies and rental on the left.
37.1 Turn right onto path leading to Nickerson State Park. Registration office is to the left. Sites are plentiful—but not held open for late-arriving cyclists. Please note: This campground fills up fast during the summer. It is open all year. You'll find all the usual amenities and shaded sites. If you need food or a laundromat, or you'd prefer a motel, ride to Orleans, a few miles away.

Nickerson State Park to Pinewood Lake Campground (44.1 miles)

Beginning at Cape Cod's curved elbow, you'll ride up its forearm, then along the narrow, outstretched fingers, to Provincetown, where you'll catch a ferry to Plymouth. Both towns warrant time spent exploring their history, their homes built in the 1700s and 1800s, and popular whale-watching tours as well.

From Nickerson State Park, pedal the Cape Cod Rail Trail, with short sections of paved road near Orleans, then it's on to the Salt Pond visitor center in Eastham where the trail ends. The route is mostly flat.

Upon entering Cape Cod National Seashore, you'll ride a bike path over rolling hills past Nauset Marsh to a gorgeous trail to the Coast

Cyclists on the bike/hike trail overlooking Nauset Marsh

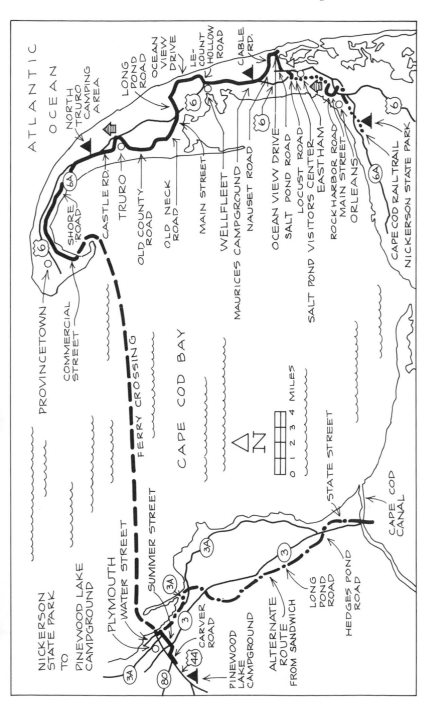

Guard Beach area. From here to Provincetown, you'll travel hilly terrain with mostly moderate grades. You'll encounter some flat sections, too, and several short but steep hills.

Roads are mostly two lanes with no shoulders, but traffic is basically light. Be prepared for heavy traffic in certain areas. You'll ride US 6, a busy highway, but there's usually a shoulder, at least along the portions of US 6 mentioned in this guide.

After ferrying over to Plymouth, you'll ride side roads to busy US 44 and on to Pinewood Lake Campground, a quiet retreat among the pines.

MILEAGE LOG

0.0 From the junction of the Cape Cod Rail Trail and the path leading to Nickerson State Park (the point upon which you entered the park), continue on, passing under Hwy. 6A.

1.5 The Bike Trail merges onto an unsigned residential street. Cycle on, following "Bike Trail" signs.

1.9 Cross over US 6. In a short distance, make a left at the bike trail sign, continuing on the Rail Trail.

2.5 The trail ends temporarily in a parking area. Make a left on Main St. If you turn right, you'll find shops and restaurants in town; all services are available in Orleans.

2.8 Road becomes Rock Harbor Rd.

3.0 Cross over US 6 again.

3.6 Make a right on Harbor Rd.

4.6 Turn left; you're back on the Rail Trail now. **SIDE TRIP**: To reach the Mid-Cape AYH, make a left on Bridge Rd., about 0.2 mile prior to this junction. Travel 0.2 mile north to Goody Hallet Dr. and turn right 100 yards to the hostel driveway. It's open mid-May through mid-September. For more information, write or call 75 Goody Hallet Dr., Eastham, MA 02642; (508) 255-2785.

7.4 End of trail. Go right on Locust Rd.

7.7 Make a left on Salt Pond Rd.; bike shop on the right.

7.8 Cross US 6. This is Eastham now. Motels are available in the area. Keep straight.

7.9 Entrance to Salt Pond visitor center, open daily from spring until early winter; rest rooms, museum, gift shop, information, films. To continue north, from the entrance go straight on the bike path, passing the signed Doane Memorial and pedaling through the Nauset Marsh en route.

10.0 Bicycle path ends at the Coast Guard Station and beach. After visiting the area, head north on Ocean View Dr., where there are some fine views of the Atlantic. Climb a short, steep hill.

11.1 Left on Cable Rd., which merges into Nauset Rd. along the way. Notice Nauset Light Beach on the right before turning.

13.1 Turn right on US 6, a four-lane highway with narrow or no shoulders. Amenities are many in this area.

13.9   Wellfleet, an early whaling town before the Revolutionary War; all services available. The road narrows to two lanes with a shoulder.

14.0   Maurices Campground on the right. In addition to the usual services, there's a general store and deli; cabins and cottages are also available.

16.5   Cross Black Fish Creek and take the Hwy. 6A exit. Pass the visitor center and general store. This is South Wellfleet.

16.7   Make a right on Lecount Hollow Rd.

17.5   Turn left on Ocean View Dr., another gorgeous drive.

19.4   Cycle left on Long Pond Rd.

21.4   Cross over US 6.

21.6   Make a right on Main St.

22.2   Public library on the left; bear right on unsigned W. Main St. and climb a steep hill.

23.2   Turn left on Old Neck Rd. Roads are roller-coasterlike as you continue.

24.4   Bear left on unsigned Old County Rd.

26.6   Junction with Fisher Rd.; keep right, climbing a steep hill.

27.1   Look to the west for a view of Cape Cod Bay.

28.0   Turn left on unsigned Hwy. 6A. **SIDE TRIP:** The Little America AYH is located nearby. Interested? Do not turn left on Hwy. 6A, but instead continue straight, crossing US 6 and then riding North Pamet Rd. for less than 1 mile. Originally a Coast Guard station, the hostel is located in the Cape Cod National Seashore and is only seven walking minutes from the beach. It's open mid-June through the Labor Day holiday; for additional information, write or call P.O. Box 402, Truro, MA 02666; (508) 349-3889.

28.1   Truro General Store on the left. All services are available in Truro.

28.2   Go left on Castle Rd.

29.4   Junction with Cornhill Rd.; keep right on Castle Rd.

30.1   Turn left on US 6; shoulder.

30.8   Junction with Highland Rd. North Truro Camping Area is to the right (east), less than 1 mile away. It offers all amenities and a store. It's open year-round.

31.3   Fork; go left on Hwy. 6A (Shore Rd.), a narrow, shoulderless road. Terrain flattens out as you pass mile after mile of cottages and motels with occasional views of the bay.

35.9   Provincetown. All services are available along the route.

36.8   Bike route takes off to the right; stay straight.

36.9   Fork; Hwy. 6A takes off to the right; keep to the left on unsigned Commercial St., a one-lane road on which bikers are allowed to travel both ways.

38.5 Downtown Provincetown, a bustling historic town with an endless variety of food and gift shops. Head left on Standish St., then curve right and go past the visitor center.

38.9 Provincetown Harbor. On November 11, 1620, the Pilgrims first landed at what is now Provincetown Harbor. They stayed 36 days before sailing across Cape Cod Bay to Plymouth. While in Provincetown, the first white child, Peregrine White, was born in the New World. Now you've reached the wooden pier from which the ferry departs. You'll have to buy tickets at the pier entrance. The ferry leaves daily during the summer at 4:30 P.M. and usually arrives in Plymouth about 6:00 P.M. There are rest rooms and snacks on board. Cost is $12 each (in 1991). Bikes are free. For more information, call the Plymouth and Provincetown Steamship Co., (617) 747-2400, or in Massachusetts, (800) 242-2469.

39.0 Plymouth Harbor. This is where the Pilgrims arrived via the *Mayflower* after spending 36 days in Provincetown. The Pilgrims lived on board the vessel during their first winter in the New World. The *Mayflower II*, a reproduction of the seventeenth-century merchant ship that brought the Pilgrims here in 1620, is on exhibit. To continue, ride through the parking area and make a left on the first street, which is Water St. Restaurants, markets, and motels are plentiful in town. Also there's a bike shop.

39.2 Plymouth Memorial State Park on the left. Plymouth Rock rests as a memorial to the Pilgrims who landed here in 1620, establishing the first permanent colony in New England. Pass the Town Brook on the right soon after.

39.3 Fork; bear right on Water St. to Sandwich St. (Hwy. 3A). Alternate route from Sandwich (described in the segment Melville Ponds Campground to Shawme-Crowell State Forest) merges onto the main route here. Head straight, curving right, then making an immediate left on Summer St. (at Governor Carver Square). The road is narrow with no shoulders; traffic can be heavy.

40.2 Cross over Hwy. 3.

41.0 Right on Carver Rd., a narrow, uncrowded road.

41.5 Junction. Head left on US 44 West. The road is two lanes, narrow, and very busy. Use caution!

41.8 Junction with Hwy. 80. This is the turnoff point for the next segment. To reach Pinewood Lake Campground for today's destination, continue straight on US 44.

43.3 Turn left on Pinewood Lane, an uncrowded road that turns to hard-packed gravel in 0.4 mile.

44.1 Registration office for 150-acre Pinewood Lake Campground; store, snack bar, restaurant. Pinewood Lake offers all services, including swimming and boating, and is open May through November.

Pinewood Lake Campground to Annisquam Campground (92.5 miles)

Although you'll never lack for amenities during this segment of the Atlantic Coast ride, campgrounds are nonexistent between the starting and ending points, thus the extra-long segment.

You'll have to choose whether to cycle straight through or stop some place in between. Some may opt for a motel, others will probably ask permission to pitch a tent in someone's yard. Another thought is the Boston International AYH, located in downtown Boston. A four-story turn-of-the-century building, the hostel is open all year.

From Pinewood Lake Campground, it's a pleasant ride (once off US 44) through lush, gentle terrain to Highway 80, where you'll pass one small country town after another. Brockton, home of Massasoit College, is a bit congested, but traffic eases up a bit until you merge onto Highway 138. As you near Boston, traffic increases but a shoulder makes the ride more bearable.

A bike path leads past Turtle Pond, part of Stony Brook Reservation. Beware of short, steep climbs along this portion of the ride.

Washington Street guides you into Boston, home of the Boston Marathon, held in April. You'll notice a significant increase in traffic, but the pedaling is relatively safe in this, the seventh-largest city in the United States. Roads are basically wide, although some narrow streets must be negotiated. Enter downtown and you'll see cyclists darting about; cycling is definitely popular here in Boston.

Of all the downtowns I traveled, Boston was a particular favorite. With its comfortable, small-town atmosphere, Boston's archaic buildings reach heavenward, blending with the newest office buildings. The best way to see the city is to walk Freedom Trail, a famous path linking sixteen important sites, including Boston Common, the oldest public park in America, and Paul Revere's House, built around 1677. Along the waterfront, at Boston Harbor, board the Boston Tea Party Ship and Museum, where visitors can toss a container of tea into the harbor. Yes, this is the same harbor where those famed chests landed in 1773.

Wider roads lead north of Boston through one small town after another. Terrain north of the city is mainly rolling hills along the Massachusetts North Shore. The ride from Beverly to Gloucester is one of magnificence as you travel parallel to Massachusetts Bay, emerging onto what is known as Massachusetts' Other Cape—Cape Ann. Cape Ann, whale-watching center of the world, consists of Manchester—a lovely town adorned with a charming harbor—Gloucester, Rockport, and Essex.

The only downside of today's ride is the lack of signed streets. If you get confused, however, you have only to stop and ask directions.

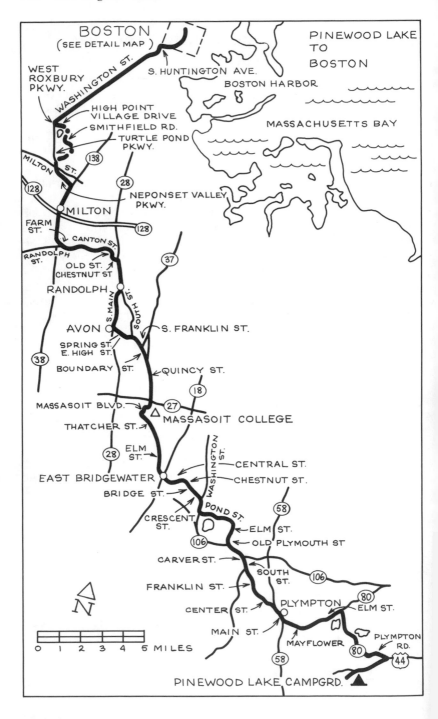

PINEWOOD LAKE
TO
BOSTON

BOSTON
(SEE DETAIL MAP)

S. HUNTINGTON AVE.
BOSTON HARBOR

WEST
ROXBURY
PKWY.

WASHINGTON ST.

MASSACHUSETTS BAY

HIGH POINT
VILLAGE DRIVE
SMITHFIELD RD.
TURTLE POND
PKWY.

MILTON ST.

138

128

28

NEPONSET VALLEY
PKWY.

MILTON

FARM
ST.

128

CANTON ST.

RANDOLPH
ST.

OLD ST.
CHESTNUT ST.

37

RANDOLPH

S. MAIN ST.

SOUTH ST.

AVON

S. FRANKLIN ST.

SPRING ST.
E. HIGH ST.

38

BOUNDARY ST.

QUINCY ST.

MASSASOIT BLVD.

18

27

MASSASOIT COLLEGE

THATCHER ST.

28

ELM
ST.

WASHINGTON ST.

CENTRAL ST.

EAST BRIDGEWATER

CHESTNUT ST.

BRIDGE ST.

WASHINGTON ST.

58

CRESCENT
ST.

POND ST.

ELM ST.

106

OLD PLYMOUTH ST

CARVER ST.

SOUTH ST.

106

FRANKLIN ST.

80

CENTER ST.

PLYMPTON

ELM ST.

MAIN ST.

MAYFLOWER

PLYMPTON
RD.

80

0 1 2 3 4 5 MILES

58

44

PINEWOOD LAKE CAMPGRD.

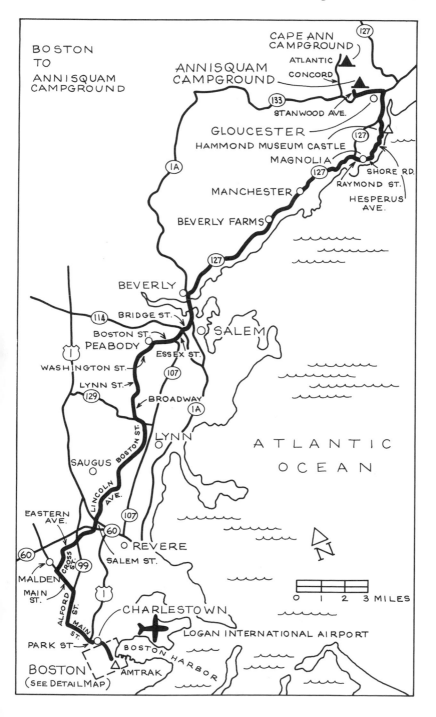

BOSTON
TO
ANNISQUAM
CAMPGROUND

CAPE ANN
CAMPGROUND

127

ATLANTIC
CONCORD

ANNISQUAM
CAMPGROUND

133

STANWOOD AVE.

GLOUCESTER

HAMMOND MUSEUM CASTLE

127

MAGNOLIA

127

SHORE RD.

RAYMOND ST.

MANCHESTER

HESPERUS
AVE.

BEVERLY FARMS

IA

127

BEVERLY

114

BRIDGE ST.

BOSTON ST.

SALEM

PEABODY

ESSEX ST.

WASHINGTON ST.

107

LYNN ST.

129

BROADWAY

IA

LYNN

ATLANTIC

SAUGUS

BOSTON ST.

OCEAN

LINCOLN AVE.

EASTERN
AVE.

107

60

60

REVERE

99

SALEM ST.

N

MALDEN

CROSS ST.

1

MAIN
ST.

ALFORD ST.

CHARLESTOWN

0 1 2 3 MILES

LOGAN INTERNATIONAL AIRPORT

MAIN ST.

PARK ST.

BOSTON HARBOR

BOSTON
(SEE DETAIL MAP)

AMTRAK

Although you'll travel many different streets today, the route really isn't as difficult as it may seem.

MILEAGE LOG

0.0   Pinewood Lake Campground office. Return the way you came.

0.8   Back at US 44. Turn right. Remember, use caution on this busy, narrow highway.

2.3   Turn left on Plympton Rd. (Hwy. 80). There's a shopping center at the junction.

3.9   Hwy. 80 curves to the right. Enter Kingston town limits.

5.9   Road is now called Indian Pond Rd., Hwy. 80, and Bishops Hwy.

6.4   T-junction; turn left on unsigned Elm St. There's no shoulder, but it's a wide, uncrowded road, like many of the roads to come. Elm St. changes to Brook St. upon entering Plympton.

8.5   Road curves to the right and becomes Colchester St., later changing to Mayflower St.

9.8   Turn right on Main St. (Hwy. 58); convenience store on the corner; shoulder now.

10.8   Turn left on Center St.; no shoulder.

12.1   Road becomes Franklin St. Enter Halifax town limits.

13.4   Road merges right onto South St.

13.8   Bear left on Carver St.

14.2   Road ends; turn left on Hwy. 106; gas station/snacks at corner; shoulder.

14.7   Turn right on Old Plymouth St. There's no shoulder, but this road, like many other area roads, sports light traffic.

15.0   Fork; head right on Elm St.

15.8   Bike repairs (private home) at 161 Elm St.

15.9   Turn left on Pond St.

16.7   East Bridgewater town limits.

17.2   Robin's Pond Park on the left.

17.8   Make a right on Washington St.

18.6   Left on Crescent St.

19.4   Road curves to the right on Bridge St.

19.5   Bear left on Chestnut St., first road after turning.

19.9   Left on Central St.; small shoulder.

20.8   East Bridgewater Veterans Memorial Park on the left.

21.1   Junction with Hwy. 18. Keep straight on Central. There are restaurants and a store in the area.

21.6   Make a right on Elm St.

23.5   Fork; bear left on Thatcher St., entering Brockton town limits.

24.8   Entrance to Massasoit College. Head right and ride straight to the college, then bear left. This is Massasoit Blvd.

25.6   Junction with Hwy. 27. Go across the highway and continue on what is now called Quincy St.; it has wide lanes. Plenty of restaurants, markets, and a motel are found here.

27.3 Road curves to the left.

27.7 Road merges right on N. Cary St.; wide lanes.

27.9 Bike shop on the left. Abington town limits.

28.3 Groceries and pizza on the right.

28.5 Make a left on Boundary St. The road is narrow with little traffic.

29.2 Road changes to Linwood St. at Holbrook town limits before reaching Hwy. 37 (S. Franklin St.). Cross Hwy. 37 and the road becomes South St. There are some services in the area, including a bike shop.

29.8 Make a left on Spring St., which becomes E. High. This is the town of Avon now.

30.1 Bear right on Hwy. 28 (S. Main St.); some services.

31.2 Randolph; bike shop in area. Lanes are wide now.

33.1 Hwy. 139 joins Hwy. 28 here. Continue on past all services; watch for heavy traffic.

34.8 Turn left on Chestnut St. **SIDE TRIP:** There's a large motel about 2 miles straight ahead on Hwy. 28.

34.9 Make a right on unsigned Old St.; shoulder now.

35.1 Make a left on unsigned Canton, which becomes Randolph St. farther along.

35.9 T-junction; keep left on Canton St.

36.1 Cross under Hwy. 24.

38.1 Go right on Farm St.; no shoulder.

38.5 Make a right on Hwy. 138, a heavily trafficked roadway. There's a wide shoulder, however.

39.7 Cross over Hwy. 128; restaurants, market just beyond.

40.7 Milton town limits.

40.8 Blue Hills Trailside Museum on the right.

41.6 Turn left on the Neponset Valley Pkwy.; bike lane on the right.

42.2 End of the bike path. Curve to the right, then left, staying on Neponset Valley Pkwy. The road is four lanes, with no shoulder. Watch for heavy traffic.

43.0 Follow bike signs; cross under old bridge.

43.1 Make a left on Milton St. Ride over John J. Hart Memorial Bridge. Exit bridge, then turn right on the Neponset Valley Pkwy.

43.4 Road curves to the left, staying on parkway; narrow shoulder.

43.7 Cross Mother Brook. Stay straight; you're now riding the Turtle Pond Pkwy.

43.8 There's a park on the right with rest rooms. Turn here, following the signs for a bike trail. The path forks once you begin pedaling; take the right fork.

44.6 Path ends. Head left on Reservation Rd.

44.7 Make a right and travel through the park via a paved unsigned road (Smithfield Rd.).

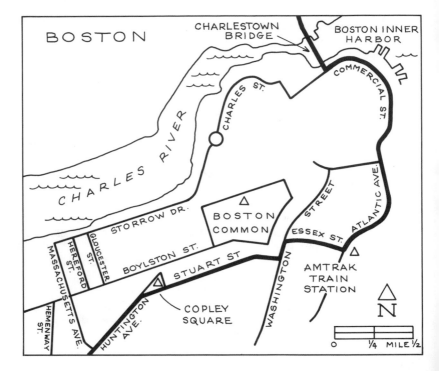

44.9 T-junction; head across the road to the Stony Brook Bike Path and bear left. Travel up and down (some are very steep grades) through Stony Brook Reservation.

46.3 Exit bike path on High Point Village Dr.; make a left, then go right on West Roxbury Pkwy.

46.4 Junction. Go right on Washington St., a wide four-lane road. There are restaurants and markets as you descend. As you near downtown Boston, traffic will increase.

48.3 Lane narrows; four lanes now; no shoulder.

48.7 Fork; keep left on South St., following the trolley tracks. The road is a bit wider now and back to two lanes.

49.3 Road changes to Centre St.

50.0 Road curves to the left and merges onto S. Huntington Ave.

50.9 T-junction; turn right on Huntington Ave. (Hwy. 9).

52.0 Pass the Museum of Fine Arts, Northeastern University, and the New England Conservatory of Music as you continue.

52.6 Junction with Massachusetts Ave. There are many enormous hotels as you continue straight to Copley Square. **SIDE TRIP:** Those interested in hosteling should turn left on Massachusetts Ave., riding north to Boylston St., then west (left) to Hemenway

St. For additional information, write or call Boston International AYH at 12 Hemenway St., Boston, MA 02115; (617) 536-9455.

53.1 Road merges onto Stuart St., a one-way street.

53.9 Turn left on Washington St.

54.0 Make a right on Essex St.

54.4 Go left on Atlantic Ave., passing numerous wharfs along Boston Harbor.

55.2 Christopher Columbus Park on the right.

55.4 Road changes to Commercial St. There are some nice views of Boston's Inner Harbor now.

56.1 Turn right onto the Charlestown Bridge; there's a separate path for pedestrians and bikers.

56.5 Exit bridge, go straight, then turn right on Park St. The USS *Constitution*, known as "Old Ironsides," is docked near here and is open to visitors. It's the oldest commissioned warship afloat in the world.

56.7 Bear left on Warren St., which becomes Main St. The lane is wide.

57.6 Stop sign; fire station straight ahead. Turn left on Bunker Hill St.

57.7 Keep to the right, traveling Alford St. (Hwy. 99) now. The highway is four lanes, with a parking lane to ride in if it's not too crowded.

57.9 Bridge over the Malden River.

59.0 Downtown Everett begins.

Boston Harbor

59.1   A Mexican restaurant is located here on the right. They make excellent burritos; in fact, they won the *Boston Magazine* award for serving the best burritos around.

59.2   Traffic rotary. Go right to the second exit, pedaling Main St. toward Malden.

60.4   As you enter Malden (there's a motel available in the area), cycle right on Cross St., which becomes Short St.

61.5   T-junction; turn right on Eastern Ave., which becomes Salem St. en route. There are plenty of restaurants.

62.1   Junction with Hwy. 99.

62.8   T-junction at large intersection; keep left and head across Hwy. 60 and continue straight.

63.1   Revere town limits.

63.2   Cross under US 1; road is wide now.

64.0   Enter Saugus and road changes to Lincoln Ave.

64.4   Rotary; bear right toward Lynn on unsigned Lincoln Ave. Shops are in town.

65.9   Cross over inlet. Just past it, the road curves to the right and becomes Boston St. in the town of Lynn. Founded in 1629, this is New England's third-oldest community. There's a bike shop in the area.

66.3   Fork; keep left.

66.6   Short, steep grade.

67.1   Unsigned triple fork; keep straight.

68.5   T-junction; go left on Hwy. 129 West.

69.0   Unsigned Broadway curves to the right.

70.8   Peabody town limits. Motels are available in the area. The unsigned road is called Lynn St.

71.1   Library on the right.

71.5   Road curves to the right and becomes unsigned Washington St.

72.1   Salem town limits; motels in vicinity.

72.8   Turn right on Main St., which becomes Boston St.; restaurants, market, et cetera.

73.8   T-junction; turn left on unsigned Essex St.

74.0   Salem Public Library on the left.

74.3   Junction with Hwy. 114. Turn left on Hwy. 114 West. Before exiting town, cruise the old section. There are lots of shops in the area.

74.4   Head right on Bridge St., following signs to Beverly on Hwy. 1A.

74.6   Traffic circle; go halfway around and continue north.

74.9   Bicycle shop on the left.

75.7   Cross the bridge over Salem Sound; excellent view out toward Massachusetts Bay.

76.0   Exit bridge and enter Beverly, birthplace of the American Navy. Go right, then straight toward Hwy. 22 North and Hwy. 127. **SIDE TRIP:** Turn left at the Hwy. 1A junction for a variety of services. There's a bike shop 1.2 miles away and a motel 3.5 miles down the highway.

76.1 Turn right on Hwy. 127 North, which sports a good shoulder.

77.0 Park and rest rooms off to the right as you cycle along Salem Sound.

78.3 Endicott College.

80.5 Town of Beverly Farms. There's a few shops in town, some restaurants, and markets.

80.7 Fork; go right. Actually the two roads meet again but the right fork hugs the water.

81.1 Roads merge together.

81.8 Manchester, a fashionable village with a picturesque harbor. Be sure to visit Singing Beach, a famous site where the sand makes musical sounds beneath one's footsteps. You'll find all services, including a bike shop, in the vicinity.

82.4 An inn on the right. Day and week lodging.

83.0 No shoulder through town.

83.2 Library on the right.

84.0 There's a shoulder once again, but you'll lose it in 1 mile.

Manchester Harbor

86.2 Turn right on Raymond St. A sign points the way to Magnolia. There's no shoulder, but the next three roads bear little traffic.

86.7 Magnolia. There's a cafe and small market. Bear right on Shore Rd., a one-way, beautiful route along the ocean.

87.4 Road seems to end but doesn't; keep straight, traveling a bumpy, narrow path.

87.6 Road ends. Head right on unsigned Hesperus Ave.; two lanes, no shoulder, little traffic.

88.6 Hammond Museum Castle. You'll find a unique collection of Roman, Medieval, and Renaissance artifacts in this, the home of Dr. John Hays Hammond, Jr., America's second greatest inventor next to Thomas Edison.

89.3 T-junction; cycle right. Back on Hwy. 127 North; shoulder.

90.1 Park on the right near the water.

90.5 Gloucester; all services (including bike shop) in area; no shoulder.

90.7 Junction. Head left on Hwy. 133 West; shoulder.

92.1 Go right on Stanwood Ave. to signed Annisquam Campground, open May through September. There's a motel just before here.

92.3 Road turns to gravel as you descend.

92.5 Annisquam Campground office; shady and open sites with tent sites along the river. There's a pool, a laundromat, rustic cottages, and a small store, in addition to the usual services.

Annisquam Campground to Camp Eaton (60.0 miles)

For the first time since your Atlantic Coast ride began, you'll have the opportunity to pedal through portions of two states and all of one state—in one day. In fact, if desired, you could have breakfast in Massachusetts, lunch in New Hampshire, and dinner in Maine.

From the Annisquam Campground, you'll head northwest through Cape Ann, named in honor of the mother of King Charles I of England. As you continue up the North Shore, a region famous for some of the world's best whale-watching opportunities, you'll travel through farm country, once again reaching the coast at Salisbury Beach.

Towns in between are small and filled with lovely old buildings. Salisbury itself is a busy place with an amusement park, a fun zone, and numerous shops and food concessions.

Enter New Hampshire, the Granite State, at Seabrook, another popular spot. Continue on and you'll wheel past a series of beautiful beaches, encompassing a mere 18 miles of coastline, and many state parks. You'll ride ocean-hugging Highway 1A where magnificent views are the norm. Favorite coastal activities include para-sailing and whale watching.

As you ride north, you'll leave commercialism behind for a while. Travel along the ocean's edge to Rye Harbor, a quaint haven where fishing and whaling tours leave port. The rest of the New Hampshire coast is relatively free of motels and restaurants, clothed instead with a variety of state parks.

Portsmouth, New Hampshire's only port, is an interesting mix of old and new, with beautiful Prescott Park overlooking the waterfront.

Enter Maine, New England's largest state, and the nation's easternmost state, at Kittery. You'll end the day at York Harbor, a fun spot with sandy beaches.

Today's segment consists of relatively flat terrain and gentle roller-coasterlike hills.

MILEAGE LOG

0.0 Annisquam Campground office. Return to the main highway.

0.4 Junction with Hwy. 133 West. Cycle right.

1.0 Market on the left.

1.5 Concord St. is off to the right. **SIDE TRIP:** It leads down to the Cape Ann Campground, open May through October. It's about 3 miles off route: 2.2 on Concord St., then another 0.5 on Atlantic. It has shady sites, all amenities, a laundromat, and a small store. This road also leads to the Wingaersheek Beach and motel.

2.0 Cross under Hwy. 128.

2.9 Motel on the right; restaurants and antique shops another mile up the road.

4.2 Country market and deli on the left.

4.6 Restaurant on the right.

5.2 Essex, noted for its 300-year tradition of shipbuilding. Settled in 1634, Essex saw the building of more two-masted ships than any other town in the world. You'll find shops and motels in town.

5.7 Junction with Hwy. 22.

8.2 Ipswich. You'll find all amenities, including a bike shop, in this town boasting more seventeenth-century structures than any other community in America.

10.2 Hwy. 1A merges onto the route. There's a motel at the junction, and a restaurant just beyond. Bear right on Hwy. 133. There's no shoulder.

11.0 Head through downtown Ipswich.

11.6 Shoulder again. Shops continue.

14.1 Hwy. 133 leaves the route. Continue on Hwy. 1A.

14.5 Motel on the right; bike shop just beyond.

14.8 Rowley, a small town settled in 1638; store and motel somewhere in the nearby area.

17.7 Newbury.

18.7 Cross the Parker River.

21.5   Exit on right to Plum Island, home of the Parker River Wildlife Refuge.

21.9   Newburyport, the smallest city in the Commonwealth (state of Massachusetts), and birthplace of the U.S. Coast Guard. It offers all services, including a bike shop; be sure to visit its restored downtown, magnificent harbor, and sunny beaches.

22.9   Turn right, merging with US 1 just prior to crossing the Merrimack River.

23.3   Top of bridge provides wonderful view of area.

23.5   Inn and restaurant on the right as you enter Salisbury, Massachusetts' northernmost town; motels in area.

25.2   Junction with Hwy. 110.

25.3   Junction with Hwy. 1A to Salisbury; market and restaurant. Go right toward the beach on Hwy. 1A.

26.0   **SIDE TRIP:** Glenwood Ave. leads to signed Pines Campground 0.4 mile away; shaded sites, hot showers, laundromat, store.

26.1   Motels/restaurants begin.

26.9   Campground on the left.

27.4   **SIDE TRIP:** Road on the right leads to Salisbury Beach State Reservation, located about 1.5 miles distant. In addition to the usual amenities (camping, showers), you'll find snacks, river fishing, and swimming opportunities also.

27.6   Turn left on Hwy. 1A. Salisbury Beach and shops are near here. Look for Pirate's Fun Park, the state's last remaining seaside amusement park, with rides, games, food, and shows. It's open daily during summer.

29.7   Seabrook, New Hampshire, at the junction with Hwy. 286; four lanes, narrow shoulder. **SIDE TRIP:** Adams Campground —a full-service facility—is about 1 mile west on Hwy. 286.

31.3   Cross bridge over the Blackwater River.

31.5   End of bridge; enter Hampton Beach. Motels and restaurants are numerous from Salisbury to Hampton Beach.

31.6   Hampton Beach State Park on the right; picnic facilities, sandy beach, bathhouse, opportunities for fishing and swimming. Hampton Marina is on the left.

32.9   Shoulder disappears.

36.2   North Hampton State Park; bathhouse, swimming; quieter than the other Hampton beaches.

39.0   Jenness State Beach; bathhouse, swimming, wonderful view stretching from Hampton to Portsmouth. Motels/restaurants/store are in the area.

40.3   Beautiful Rye Harbor Marina on the right; terrific spot from which to board a whale-watching tour. Motels/restaurants are nearby.

40.7   Rye Harbor State Park on the right; picnic area, rest rooms, and fishing.

42.5   Additional motels and restaurants in this area.

Rye Harbor

43.0 Wallis Sands State Park on the right; bathhouse, snack bar, and swimming.
44.4 Bike path on the right. At this point, Hwy. 1A narrows; there's no shoulder. A sign points to Odiorne Point State Park, site of the first European settlement in New Hampshire. It was settled in 1623 when Scottish fishermen landed here.
44.6 Entrance to 137-acre Odiorne Point State Park on the right, which

includes the largest undeveloped span of shore on New Hampshire's coast. There are picnic facilities, nature trails, and a visitor center.

45.3 Another entrance to the state park.

45.5 Cross Seaveys Creek. The bike lane ends; the road continues to be shoulderless.

46.5 Foyes Corner; market here. At the junction, make a right, continuing on Hwy. 1A.

47.1 Restaurant on the right just before crossing Sagamore Creek. There's a shoulder over the bridge, with the road widening just after.

47.7 Little Harbor Rd. **SIDE TRIP:** Make a right turn 0.7 mile to the Wentworth-Coolidge Mansion, an eighteenth-century 42-room mansion, once home to Benning Wentworth, New Hampshire's first Royal Governor. Purchased in 1886 by John Templeman Coolidge III of Boston, it was carefully restored and given to the state in his memory in the 1950s. It is listed on the National Register of Historic Houses, and is open daily mid-June through Labor Day and on weekends in the spring.

48.1 Turn right on South St. as you enter Portsmouth; all services in area, including a bike shop.

48.8 T-junction; go left on unsigned Pleasant Rd., then make an immediate right on Marcy St., passing the Children's Museum in 0.1 mile. Children will enjoy the hands-on exhibits involving lobsters, computers, and so on.

49.0 Prescott Park on the right. A great place for a rest, it has more than 500 varieties of flowers throughout the impressive gardens overlooking the Piscataqua River. Strawberry Banke is to the left. Open daily from May through October, this is one of America's oldest neighborhoods, with thirty-five historic homes built anywhere from the seventeenth to the twentieth century. Sheafe Warehouse Museum and Portsmouth Heritage Museum are located in this area as well.

49.1 Cycle left on Court St.

49.2 Make a right on Atkinston St., then make an immediate right on State St. and in 200 feet or so begin crossing the Piscataqua River on the Memorial Bridge (US 1). The bridge is dedicated to the sailors and soldiers of New Hampshire who participated in World War I. (Consider walking your bike on the walkway, as the grated pathway is very slippery.) Special note: Before crossing the bridge into Maine, be sure to cycle around downtown Portsmouth. If you feel like walking, you can stroll along the Portsmouth Trail, which passes six homes built in the eighteenth and nineteenth centuries.

49.6 Exit bridge. Continue on US 1. Enter Kittery, Maine's oldest city, established in 1647. A shipbuilding community for more than two centuries, it was here that shipbuilders produced the *Ranger*, the first ship to fly the Stars and Stripes. It was commanded by John Paul Jones. You'll find all services, including a bike shop, in the area.

50.0 Junction with Hwy. 103.

50.4 Hwy. 103 bears to the left; market, restaurant, library near the junction.

50.6 Shoulder now.

50.8 Junction with Hwy. 236 North. Continue right on Hwy. 103, a shoulderless road.

51.9 Bridge over Spruce Creek.

52.5 Fort McClary State Memorial entrance on the right; picnic area, 1846 blockhouse.

53.5 Turnoff to Fort Foster Park (Chauncey Creek Rd.) on the right. Historical war barracks, a playground, a picnic area, and a pier exist at the 80-acre park.

57.6 Pass through Wheeler Wildlife Refuge, a mudflat area.

57.9 Cross the York River and enter York Harbor.

58.3 Turn right on Hwy. 1A North; shoulder now.

59.5 Shoulder ends, but road is fairly wide all the same.

60.0 Camp Eaton on the left, Libby's Oceanside Camp on the right. Both camps boast of all services, with Camp Eaton offering a discount for the lone bicyclist. In addition, it always keeps a site open for late-arriving bikers on jam-packed weekends. Camp Eaton is open May through September.

Camp Eaton to Guay's Village and Campground (47.5 miles)

The ride from York Harbor is one wrought with motels and restaurants, accommodations for the influx of tourists who flock to the summer resorts of the Yorks, as they are known: York Harbor, York Beach, York Village, and Cape Neddick. Ogunquit and Wells, also historic resort towns, see an enormous increase in their summer population as well.

These southern beaches are popular, as the majority of Maine's fine sandy beaches are located in the southeast corner. Northern Maine consists mainly of beautiful, yet rugged, rocky shores.

Comprised of numerous inlets, bays, and channels, Maine's coastline, with its extreme irregularity, stretches to a total of about 2,400 miles. This is more than ten times the distance from Kittery to Eastport.

Heading north, however, you'll travel through residential areas where beautiful homes sit among the trees, rest near grassy plains, or

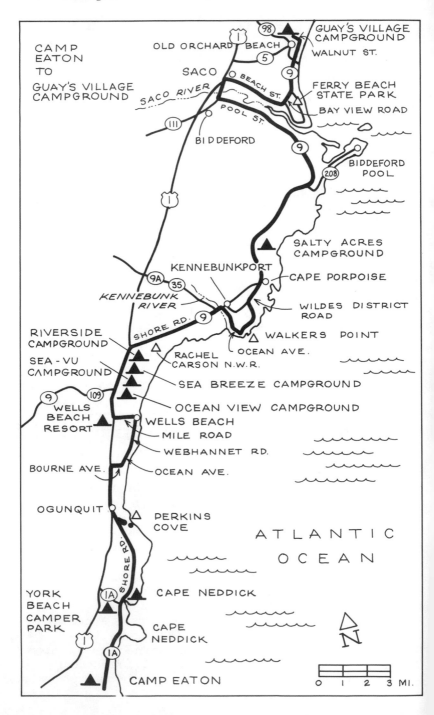

CAMP
EATON
TO
GUAY'S VILLAGE
CAMPGROUND

OLD ORCHARD BEACH

GUAY'S VILLAGE CAMPGROUND
WALNUT ST.

SACO

FERRY BEACH STATE PARK

BEACH ST.

BAY VIEW ROAD

SACO RIVER

POOL ST.

BIDDEFORD

BIDDEFORD POOL

SALTY ACRES CAMPGROUND

KENNEBUNKPORT

CAPE PORPOISE

KENNEBUNK RIVER

WILDES DISTRICT ROAD

SHORE RD.

RIVERSIDE CAMPGROUND

WALKERS POINT

OCEAN AVE.

SEA-VU CAMPGROUND

RACHEL CARSON N.W.R.

SEA BREEZE CAMPGROUND

OCEAN VIEW CAMPGROUND

WELLS BEACH RESORT

WELLS BEACH

MILE ROAD

WEBHANNET RD.

BOURNE AVE.

OCEAN AVE.

OGUNQUIT

PERKINS COVE

ATLANTIC
OCEAN

SHORE RD.

YORK BEACH CAMPER PARK

CAPE NEDDICK

CAPE NEDDICK

N

CAMP EATON

0   1   2   3 MI.

perch near the rocky shore. Along the sea at Walkers Point, you'll view the summer home of former president George Bush and his family. From there it's a nice ride on to Biddeford and over the Saco River to Saco.

Terrain for most of the ride consists of flatlands or rolling hills. Although some of the roads are shoulderless, most of the time shoulders exist where traffic is moderate. Shoulders usually line busier portions of the roadway. The segment ends in Old Orchard Beach, a tourist-oriented town of 10,000 year-round residents, where the population swells to more than 100,000 on balmy summer days.

MILEAGE LOG

0.0 From Camp Eaton, continue north on Hwy. 1A. Pass all services as you pedal parallel to Long Sands Beach.

2.5 Downtown York Beach, a summer resort since shortly after the Civil War. You'll find all services, including a bike shop, in this popular area.

2.8 York Beach Camper Park entrance on the left; all amenities, including store and laundromat.

3.1 Fork; head right on Shore Rd.; no shoulder; market on left just past junction; services cease.

3.4 Cape Neddick, a full-service campground (including a store) on the right. There's a restaurant nearby.

7.5 Lodging in area again.

7.8 Perkins Cove turnoff on the right. **SIDE TRIP:** Go about 0.5 mile past an array of shops to the picturesque waterfront area, popular with artists since the turn of the century.

8.3 Ogunquit Library on the left, in downtown Ogunquit, another popular town known for its clean, sandy beaches.

8.7 Road merges onto US 1; shoulder. Motels and other services continue for another 1.5 miles.

10.6 Turn right on Bourne Ave.

11.3 T-junction; bear left on unsigned Ocean Ave., traveling through a residential area.

12.5 Turn right on Webhannet Rd.

13.0 Series of motels and restaurants along the beach.

13.8 Turn left on unsigned Mile Rd.; shoulder. Wells Beach is to the right.

14.7 Turn right on US 1; shoulder. Wells Beach Resort, a full-service facility, is across the street. In addition, there's a pool and recreation room with limited groceries available. There are numerous supermarkets, restaurants, and motels in the area.

16.0 Junction with Hwys. 9 and 109. Hwy. 109 joins the route at this point. Keep straight on US 1 and Hwy. 9. **SIDE TRIP:** Just past the junction you'll see unsigned Lower Landing Rd. on the right.

Ocean View Campground is a short 0.3 mile away; all amenities, laundromat, store.

16.4   Sea-Vu Campground on the right. Again, there are all services, with a laundromat and store.

17.2   Sea Breeze market, motel, and campground on the right. There's a deli, as well as cabins, a pool, and a laundromat, in addition to the usual amenities.

17.8   Riverside, an all-service campground on the right; store. Just past the campground, turn right on Hwy. 9 (Shore Rd.); no shoulder.

18.5   Rachel Carson National Wildlife Refuge on the right. The 750-acre refuge, named for environmentalist Rachel Carson (1906–64), author of *Silent Spring*, a book destined to alert the public to the dangers of pesticides in our environment, is a haven for migratory birds.

18.6   Shoulder for 0.8 mile, then it disappears.

19.9   Motel on the left.

20.2   Cross bridge; vast drainage surrounds area.

20.8   Junction to Kennebunk Beach. Unsigned road (Sea Rd.) leads to the beach. There's a variety of shops and services as you continue.

22.1   Junction with Hwys. 9A and 35; keep straight on Hwy. 9. There's an information center on the left, and several shops here.

22.3   Cross the Kennebunk River and enter Kennebunkport, where many visitors enjoy the boutiques and galleries housed in restored historic buildings in Dock Square.

22.4   Turn right on Ocean Ave. Cycle past the marina, then continue through a residential area.

24.6   Walkers Point off to the right. Former president George Bush's 11-acre family estate is easily viewed from the road.

26.1   Wildwood Fire Company on the right. Make an acute right on unsigned Wildes District Rd.

27.2   Three-way unsigned junction; stay straight.

27.5   Junction with Hwy. 9 at Cape Porpoise, a quiet fishing village. Make a left on Hwy. 9 East. In addition to a library, there are several shops and motels in the area.

29.4   Shoulder begins. Head inland now. This is a nice open area with deep green, grassy meadows.

30.1   Salty Acres Campground and market on the right; motel and restaurant on the left, with another just ahead.

34.3   Hwy. 208 joins the route now.

35.2   University of New England.

35.9   Sandwich shop. Now you travel along the Saco River, obscured by homes most of the time, but you'll catch a glimpse of it now and then.

38.5   Shoulder ends.

39.2   Fork; keep to the left on what is called Pool St. upon entering

Cyclist in downtown Kennebunkport

downtown Biddeford, a community where textiles still command the city's economic base. Full services are in the area.

39.5 Junction with Hwy. 111 to the left. Go right on Hwy. 9.

40.2 Bridge over the Saco River. There's a bicycle shop as you head through downtown.

40.9 Turn right on Beach St., which is also Hwy. 9 and later becomes Ferry Rd. US 1 is straight ahead before turning. Pass through a residential area now.

41.8 Bike path begins on the right.

43.8 Go left on Bay View Rd.; bike lane continues; shoulder as well.

44.1 Ferry Beach State Park on the right; trails, picnic area, sandy beach. If you're into tupelo trees, a member of the sour gum family and sometimes grown as an ornamental, there's a stand in the 100-acre park. Prized for their brilliant scarlet autumnal foliage, tupelo trees are rare for this latitude.

44.4 Merge back onto Hwy. 9, turning left and traveling through a residential area. There's no shoulder.

45.6 Turnoff to Ocean Park (Temple Ave.). Shops and motels near the junction extend along the roadway as you proceed to Old Orchard Beach, a popular potpourri of sandy beaches, amusement parks, and an ocean pier.

46.8 Junction of Hwys. 5 and 9 in the middle of Old Orchard Beach. Continue straight on Hwy. 9.

47.2 Turn left on Walnut St.

47.5 Guay's Village and Campground on the right. It is open from Memorial Day through Labor Day. Located on five acres, the grounds are a quiet retreat from Old Orchard Beach. Besides tent sites and the usual amenities, you'll find cabins, a laundromat, and a swimming pool.

Guay's Village and Campground to Flying Point Campground (48.3 miles)

As you continue through Old Orchard Beach, named for an apple orchard that served sailors as a welcome landmark, remain on Highway 9, a heavily trafficked road leading to Pine Point and inland to West Scarborough. Going northwest from there, you'll head onto US 1 to continue north.

Pedal toward Cape Elizabeth after going inland around the inlet at Scarborough, visiting Higgins Beach en route to Portland Head Light. You'll occasionally see the coast.

Head through downtown Portland via an easy path, following Back Cove as you pedal north. Quiet Highway 88 merges onto US 1 just south of Freeport, home of L. L. Bean, the internationally known mail-order sporting goods outfitter. Countless outlet stores have joined L. L. Bean in expanding the town.

After a day of riding gentle terrain consisting of easy ups and down, with a few steeper grades thrown in for good measure, you'll spend the night at Flying Point Campground, along Casco and Maquoit Bays.

MILEAGE LOG

0.0 Guay's Village and Campground entrance. Head back the way you came on Walnut St.

0.3 Junction. Turn left on Hwy. 9.

1.6 Scarborough.

2.2 Turn left on Pine Point Rd. (Hwy. 9); all services in Pine Point; shoulder now.

2.9 On the left is Bayleys Camping Resort with the usual services. Just ahead is Scarborough Marsh, Maine's largest salt marsh. Maintained by the Maine Audubon Society, there are exhibits, a small museum, a gift shop, an information center, nature trails, and canoe rental. It's open daily mid-June through Labor Day.

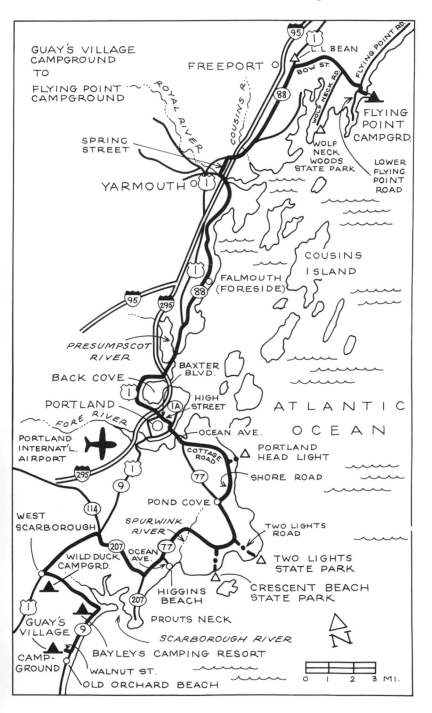

GUAY'S VILLAGE CAMPGROUND TO FLYING POINT CAMPGROUND

FREEPORT

L.L.BEAN

BOW ST.

WOLF NECK RD.

FLYING POINT RD.

FLYING POINT CAMPGRD.

ROYAL RIVER

COUSINS R.

SPRING STREET

WOLF NECK WOODS STATE PARK

LOWER FLYING POINT ROAD

YARMOUTH

COUSINS ISLAND

FALMOUTH (FORESIDE)

PRESUMPSCOT RIVER

BAXTER BLVD.

BACK COVE

A T L A N T I C

O C E A N

PORTLAND

FORE RIVER

HIGH STREET

OCEAN AVE.

PORTLAND HEAD LIGHT

PORTLAND INTERNAT'L. AIRPORT

COTTAGE ROAD

SHORE ROAD

POND COVE

WEST SCARBOROUGH

SPURWINK RIVER

TWO LIGHTS ROAD

WILD DUCK CAMPGRD.

OCEAN AVE.

TWO LIGHTS STATE PARK

CRESCENT BEACH STATE PARK

HIGGINS BEACH

GUAY'S VILLAGE

PROUTS NECK

N

CAMP-GROUND

BAYLEYS CAMPING RESORT

SCARBOROUGH RIVER

WALNUT ST.

OLD ORCHARD BEACH

0   1   2   3 MI.

5.1 Dunstan Landing Rd. exit. **SIDE TRIP:** Turn off to Wild Duck Campground, about 0.5 mile to the left, for the usual amenities, as well as a laundromat and pond.

5.4 Hwy. 9 merges with US 1 in West Scarborough; make a right.

8.5 Exit US 1 and Hwy. 9. Turn right on Hwy. 207. Motels, restaurants, groceries are at the junction. The shoulder continues. Travel past scattered homes, farms, and marshland for the most part, then skirt a rocky headland with views of the Atlantic before heading west to Portland.

11.5 Turn left on Hwy. 77 to Cape Elizabeth.

12.6 Turnoff to Ocean Ave. and Higgins Beach. Continue on Hwy. 77.

13.6 Restaurant at this point.

16.1 Road leads to Crescent Beach State Park on the right. **SIDE TRIP:** Reach the beach in about 1 mile. One of Maine's finest beaches, it has picnic facilities, a bathhouse, and a snack bar.

16.9 Snack stand on the right.

17.2 Junction with Two Lights Rd. There's a diner on the left at the junction. **SIDE TRIP:** Two Lights Rd. leads right to Two Lights

Laughing gulls

State Park in about 1 mile. At the park, enjoy a wonderful view of Casco Bay while strolling along the rocky headland. There are picnic facilities.

18.6 Pond Cove; grocery store, pizza shop, et cetera.

18.9 Turn right on Shore Rd.; no shoulder now.

21.3 Fort Williams Park on the right. **SIDE TRIP:** Go 0.5 mile to Portland Head Light, erected during the George Washington administration in 1791. Picnic facilities and premier ocean views exist here. There's a shoulder now.

22.3 South Portland; markets, restaurants.

22.9 Shore Rd. turns to Cottage Rd.

23.2 Fork; bear right on Cottage Rd.; no shoulder.

23.5 Cottage Rd. merges onto Ocean Ave. (Hwy. 77). Turn right.

23.9 Shoulder begins.

24.0 Begin crossing South Portland Bridge spanning the Fore River. As you cross you'll see the Portland International Marine Terminal. Ferries depart from this point for Nova Scotia.

24.4 Exit bridge. Enter Portland, Maine's largest city with 65,000 inhabitants; all services in area.

24.7 Junction of Hwy. 77 and Hwy. 1A. Turn left on Hwy. 77 (High St.) and head up the hill. The lane is wide. **SIDE TRIP:** Before entering downtown Portland, be sure to visit the waterfront district (stay on Hwy. 1A), first settled between 1632 and 1633. It's one of the oldest ports on the eastern seaboard, and visitors often admire cobblestone streets and gas street lamps while exploring the wharfs, fish markets, and restaurants.

25.0 Downtown Portland. Follow signs to Hwy. 77. There are some motels in downtown, although most are near I-295.

25.3 Hwy. 77 ends. Continue on US 1 North.

25.8 Follow signs. Turn right on US 1 (Baxter Blvd.). The road follows a jogging/walking path along Back Cove. No trucks are allowed. There's a bike shop at the junction.

27.6 Payson Park on the left.

28.2 Pass over I-295, then merge onto the highway for a short distance.

28.4 All bikes must exit I-295, and now ride US 1 via Exit 9. Cross the Presumpscot River to your left; Casco Bay is on the right.

28.9 No shoulder, but there's a bike path.

29.1 Bridge crossing. Enter Falmouth town line.

29.4 End of bridge; shoulder now.

30.6 Head right on Hwy. 88; narrow shoulder, sometimes none. Fortunately, there should be little traffic as you pass some beautiful homes with an occasional view of Casco Bay through the trees.

31.4 Bike lane now.

33.0 A market on the right. The bike lane disappears; the road offers a narrow shoulder, but sometimes there's none.

33.5 Cumberland town limits.

37.3　Yarmouth, an attractive town built along the Royal and Cousin Rivers. Watch for Yarmouth's famous annual Clam Festival, always held the third weekend in July. The road forks; keep to the left. There are two motels in the area.

37.6　Restaurant/inn on the right.

38.2　Cross under bridge (I-95) and go right at first fork; this is still Hwy. 88.

38.6　Fork; head right on Spring St. (Hwy. 88).

39.1　Hwy. 88 joins US 1; narrow shoulder.

39.5　Visitor information center on the left; wide shoulder.

40.6　**SIDE TRIP:** Turnoff to Winslow Memorial Park, which is 3 miles away. This small town-maintained park offers camping and a sheltered swimming area. Motels/restaurants begin.

41.5　Bicycle shop on the left with an occasional outlet store as you pedal toward the outlet haven of Freeport.

42.7　Shoulder disappears, but reappears in 0.7 mile.

42.8　Junction with Desert Rd. Stay on US 1.

44.4　Junction with Bow St.; L. L. Bean is on the left. Turn right on Bow St.; no shoulder, but traffic isn't too bad. (Bow St. turns into Flying Point Rd. some place along the route.) L. L. Bean's retail store is open 24 hours a day, 365 days a year. There are numerous other outlets, restaurants, and bed-and-breakfast inns in town. **SIDE TRIP:** The cheapest motel is straight ahead on shoulderless US 1 for another 2.5 miles.

44.8　Market on the left. Continue on roller-coaster hills to the campground.

46.7　Turnoff to Wolf Neck Rd. on the right; keep straight. **SIDE TRIP:** The road leads to Wolf Neck Woods State Park, a scenic park on Casco Bay and the Harraseeket River. Picnic facilities and hiking trails are available.

48.0　Turn right on unsigned Lower Flying Point Rd., then make an immediate left on a hard-packed gravel road. There's a sign pointing the way to the campground.

48.3　Flying Point Campground office. At this full-service camp, open May through October 15, you'll find a gift shop, but no snacks, and there are wonderful views of both Casco and Maquoit bays.

Flying Point Campground to Loons Cry Campground (51.6 miles)

Although you'll be riding coastal lowlands today, you won't actually see Maine's coastline. Numerous bays, inlets, and channels prohibit riding directly along the sea. If you want to explore the coast, however, consider riding south along one of many peninsulas, a maze of fingers stretching to the Atlantic.

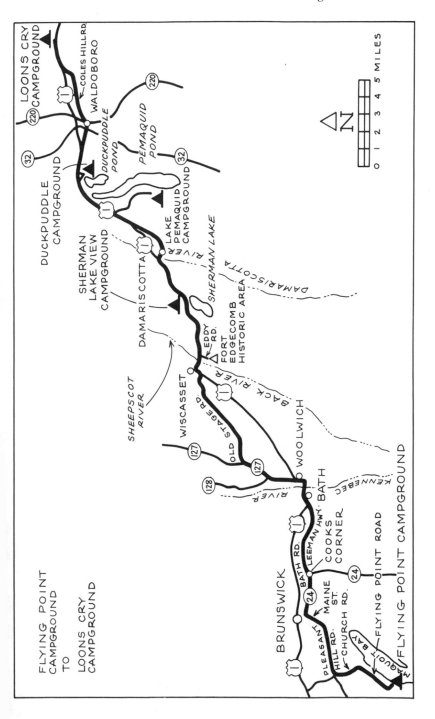

The ride won't necessarily be water-free, however, as there are several beautiful rivers to cross, including the Kennebec, just east of Bath, and the Damariscotta River, which flows through the quaint town of Damariscotta.

The day begins with a grand ride through gentle rolling hills and farmland, and on to the tree-lined streets of Brunswick. The route is virtually traffic-free.

Highway 24 from Brunswick to Bath is another story. Although it's more crowded than the roads prior to Brunswick, and is a bit congested at times, the traffic is tolerable, as US 1 carries most of the heavy traffic.

Bath, often called the cradle of shipbuilding in Maine, has launched more than 4,000 ships in the course of its long history. This includes nearly half of all the wooden sailing vessels produced in the United States between 1862 and 1902. You'll travel rural uncrowded roads to Wiscasset. Quaint shops are popular in this scenic village, also once a great shipbuilding center.

From there, pedal busy US 1. Fortunately, there's a wide shoulder for the most part. In Waldoboro, a quiet and charming community offering many bed-and-breakfast inns, you'll travel through downtown via some *very* steep hills and valleys.

At the end of the day, you'll rest your eyes at beautiful North Pond, and Loons Cry Campground, where loons call and jays chatter.

Sunrise at North Pond

MILEAGE LOG

0.0 Flying Point Campground office. Head back the way you came.

0.3 Back at Flying Point Rd., cycle right along some gentle rolling hills. Although shoulderless, the road is uncrowded.

3.0 Cross Bunganuc Brook, then it's up a steep hill to a fork in 0.1 mile. Bear left on Church Rd.

5.1 Junction. Turn right on unsigned Pleasant Hill Rd., again cycling gentle rolling hills.

6.9 T-junction; turn left on unsigned Maine St., a wide road.

7.5 Market on the left as you enter Brunswick; all services, including a bike shop.

8.1 Turn right on Hwy. 24 (Bath Rd.), cycling past Bowdoin College. Alumni include Henry Wadsworth Longfellow and Arctic explorers Admiral Robert E. Peary and Donald B. MacMillan.

8.3 Junction with Hwy. 123; keep straight. There's a shoulder and restaurants along the route now.

9.5 Airport on the right.

10.5 Cooks Corner. There's a shopping center, laundromat, and restaurants at the junction. Keep straight on Bath Rd., which turns into Leeman Hwy.; shoulder disappears. Hwy. 24 heads south to Bailey Island.

11.0 Shopping center on the right.

11.4 Motel on the left; there's another 1 mile ahead.

12.8 Market on the left, with an inn and restaurant in 0.3 mile.

15.4 Bath; all services in area. Merge onto US 1 (narrow shoulder), then exit to the business district. Stay straight, paralleling US 1, then reenter US 1 via a bikeway/sidewalk. Bath, the "City of Ships," launched America's first trans-Atlantic sailing ship, building thousands of boats of every shape and size since. Visit the Maine Maritime Museum & Shipyard, 243 Washington St., and relive shipbuilding history. On the banks of the Kennebec River, the museum is open daily, year-round.

16.0 Begin riding sidewalk across bridge over the Kennebec River.

16.7 End of bridge; keep straight on US 1 through Woolwich.

17.1 Turn left on Hwy. 127 North; narrow road; traffic is fairly light. Terrain is hilly and roller-coasterlike, with some steep grades.

19.0 Junction with Hwy. 128; stay straight on Hwy. 127.

21.0 Turn right on Old Stage Rd.

21.7 Fork; keep straight.

22.0 Top of hill.

24.5 Stop sign; go left on (unsigned) Mountain Rd., past a cemetery.

24.7 Bear right, staying on Old Stage Rd.

25.5 Creek crossing.

26.3 Stop sign; head left on unsigned road.

27.2 Turn left on US 1; no shoulder; heavy traffic.

27.5   Wide shoulder as you enter the town of Wiscasset, nineteenth-century home port for many prosperous sea captains and merchants. Many of their grand homes—of Federal, Georgian, and Victorian architecture—still stand. You'll find shops, restaurants, and bed-and-breakfast inns in town.

28.2   Cross Donald E. Davey Bridge over the Sheepscot River. **SIDE TRIP:** Before crossing, skirt the west bank and see the hulks of the four-masted schooners *Hesper* and *Luther Little*. Beached in 1932, these World War I schooners served as cargo vessels during the 1920s.

28.7   Exit bridge. Edgecomb Inn is near here. **SIDE TRIP:** Eddy Rd. (to the right) leads to Fort Edgecomb Historic Area in 0.5 mile. Built in the early 1800s to protect Wiscasset, the most important shipbuilding center north of Boston at that time, its restored fortifications overlook the Sheepscot River, where harbor seals are often seen. There are picnic facilities and opportunities for fishing.

28.9   Market on the left.

29.6   Junction with Hwy. 27; keep straight. There are several motels in the area. Hwy. 27 leads south to the Boothbay Harbor area.

31.8   Cross Sherman Lake; rest area just beyond.

32.3   Sherman Lake View Campground entrance on the left: all-service facility, and there's a laundromat as well.

34.1   Market/restaurants; visitor information center.

34.9   Exit on Business US 1.

35.6   A bridge over the Damariscotta River leads into downtown Damariscotta, a pretty community with tree-lined streets and a series of small shops. There's a laundromat, in addition to the usual amenities.

35.8   Junction with Hwys. 129 and 130 to Bristol and south to Christmas Cove and Pemaquid Point. Remain on US Business 1, a shoulderless path along gentle to moderate rolling hills. There's a visitor information center just beyond the junction.

36.2   Market on the left with another market and two motels within the next mile.

38.4   Restaurant on the right. Merge onto US 1 just beyond. There's a shoulder again.

39.8   Turnoff to Lake Pemaquid Campground. **SIDE TRIP:** Located less than 4 miles away, the campground has all amenities, including a laundromat, limited groceries, fishing, and swimming in the lake.

41.6   Motel on the right.

41.7   Exit for Duckpuddle Campground. **SIDE TRIP:** 1.5 miles distant on Pemaquid Lake or Pond, whichever you prefer, it has all services, including a laundromat, limited groceries, and lake swimming and fishing opportunities.

42.3   This road also leads to Duckpuddle Campground.

A beached World War I schooner along the Sheepscot River

43.2 Waldoboro town line and the beginning of some steep hills.

44.4 Top of hill.

44.8 Turn right on unsigned old US 1. Beforehand there are signs for a variety of bed-and-breakfast inns. Steep climbs and descents begin shortly.

46.0 Cross Hwy. 32.

46.4 Head straight on Hwy. 220 North, which is also Main St. Climb a steep grade past a few shops, including a cafe. Other portions of town exist closer to US 1, about 0.5 mile to the north.

46.9 Turn right on unsigned Coles Hill Rd. for a very steep climb.

47.1 Cabins on the left near top of hill.

50.1 Merge onto US 1; wide shoulders.
50.3 Pizza house/restaurant on the right.
50.5 Convenience store on the left.
50.8 Motel on the right.
51.6 Entrance to Loons Cry Campground, a wonderful spot with all amenities and tent sites on the shore of North Pond. It's a beautiful lake, blessed with loons and their unique song, and you'll find canoe and kayak rentals available, as well as some snack items. Loons Cry Campground is open all year.

Loons Cry Campground to Flying Dutchman Campground (52.6 miles)

Wake up this morning and know that Highway 90 traverses gentle to moderate hills across green pastures, past rural homes, and through small towns, escorting you to the lovely coastal city of Rockport. Upon viewing Rockport's deep harbor village, it's not hard to imagine why the area has long attracted artists and musicians.

From Rockport to Camden, the highway offers enchanting views now and again, with Camden an obvious delight to those who flock here by the thousands. Known as the windjammer capital of the world, Camden boasts a charming and busy harbor, wonderful shops, and restaurants. Pedal into town on a Saturday, and you may see a fleet of tall-masted schooners arriving after a week's cruise on coastal waters. On Monday morning, they set sail again.

Leave Camden via US 1, a road with wonderful views and no shoulders for the first 8 miles. Although traffic may be heavy, pedaling the

Belfast Bay, Belfast

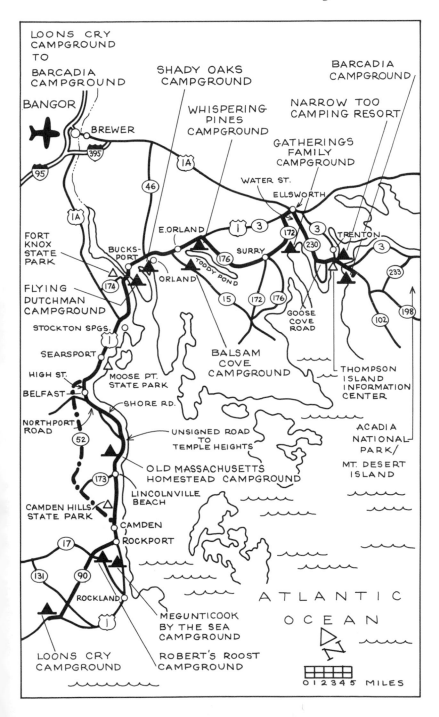

LOONS CRY CAMPGROUND TO BARCADIA CAMPGROUND

BANGOR

BREWER

SHADY OAKS CAMPGROUND

WHISPERING PINES CAMPGROUND

BARCADIA CAMPGROUND

NARROW TOO CAMPING RESORT

GATHERINGS FAMILY CAMPGROUND

WATER ST.

ELLSWORTH

TRENTON

FORT KNOX STATE PARK

E. ORLAND

BUCKS-PORT

SURRY

TODDY POND

ORLAND

FLYING DUTCHMAN CAMPGROUND

STOCKTON SPGS.

GOOSE COVE ROAD

SEARSPORT

HIGH ST.

BELFAST

MOOSE PT. STATE PARK

BALSAM COVE CAMPGROUND

THOMPSON ISLAND INFORMATION CENTER

SHORE RD.

NORTHPORT ROAD

UNSIGNED ROAD TO TEMPLE HEIGHTS

ACADIA NATIONAL PARK/ MT. DESERT ISLAND

OLD MASSACHUSETTS HOMESTEAD CAMPGROUND

LINCOLNVILLE BEACH

CAMDEN HILLS STATE PARK

CAMDEN

ROCKPORT

ATLANTIC OCEAN

ROCKLAND

N

MEGUNTICOOK BY THE SEA CAMPGROUND

LOONS CRY CAMPGROUND

ROBERT'S ROOST CAMPGROUND

0 1 2 3 4 5 MILES

coast makes the trip worthwhile. However, those who'd rather bypass US 1 can take Highway 52 from Camden to Belfast, a total of about 18 miles. This route boasts of fewer cars and great scenes.

From Belfast, known for its superb examples of nineteenth-century residential and commercial architecture, it's a pleasant ride across rolling hills to the Penobscot River, site of Fort Knox, Maine's largest fort. The perfectly preserved fort sports granite walls 20 feet high and 40 feet thick. Original cannons still stand in place.

From Fort Knox, you'll cycle across the Penobscot River to Flying Dutchman Campground, your camp for the night.

Penobscot River crossing near Fort Knox State Park

MILEAGE LOG

0.0 Loons Cry Campground entrance on US 1. Continue north.

0.2 Turn right on the first unsigned road. There's a short climb to a fork in 0.1 mile. Head left.

0.7 Merge back onto US 1; cycle right. There's a shoulder again. **ALTERNATE ROUTE**: Upon cycling this portion of the roadway, I was urged to exit US 1, riding the unsigned road, due to construction in progress. The construction complete, US 1 now offers a shoulder, so you can stay on the main road if you so desire.

1.3 Head left on Hwy. 90, traveling moderate rolling hills. There's a wide shoulder.

2.1 Market on the left.

2.3 Bridge over the St. George River.

2.6 Junction with Hwy. 131.

8.7 Variety store on the right.

9.5 Junction with Hwy. 17.

9.8 Restaurant on the right.

10.3 Robert's Roost Campground, a quiet, shady campground with all amenities and a laundromat.

10.6 Restaurant on the left.

10.9 Pizza shop on the left.

12.2 Junction with US 1; deli at junction. Go straight on West St. **SIDE TRIP**: Megunticook by the Sea Campground is 2 miles to the right on US 1. Open May 15 through October 15, the camp offers the usual services plus a laundromat, limited groceries, and a game room.

12.5 T-junction; make a left on unsigned Pascal St.

12.8 Cross bridge over inlet, going right, then left on Central through downtown Rockport; all services in area. **SIDE TRIP**: Before crossing the bridge over the inlet, visit Rockport Marine Park on the right just before the bridge. There's a great view of Rockport Harbor from the well-kept park that has picnic facilities and three restored lime kilns. At one time, Rockport was a leading producer of lime. Close to the park, on Sea St., is Rockport Apprenticeshop, where they pass on traditional wooden boat-building techniques to students. Visitors are welcome.

13.0 Fork; go right on Russell Ave., following all shoulderless roads to Camden; the road becomes Chestnut St. Traffic is usually light. Look for the country's first herd of Belted Galloways, Camden's famous "Oreo cows," along the route.

14.1 Turn right on Bayview St., a beautiful ride past farms and country homes.

15.3 Laite Beach Park on the right; picnic facilities, rest rooms, good view of Camden Bay.

15.6 Downtown Camden; all services in the area.

15.8 Main St. (Junction with US 1); turn right. There's no shoulder; the road is heavily trafficked. There are many popular shops here and at the nearby harbor, where you'll find the visitor center. As you continue, US 1 is a moderate roller-coaster assortment of hills, with a few steeper grades.

16.0 Library on the right.

16.3 Junction with Hwy. 52. **ALTERNATE ROUTE:** Although US 1 is the most scenic route to Belfast, it's also the busiest. For lighter traffic, ride Hwy. 52 to Belfast. It's about 18 miles to town.

17.4 Motel/food stand.

17.6 Camden Hills State Park on the left, picnic area on the right. The state park has a camping area with hot showers, a road leading to Mount Battie where there's an unsurpassed 360-degree view of the islands in Penobscot Bay, and a trail leading to the top of Mount Megunticook, highest of the Camden Hills. The park is open from May 15 through October 15.

18.7 Motels/cabins stretch off and on for several miles.

21.7 Junction with Hwy. 173 and the community of Lincolnville Beach. Known for its lobster restaurant, there's a market, restaurants, and one of the area's few stretches of sandy beach. This is also the takeoff point for the ferry to Isleboro. The *Margaret Chase Smith* makes scheduled 20-minute runs to the island, with passengers disembarking near the Grindle Point Lighthouse, home of the Sailor's Memorial Museum.

22.9 Bridge over Ducktrap River.

23.8 Old Massachusetts Homestead Campground is on the left; a laundromat, snacks, shaded sites, usual services.

24.3 Shoulder now.

26.5 Diner on the right; motel just ahead.

26.8 Junction for Temple Heights. Go right on a narrow, unsigned road with little traffic. Descend the first hill and bear to the right up a short, steep hill. There are wonderful views of West Penobscot Bay along the roadway, now called Shore Rd. although you'll have to work to get them. A few steep climbs (all short) are in order.

28.6 Road turns to hard-packed gravel.

29.3 Back on pavement.

31.7 Store/deli on the left.

31.8 Merge onto US 1 North (right); shoulder. There's a restaurant on the corner.

33.6 Exit on Northport Rd.; no shoulder, but lane is wide.

33.8 Hamburger stand on the right.

34.1 Belfast City Park on the right.

34.6 Small store on the right.

34.8 Road changes to High St.

35.1 Cross Main St. in downtown Belfast; all services in area. Continue straight. As with many coastal Maine communities, Belfast, established in 1770, is steeped in shipbuilding history. Its downtown and waterfront are filled with fine examples of Greek Revival architecture and many of the sea captains' homes have been transformed into lovely bed-and-breakfast inns.

35.7 Turn onto US 1 North and Hwy. 3 East. Those riding the Hwy. 52 alternate route meet up with the main route here. Pedal the bridge spanning the Passagassawakeag River.

36.3 Wide shoulder after exiting bridge. There are motels and restaurants in the East Belfast area.

37.0 Country store/deli/grill on the left.

39.4 Moose Point State Park on the right. A nice place for a picnic, it has terrific views of Penobscot Bay.

41.2 Searsport, Maine's second-largest deepwater port and a small community with one of the richest maritime histories in The Pine Tree State. You'll find all amenities in the self-described antiques capital of Maine, including bed-and-breakfast inns.

41.5 Penobscot Marine Museum on the left; information center just beyond.

42.4 Shoulder ends.

42.5 Bicycle shop on the left; market, restaurant, motel as you leave town. Be prepared for great views (off and on) of Penobscot Bay and the Penobscot River throughout your trip to Bucksport.

42.7 Shoulder again.

44.5 Motel/restaurant on the left.

45.2 Motel/restaurant as you enter Stockton Springs.

45.9 Junction with Hwy. 1A on the left. Keep right and continue on US 1 and Hwy. 3.

46.3 Food stand on the right.

46.5 Market on the right.

48.1 Motel on the left.

51.2 Prospect town line.

51.7 Scenic overlook; good view of Bucksport, Penobscot River, and Verona Island.

52.0 Restaurant on the right; nice view of the river, good prices.

52.1 Bear right and cross Waldo-Hancock Bridge; narrow shoulder. **SIDE TRIP:** Before crossing the bridge, ride to Fort Knox State Park; picnic facilities, rest rooms. Pedal straight on Hwy. 174 for 0.2 mile. Construction of Fort Knox, a fortification known for its fine granite craftsmanship, began in 1844 and continued for twenty years. The fort was manned during the Civil and Spanish American Wars.

52.5 Verona town line/end of bridge. Follow signs to the right to the Flying Dutchman Campground, located along the Penobscot River.

52.6   Flying Dutchman Campground office; all services, shady and sunny sites. The campground is open Memorial Day through October 15.

Flying Dutchman Campground to Barcadia Campground (37.1 miles)

This segment spans typical coastal Maine terrain—rolling hills with a few steep grades—leaving plenty of time for resting or exploring once you reach the day's destination on Mount Desert Island at Acadia National Park. Encompassing nearly 35,000 acres, Acadia National Park consists of portions of Mount Desert Island, Isle au Haut, and Schoodic Peninsula, although most of the park rests on Mount Desert Island.

Upon leaving Flying Dutchman Campground, you'll travel through Bucksport, heading Down East, as it is often termed. Down East Maine consists of the easternmost and northernmost counties of the state, from the mouth of the Penobscot River at Bucksport to the St. Croix River in Calais, and from the awesome beauty of Acadia National Park to the spacious potato fields of Arrostook County.

This is a land of unsurpassed beauty, with mountains, lakes and rivers, small streams and ponds, peninsulas and islands, towering headlands and endless vistas. The following route is just a sample of the splendor of Down East Maine.

Although you'll pedal US 1 for a portion of the ride, Highways 176 and 172 will lead you along uncrowded roads through farmland and rural Maine.

The entire ride is one of pure pleasure en route to Barcadia Campground on Mount Desert Island. This segment ends at Barcadia, but there are many other Mount Desert Island campgrounds from which to choose.

There are two national park campgrounds and ten private ones. All but one are open from about May to October. Blackwoods, a national park campground, is open year-round. The private campgrounds offer hot showers; the national park facilities do not. Some of the private facilities also offer laundromats and pools.

A side trip allows but a small sampling of Acadia National Park and Mount Desert Island. If time permits, you can explore the island to your heart's content, spending days cycling the 108-square-mile island.

Upon visiting Mount Desert Island, the third-largest island in the continental United States (Long Island and Martha's Vineyard are larger), it's easy to see why the first tourists came here nearly 6,000 years ago. In the early years, Abenaki Indians came here to fish and hunt, eat berries, and dig for clams. Today, more than 4 million people come annually to Acadia National Park to hike, bike, ride horses, kayak, fish, shop, relax, and sightsee, making it second only to the Great Smoky Mountains in popularity among national parks.

MILEAGE LOG

0.0 Flying Dutchman Campground office. Return to the main road.

0.1 Back on US 1 and Hwy. 3, cycle right; no shoulder.

0.2 Rest area on the right; picnic facilities, outhouses.

0.3 Market/food stand on the right.

0.7 Market on the right.

0.9 Shoulder again.

1.0 Junction of US 1 and Hwys. 3 and 15; cross the bridge into Bucksport; all services as you head out of town by turning right on US 1. Bucksport's history includes shipbuilding and lumbering. As you cycle around town, look for the Jed Prouty Inn, a Maine landmark. It was built in 1798 as a stagecoach stop, and several mid-nineteenth-century presidents stopped here, including Martin Van Buren, Andrew Jackson, John Tyler, and William Henry Harrison.

2.4 Junction with Hwy. 46 on the left.

3.0 Shady Oaks Campground to the right of this junction; all amenities, including a laundromat.

3.5 Cross the Orland River, its banks a splendid home for the serene village of Orland.

4.3 H.O.M.E. Village on the right. H.O.M.E., which stands for Orland's Homemakers Organized for More Employment, is an unusual cooperative venture with a variety of crafts workshops featuring the work of Maine artisans. Crafts include pottery, weaving, leatherwork, and woodworking; there's even a market with fresh produce, a craft museum, and a gift shop. H.O.M.E. is open daily; look for H.O.M.E.'s annual country and crafts fair in August.

5.7 Junction with Hwy. 15; convenience store. **SIDE TRIP:** Balsam Cove Campground is located 2 miles to the right; all services, store, laundromat.

7.0 Convenience store in East Orland; all services in area; country store/post office/deli here.

7.3 This unsigned road also leads to the Balsam Cove Campground.

7.4 Notice Toddy Pond on the right, which stretches for 9 miles.

7.9 Restaurant/cottages.

8.0 Whispering Pines, a full-service campground, on the right; some shady sites.

9.0 Small market on the left; top of biggest hill of the day.

9.9 Junction; go right on Hwy. 176 West; no shoulder, but road is uncrowded. You'll see Toddy Pond off and on as you cycle south past farmland and an occasional home. It's a place where wild-flowers line portions of the roadway in the summer.

15.2 Nice view of surrounding area from this point.

19.3 T-junction at the town of Surry; go left on Hwy. 172; shoulder.

19.6 Market on the left.

21.4 Bridge crossing.

21.5 Dining and lodging on the right.

21.9 The Gatherings Family Campground on the right; a gravel road leads to the office of this full-service facility, which includes a laundromat and limited groceries. Shady sites are situated on the shore of Union River Bay.

23.1 Ellsworth town line.

25.0 Market on the right.

25.8 Merge back onto US 1/Hwy. 3. Bear right.

26.0 Cross Union River and make a right on Hwy. 230 South (Water St.) just beyond. This is downtown Ellsworth, where you'll find all services. Although the road is shoulderless, traffic is relatively light as you head out of town. Known as the Gateway to Mount

Cyclists enjoying the view of Frenchman Bay, Acadia National Park

Desert Island and Acadia National Park, Ellsworth is the commercial center of Hancock County. Downtown Ellsworth offers interesting shops and restaurants; the outskirts provide shopping malls, campgrounds, accommodations, and restaurants.

26.5 Bicycle shop on the right.

32.5 Go left on Goose Cove Rd.

34.3 Back on Hwy. 230; pedal left.

35.8 Junction with Hwy. 3 in Trenton; cycle right; shoulder now. Motels and restaurants in area; Narrow Too Camping Resort across the street; all services, gift shop, laundromat.

36.4 Mount Desert Bridge crosses Mount Desert Narrows and leads to Mount Desert Island.

36.7 Thompson Island information center on the right; Thompson Island picnic area on the left. The information center offers information on both Mount Desert Island and Acadia national parks.

37.1 Barcadia Campground; a full-service facility on Western Bay, it has both shady and sunny sites.

Side Trip: Bar Harbor/Northeast Harbor Loop

Those cycling this 45-mile loop will find premier ocean viewing at its best, although you will travel an interior route to the coast. From the Barcadia Campground it's a 12-mile ride to Bar Harbor, Mount Desert Island's largest and most popular town. You'll pass two campgrounds en route. The entire loop is a continual series of ups and downs, roller-coaster thrills where rocky shores abound, waves splash on shore, and peregrine falcons dive, raising their young on precipitous cliffs.

You'll pedal past extravagant homes and yacht-bound harbors, scenes where wild roses border the landscape and beavers work building ponds.

The best route travels south from Barcadia Campground along Hwys. 102 and 198, then left (east) on Hwys. 3 and 198. You'll make another left on Hwy. 233 before reaching downtown Bar Harbor. All roads sport shoulders.

If you want to climb 1,532-foot Cadillac Mountain, the park's highest mountain and the highest point on the Eastern seaboard, you'll pass the turnoff to the mountain at the 10.3-mile mark. There's a spectacular view from atop the mountain.

Bar Harbor, first called Eden when it was founded in 1796, was named for its ideal setting on shimmering Frenchman Bay. Located at the base of the island's attractive mountains, Bar Harbor offers a wide choice of accommodations, including the Mount Desert Island AYH, located in downtown Bar Harbor on Kennebec St. It's closed August 31 through June 14; for more information, write or call P.O. Box 32, Bar Harbor, ME 04609; (207) 288-5587.

Downtown Bar Harbor is a shopper's delight, with many fine

Bar Harbor area, Mount Desert Island

specialty shops and boutiques, gift shops, galleries, museums, and excellent restaurants.

Be sure to visit the Bar Harbor town pier, a stunning spot from which you can board a whale-watching, sunset, fishing, or nature cruise. From June to September, the cruise ship *Bluenose* departs from the Bar Harbor ferry terminal each morning en route to Yarmouth, Nova Scotia, 6 hours away. You can return the same day, or spend the night and return the next evening.

After visiting the shops and pier, go south on Hwy. 3. From Bar Harbor, Hwy. 3 is shoulderless, but you'll soon ride 20-mile Park Loop Rd., where you'll travel Ocean Ave., a two-lane one-way road (at least it is along the portion of road you'll follow), where scenes are one delight after another.

Excellent views are yours for the asking. Stop at Thunder Hole, a natural chasm formed by the awesome forces of the sea. Visit after a large storm has passed, and large waves will sweep into the chasm, sounding a thunderous clap and creating an enormous sea spray, as the waves have nowhere to go but up.

After passing Otter Point, Otter Cove, and so on, merge back onto Hwy. 3, taking the unsigned road out to Ingraham Point. Next you'll pass Seal Harbor and continue on Hwy. 3 again to Northeast Harbor, a quiet community and home base to the *Sea Queen* ferry serving the Cranberry Isles. Sightseeing and whale-watching excursions are also available.

Town highlights include the Great Harbor Collection Museum on Main St., Thuya Gardens, and Asticou Gardens, where you'll view rare azaleas. In addition to a luxurious waterfront motel, Northeast Harbor offers charming inns, restaurants, a deli, and a bakery.

Take Sargent Dr. north along Somes Sound—the only fiord on the Eastern seacoast—for more outstanding views. Merge back onto Hwys. 3 and 198 along Somes Sound to complete the loop.

Numerous other side trips await exploration. Perhaps you'd like to explore Southwest Harbor and/or Bass Harbor (where you can catch the ferry to Swans Island), or maybe you'd rather ride a series of carriage roads.

There are 57 miles of carriage roads, a network of woodland paths free of motor vehicles, enjoyed by bicyclists, hikers, horseback riders, and carriages. The easy-to-ride gravel roads were built between 1915 and 1933, directed and financed by John D. Rockefeller, Jr.

In addition to the carriage roads, there are more than 120 miles of trails in the park. They range from short, easy walks to steep trails.

Barcadia Campground to Bangor International Airport (39.3 miles)

There are several ways in which you can end your ride. You can cycle back home, you can take a bus to Bangor International Airport, or you can cycle to the Bangor airport if you'd like. This segment describes the latter.

For those who'd rather bus than pedal, Greyhound Bus Lines offers summer service between Bar Harbor and Bangor International Airport. Bicycles are allowed as long as they are boxed. Call Greyhound at (207) 945-3000 for more information.

If you decide to ride to Bangor, be prepared for heavy traffic from Ellsworth to Brewer when shoulders are usually narrow or nonexistent. You'll ride moderate terrain, with some steeper climbs and descents.

If you'd rather not end your ride, why not continue your trip Down East, with Lubec your destination? You'd arrive in Lubec, about 100 miles to the northeast, via US 1, US 1A, Highway 191, and Highway 189. Lubec, once dubbed the Sardine Capital of the World, is the country's easternmost town. There's bus service between Bangor and Lubec. Contact St. Croix Bus Lines at (207) 454-7526 for additional information.

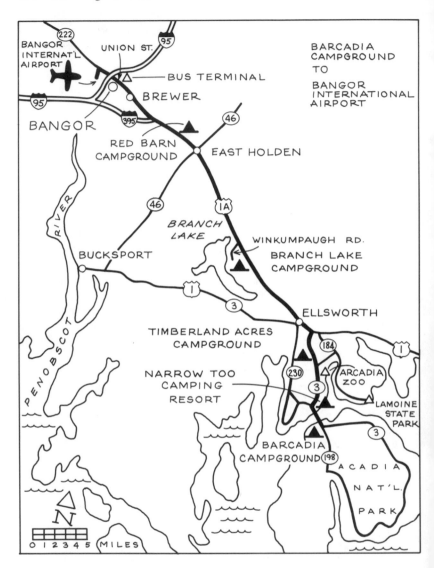

MILEAGE LOG

0.0 Barcadia Campground entrance. Go left on Hwy. 3; shoulder. The ride from here to Ellsworth is gentle rolling hills.

1.3 Junction with Hwy. 230. Keep straight on Hwy. 3, riding through Trenton, where there are restaurants and motels.

1.9 Supermarket on the left.

2.2 Restaurant with excellent prices on the right. There's a motel, too.

4.6 Arcadia Zoo on the right. Open daily in the summer, this non-profit preserve features more than 150 native and exotic animals, including moose, zebras, and peacocks.

4.9 Junction with Hwy. 204; stay on Hwy. 3. **SIDE TRIP:** Hwy. 204 leads to the right to Hwy. 184 and Lamoine State Park, about 8 miles away, which provides camping and picnicking on Frenchman Bay.

6.5 Timberland Acres Campground on the left. Open from mid-May through mid-October, this full-service facility offers a laundromat, a pool, and limited groceries. Campsites are located in a wooded area.

6.8 Ellsworth town line.

8.4 Bike lane ends; narrow shoulder.

9.0 Information center on the left.

9.7 Junction with US 1A and US 1. Go straight on US 1A. There's no shoulder; beware of heavy traffic.

11.5 Shoulder begins, and ends in 0.2 mile. Cross river just beyond.

14.7 Rest area on the right; picnic facilities, outhouse.

15.3 Shoulder. (This narrows in 1.3 miles, but at least there's still a shoulder.)

17.2 General store on the right.

20.4 Shoulder disappears at top of hill. Turnoff on left to Branch Lake Campground. **SIDE TRIP:** Make a left on Winkumpaugh Rd., then ride southwest for 0.5 mile to Hanson Landing Rd., and make another left, traveling 1 mile to the campground. In addition to the usual services, there are limited groceries, with swimming and fishing opportunities as well.

21.9 Wide shoulder now.

24.7 Top of another hill. Restaurant and guest rooms on the left, overlooking Phillips Lake.

27.5 Descend to East Holden; market/pizza shop.

27.7 Junction with Hwy. 46.

28.0 No shoulder as you pedal what is now gentle roller-coaster hills.

28.7 Narrow shoulder widens in about 1 mile.

29.6 Red Barn Campground on the right; laundromat, snack bar, store, swimming pool, shaded sites, recreation room, and usual amenities.

30.2 Motel on the left.

33.1 Junction with US 395; stay on Hwy. 1A.

33.2 Brewer, a full-service town.

34.8 Fork; head left on Wilson St.

34.9 Bike shop on the left. There's another bike shop off the right fork (State St.) at the Twin City Plaza.

35.8 Junction with Hwy. 15. Head straight to Bangor on US 1A.

35.9 Begin crossing the Chamberlain Bridge over the Penobscot River. Enter Bangor halfway across. There's a wide walkway for riding bikes.

36.3 Greyhound bus terminal on the right. Stay straight on Union St., which is also Hwy. 222. Lanes are wide for biking.

37.5 Cross over I-95.

38.6 Turn left at entrance to Bangor International Airport and the Hilton Inn. There are plenty of restaurants/shops in this area, and motels in the nearby area.

39.3 Bangor International Airport terminal.

RECOMMENDED READING

Bicycle Touring

Bridge, Raymond. *Bike Touring: The Sierra Club Guide to Outings on Wheels*. San Francisco, CA: Sierra, 1979.

Editors of *Bicycling*. "Bicycle Touring." Emmaus, PA: Rodale Press, 1985.

Van der Plas, Rob. *The Bicycle Touring Manual*. Mill Valley, CA: Bicycle Books, Inc., 1988.

Area Bicycle Tour Guides

Franey, Michael. *New England over the Handlebars*. Boston, MA: Little, Brown & Co., 1975.

Mullen, Edwin, and Jane Griffith. *Short Bike Rides on Cape Cod, Nantucket & the Vineyard*. Chester, CT: Globe Pequot, 1991.

Thomas, Paul. *The Best Bike Rides in New England*. Chester, CT: Globe Pequot, 1990.

Bicycle Maintenance/Miscellaneous

Cuthbertson, Tom. *Anybody's Bike Book*. Berkeley, CA: Ten Speed Press, 1990.

Cuthbertson, Tom, and Rich Morrall. *The Bike Bag Book*. Berkeley, CA: Ten Speed Press, 1981.

Editors of *Bicycling*. "Basic Maintenance and Repair." Emmaus, PA: Rodale Press, 1990.

———. "700 Tips for Better Bicycling." Emmaus, PA: Rodale Press, 1991.

Forester, John. *Effective Cycling*. Cambridge, MA: MIT Press, 1983.

INDEX

About the author

Donna Ikenberry Aitkenhead sold her home and most of her belongings in 1983 to pursue "life on the road" as a full-time writer and photographer. The author of *The Hiker's Guide to Oregon* and other books on the Oregon wilderness, her work has appeared in many publications. An avid bicyclist, she has cycled over 26,000 miles along the Pacific and Atlantic coasts. Donna spends her winters in southern California writing about her adventures.

THE MOUNTAINEERS, founded in 1906, is a nonprofit outdoor activity and conservation club, whose mission is "to explore, study, preserve, and enjoy the natural beauty of the outdoors...." Based in Seattle, Washington, the club is now the third-largest such organization in the United States, with 12,000 members and four branches throughout Washington State.

The Mountaineers sponsors both classes and year-round outdoor activities in the Pacific Northwest, which include hiking, mountain climbing, ski-touring, snowshoeing, bicycling, camping, kayaking and canoeing, nature study, sailing, and adventure travel. The club's conservation division supports environmental causes through educational activities, sponsoring legislation, and presenting informational programs. All club activities are led by skilled, experienced volunteers, who are dedicated to promoting safe and responsible enjoyment and preservation of the outdoors.

The Mountaineers Books, an active, nonprofit publishing program of the club, produces guidebooks, instructional texts, historical works, natural history guides, and works on environmental conservation. All books produced by The Mountaineers are aimed at fulfilling the club's mission.

If you would like to participate in these organized outdoor activities or the club's programs, consider a membership in The Mountaineers. For information and an application, write or call The Mountaineers, Club Headquarters, 300 Third Avenue West, Seattle, Washington 98119; (206) 284-6310.

Send or call for our catalog of more than 200 outdoor books:
The Mountaineers Books
1011 SW Klickitat Way, Suite 107
Seattle, WA 98134
1-800-553-4453